PITT LATIN AMERICAN SERIES

They Eat from Their Labor

Work and Social Change in Colonial Bolivia

•

ANN ZULAWSKI

•

UNIVERSITY OF PITTSBURGH PRESS
Pittsburgh and London

Published by the University of Pittsburgh Press, Pittsburgh, Pa., 15260

Copyright © 1995, University of Pittsburgh Press

All rights reserved

Manufactured in the United States of America

Printed on acid-free paper

Library of Congress Cataloging-in-Publication Data

Zulawski, Ann
  They eat from their labor : work and social change in colonial Bolivia / Ann Zulawski.
    p. cm. — (Pitt Latin American series)
  Includes bibliographical references and index.
  ISBN 0-8229-1183-3
  1. Labor—Bolivia—History. 2. Social change—Bolivia—History.
3. Indians of South America—Bolivia—Employment—History.
4. Bolivia—History—To 1809. I. Title. II. Series.
HD8275.Z84 1994
306.3'6'0984—dc20   94-33040
                                                                                                           CIP

A CIP catalogue record for this book is available from the British Library. Eurospan, London

Part of chapter 4 was originally published in "Wages, Ore Sharing and Peasant Agriculture: Labor in Oruro's Silver Mines, 1607–1720," *Hispanic American Historical Review* 67:3 (1987), 405–30. An earlier version of chapter 6 was published as "Social Differentiation, Gender, and Ethnicity: Urban Indian Women in Colonial Bolivia, 1640–1725," *Latin American Research Review* 25:2 (1990), 93–113. A section of chapter 7 was published in "Frontier Workers and Social Change: Pilaya y Paspaya (Bolivia) in the Early Eighteenth Century," in *Migration in Colonial Latin America*, ed. David Robinson (Cambridge: Cambridge University Press, 1990).

This book is dedicated to my parents,
Gladys Kidwell Lachenbruch and David Lachenbruch

Contents

	List of Illustrations	ix
	List of Tables	xi
	Acknowledgments	xiii
	Introduction	3
1	Societies in Transition: *Iberians and Andeans*	11
2	Colonial Economy and the Organization of Labor	37
3	Indian Population and Migration in Upper Peru in the Sixteenth and Seventeenth Centuries	62
4	A Colonial Andean Mining Center: *Oruro, 1607–1720*	85
5	The Indian Labor Force of Oruro in 1683	114
6	Gender and Social Differentiation: *Women and Their Families Confront Colonialism*	150
7	Labor in an Agrarian Frontier Zone: *Pilaya y Paspaya, 1646–1725*	168
	Conclusion	199
	Appendixes	207
	Notes	217
	Glossary	253
	Bibliography	257
	Index	277

List of Illustrations

Map 1	Bolivia	14
Map 2	The Aymara Kingdoms	15
Map 3	Provinces of Upper Peru	66
Map 4	Oruro and Environs	90
Map 5	The Province of Pilaya y Paspaya	171
Figure 1	Estimated Total Peruvian and Potosí Silver Production, 1560–1800	49
Figure 2	Quinto Real, Oruro, 1611–1730	100

List of Tables

3.1	Estimated Monthly Living Costs for a Mitayo in Potosí, 1596	69
3.2	Variation in Originario Population and Tributary Population in Sixteen Provinces of Upper Peru, 1573–1683	72
3.3	Categories of Male Indians in Upper Peru in 1645	82
4.1	Mining and Refining Expenses for Two Weeks, Oruro, 1607	95
4.2	Occupations and Enterprises of Spanish Men, Oruro, 1607	98
5.1	Indian Males in Oruro, 1683	119
5.2	Indian Families in Oruro, 1683	121
5.3	Occupations of Male Forasteros and Yanaconas in Oruro, 1683	122
5.4	Birthplaces of Male Forasteros in Oruro, 1683	128
5.5	Years of Residence in Oruro, Forasteros, 1683	130
5.6	Birthplaces and Origins of Forasteros in Oruro, 1683	132
5.7	Birthplaces and Origins of Yanaconas in Oruro, 1683	136
5.8	Mita Obligations by Male Forasteros in Oruro, 1683	141
5.9	Tribute Payments by Indian Males in Oruro, 1683	143
7.1	Ownership of Estates in Pilaya y Paspaya, 1725	175
7.2	Adult Male Indian Population of Pilaya y Paspaya, 1646, 1684, and 1725	179
7.3	Origins of Male Forasteros in Pilaya y Paspaya, 1646	182
7.4	Age of Indian Males in Pilaya y Paspaya, 1725	189

7.5	Origins of Male Forasteros in Pilaya y Paspaya, 1725	190
7.6	Marital Status of Indian Women Listed Separately in Pilaya y Paspaya, 1725	192
7.7	Age and Marital Status of Missing Male Yanaconas, Pilaya y Paspaya, 1725	193
Appendix 1	Quinto Real, Oruro, 1611–1730	209
Appendix 2	Population Distribution by Place of Residence, Pilaya y Paspaya, 1725	211

Acknowledgments

I have been aided by many people and institutions in the time I have been working on this book. A Fulbright-Hayes Fellowship and a summer stipend from the Tinker Foundation and Columbia University allowed me to do the initial research; two faculty grants from the University of New Hampshire made possible additional trips to archives in Bolivia. A Picker Fellowship from Smith College gave me course release time to work on the book and Smith's generous sabbatical policy finally allowed me to finish writing it.

I thank the directors and staffs of the Archivo General de la Nación (Buenos Aires), the Archivo General de Indias (Seville), the Archivo Histórico de La Paz, the Biblioteca Municipal de Oruro, the Biblioteca Nacional de España and the Biblioteca Nacional del Perú for their professional assistance. I am particularly indebted to the late Gunnar Mendoza, former Director of the Archivo Nacional de Bolivia, for helping me over the years with important research suggestions and historical insights.

I gratefully acknowledge the guidance of my professors from graduate school, Herbert Klein, Nicolás Sánchez-Albornoz, and Kenneth Maxwell. Lesley Gill, Brooke Larson, Enrique Tandeter, Maria Lagos, Clara López-Beltrán, Carola Echalar, Ramiro Condarco Morales, Karen Powers, Rene Arze, Harvey Lyons, and Benjamin Brody, provided many useful commentaries and suggestions while I was researching, writing, and revising this book. The final product has also benefited from careful readings by Erick Langer and Susan Ramírez, whose efforts I sincerely appreciated and took to heart. I also thank Jane Flanders, my editor at the University of Pittsburgh Press, for her meticulousness and sense of style.

Finally, this book might not ever have been imagined if my parents, Dave and Gladys Lachenbruch, hadn't loved to travel and introduced me to Latin America. It certainly would have been more difficult to complete if my husband, Dan, hadn't truly valued and respected my interests and commitments and gotten excited about them himself.

"They Eat from Their Labor"

Introduction

IN THE 1970s Raymond Williams observed that although political or cultural hegemony can never be totally pervasive and controlling, neither can most alternate forms of expression, or even protest, be considered truly independent of the dominant society.[1] Locked in an inescapable embrace with the governed, the ruler must accommodate in order to stay in power, while only rarely can the dominated really break free of the oppressor's clutches. Although Williams is discussing advanced capitalist society, his point is equally applicable to colonial Latin America. Over the course of several centuries, colonial powers did incorporate much of the material culture and world view of the colonized and even indigenous opposition eventually became structured by the new social system.

This book studies the development of an indigenous labor force in Upper Peru—present-day Bolivia—during the seventeenth and early eighteenth centuries. This subject is fundamental to the economic history of colonialism because changes in relations of production and the transformation of Andean conceptions of property were both the result of European colonization of the Andes and essential for the success of Spain's mercantile project. The study of labor also illuminates the process of cultural conflict inherent in colonialism. As with other aspects of colonial social life, the nature of work, its meaning, who was to do it, and under what circumstances, might have appeared obvious to the Spaniards but could not simply be imposed on the new society according to a Spanish template. Rather, forms of labor and relations of production evolved because of complex interactions and struggles between Spanish and Andean economic imperatives and ideologies. Some of the results of this unequal contest resembled Spanish institutions, others appeared Andean but had been transformed for Spanish purposes, and all were in some ways colonial amalgams controlled by the Spanish but also shaped by circumstances beyond their control.

My interest in labor in the Andes began when I first read about the *mita* system of forced labor for the Potosí mines. I was horrified by the sheer exploitation entailed in the labor draft that mobilized native people from sixteen provinces in Upper Peru and made them spend one year in seven mining silver in one of South America's bleakest regions.[2] However, the mita was only one way whereby a governmentally privileged group of Upper Peruvian entrepreneurs captured a work force, and its morality and practicality were frequently debated. Moreover, the mita was often a focus of a much larger philosophical and political debate about human nature, the use of force, and the development of a free market. These issues, already important in Spain before the settlement of America, took on new meaning when the Spaniards colonized the Andes. Now one society that had begun the transition to capitalism confronted another in which labor was not conceived of as a commodity and where markets generally had not developed.

Of course, the mita, or more generally the issue of extra-economic coercion, is also crucial to a more contemporary debate about the development of the world capitalist system and the role of nonwage labor in the colonial periphery in that development. This controversy has not arisen primarily over whether various forms of coerced and nonwage labor in the periphery were essential to the capital accumulation necessary for Europe's transition to a capitalist economy; most scholars agree that they were. Rather, the theoretical and political discussion has centered on the nature of the Latin American societies that played this role in the international system. Could they be considered capitalist while relations of production other than wage labor predominated? Could they be considered feudal while they were so obviously part of an international mercantile system, had no tradition of feudalism as it existed in Europe, and, even in the early colonial period, included members who were as least partially proletarianized?[3] Using various theoretical constructs, scholars have attempted to resolve this contradiction, often by explaining how modes of production "articulated" to create the multilayered, mixed economic systems of Spain's American colonies.[4]

Seeking to understand the colonial Latin American economy continues to be an important intellectual project because its development is central to the transformations of consciousness and identity that Andean people experienced as a result of colonialism. Furthermore, the dependency debate, in one form or another, is bound to last as long as the region remains underdeveloped. Whether one locates Latin America's transition to capitalism in the sixteenth century or in the late nineteenth and early twentieth centuries,[5] the emergence of a market economy, the types of relations of production, and the social differentiation that occurred in the colonial period were obviously crucial in creating the societies that exist in the region today. Some understanding of how underdevelopment evolved is still essential to changing the situation.

My research for this book has not convinced me that the colonial economic system in the Andes was capitalist: too many of the "workers" still had access to, or had control of, the means of production and therefore could not easily be converted into wage laborers. Nor would colonial entrepreneurs necessarily have found wage labor to be the most economical system. On the other hand, the economy was highly mercantilized, and a variety of new economic and social relations emerged that, although clearly not capitalist, had also never existed in the same configurations in precapitalist Europe. They were the result of the interaction and confrontation of the colonists' evolving capitalist project with the Andeans' own changing system of social and economic organization. It is this interaction and its varied outcomes that are the main subjects of this book.

A related focus is acculturation and the myriad possible changes in identity that resulted as Andean workers were drawn into a market economy. In the seventeenth century, many workers were immigrants who left the kin groups, or *ayllus*, through which they had access to land and community support and in which they participated in the spiritual rituals intrinsic to social life.[6] While certainly in some instances emigrating and working on a commercial estate or in a mining center meant completely severing ties with these communities of kin and becoming totally Hispanicized,[7] this was not invariably the case. Nor is it logical to assume that it should have been. For one thing, if that had occurred, large numbers of migrants would have played only very limited roles in shaping the colonial economy if their only option was to become workers and adopt Spanish customs. Second, reading backward, we know that even in the twentieth century highly class-conscious, politicized Bolivian mine workers have maintained strong ethnic identification.[8]

In fact, ethnohistorical studies show that rather than always representing a separation from ayllu and land, migrating and entering the labor force may have been a collective response among indigenous peoples to the disruptions of colonialism and a means of obtaining resources essential to reproducing community life. For example, Thierry Saignes has found instances in which seventeenth-century migrant laborers functioned as *mitimaes* and *llacturunas*, pre-Columbian agricultural colonists who provided highland ethnic groups with products from the lowlands.[9] What occurred, then, was something more intricate and convoluted than a simple progression from Andean society to Bolivian society (a process that is not even complete today). Acculturation there was, but sometimes in unexpected circumstances, often of unpredictable types, and certainly many people devised ways to maintain their ritual life and ethnic networks and used them to conspicuous advantage in newfound situations.

I explore these issues and others by studying two areas that were representative of the places migrants headed for during the seventeenth century: Oruro, an important silver mining center, and Pilaya y Paspaya, an agricultural province that was developed in response to market demand in Upper Peru's cities, particularly Potosí. I have chosen the years between 1600 and 1725 for this study because this period saw a mining boom and the creation of a regional commercial network in the Andes, followed by a severe decline in silver production and economic stagnation. Thus it is possible to examine the effects of these changes on demand for labor and how the Andean people coped with the vicissitudes of the market. Oruro and Pilaya y Paspaya also provide interesting comparisons over time because, while both were poles of attraction for immigrants, they were also quite different in the types of relations of production that developed, the impact of migration on the people who settled in each area, and how they tried to negotiate the situations to minimize their exploitation.

Oruro was a mining center that never had allotments of Indian forced laborers assigned to it. Its workers were not directly coerced, but responded to various types of economic pressures in going to work there. Potosí and Oruro were the only important seventeenth-century mining centers that were referred to as cities. Carangas, Porco, Esmoraca, San Antonio de Nuevo Mundo, each of which enjoyed a period of producing significant quantities of silver during the 1600s, could at most be considered towns, and were usually simply called mining camps. In 1607, a year after its official founding, Oruro was said to have an Indian population of about 18,000,[10] while in 1613 even the viceregal capital at Lima had a population of only 14,000.[11] The total population of La Paz in the early seventeenth century is not known, but in 1628 it was said to have only 200 adult male Spanish residents.[12] This was fewer than the 520 who lived in Oruro in 1607.[13]

Part of the reason for Oruro's growth was that it was a commercial center on the road that linked Potosí to the Pacific port of Arica, from which silver was shipped to Lima. Another overland route linked the city to Lima via La Paz, Puno, and Cuzco. Oruro's geographical situation in the center of Upper Peru on the *altiplano*, or high plateau, was ideal for promoting contacts among the different groups that made up colonial society. The city was a hub for colonial mercantile activity but also central to the Andean world; it lay in an area that had been the heart of the Aymara kingdom of the Quillaca-Asanaques before the Inca conquest and then became a strategic stronghold for the Incas. (See chapter 1.) The economic opportunities and variety of people in Oruro promoted a rich urban life in which acculturation was common and social differentiation was pronounced, but the proximity to important areas of indigenous culture also enabled the Indians to maintain ties with their kin on the altiplano and to participate in communal landholding and religious rituals. All of this meant that there was considerable variety as well in the extent to which native people depended on remunerated labor and in their leverage with Oruro's mine operators.

Today the section of the Bolivian department of Chuquisaca that was the province of Pilaya y Paspaya during the colonial period seems amazingly remote from Oruro and the high plateau. The distance must have seemed even greater in the seventeenth century; yet, since the Inca period at least, colonists from ethnic groups near Oruro had used land in northern Pilaya y Paspaya to provide their communities with food that could not be grown in the highlands.[14] Outside this northern area, however, the Incas had considered the region a perilous frontier zone because it was home to people, referred to as Chiriguanos, whose economy was based primarily on hunting and gathering and whose military resistance had prevented Inca domination. The Spaniards were hardly more successful in imposing their rule in the area until the Peruvian viceroy, Francisco de Toledo, initiated a concerted pacification program in the 1570s.

In the early seventeenth century, after the development of silver mining in Potosí, Pilaya y Paspaya's southern valleys became valuable commercial property as landowners began producing wine to sell in the mining center. Like mine owners and refiners in Oruro, *hacendados* in the area were never favored by the government with labor drafts, but they were able to capture a work force of Andean migrants fleeing the mita of Potosí or looking for a means of earning the money necessary to pay their tribute to the government.

Once in the province, immigrants came into contact not only with other Andean migrants similar to themselves but also with black and mulatto slaves and free people of color. They also encountered "acculturated" Chiriguanos and their descendants who had settled down in the area as renters and farm laborers. Pilaya y Paspaya was well integrated into the internal colonial economic circuit, while still retaining many characteristics of a frontier area. Life and work in this type of setting, where contact among a number of ethnic groups was common, ultimately resulted in acculturation and miscegenation for many of the descendants of migrants to the region. In fact, these were among the defensive strategies used for coping with hacendados (and the colonial officials who supported them) who, if not rewarded with contingents of coerced workers, did everything in their power to enserf the ones who came voluntarily.

This book presents Pilaya y Paspaya and Oruro as case studies within a larger historical and conceptual context. Chapter 1 discusses the Andean and Iberian worlds on the eve of the Spanish invasion of the Western Hemisphere. Particularly, it focuses on each society's political economy and ideologies of labor and gender as crucial to understanding the evolution of relations of production in the colonial setting. I include a discussion of gender because conceptions about the appropriate roles of men and women are shaped by economic organization, and in turn influence it. This was especially true in the Andes, where the household was the basic economic unit in the pre-Columbian period and remained crucial to social reproduction after the conquest.

The next two chapters explore what happened when Iberians and Andeans met on the uneven ground of colonialism. Chapter 2 studies the development of the colonial economy in the Andes and the various approaches to organizing labor adopted by the colonists. In some respects, these turned out to be compromises between the philosophical proposals of Spanish intellectuals and the crude demands of colonial entrepreneurs. But, more significantly, they were elaborated in the process of struggle and accommodation that went on between Andeans and Europeans. Chapter 3, on the patterns and causes of the massive indigenous migrations that occurred in the seventeenth century, looks more specifically at native responses to colonial economic and social policy.

Oruro is the focus of chapters 4 and 5. Chapter 4 studies labor in the mining industry over a little more than a hundred years, focusing on workers' connections to the land and their kin groups and how these affected their efforts to resist proletarianization. Chapter 5 examines the composition of the city's Indian population in 1683, the year of an important colonial census, and specifically compares two groups of migrants to the city, the *yanaconas* and the *forasteros*, in terms of their economic activity, dependence on paid labor, and apparent separation from Andean society.

Chapter 6 takes a close look at Andean women and how their participation in the market reflected the growing class division among urban Indians. It finds that social stratification based on class was related to family and community support; those with the most extensive kin networks were also most likely to succeed in the colonial economy.

Finally, the last chapter examines Pilaya y Paspaya and changing patterns of migration and labor in the province between the 1640s and the 1720s. Compared with Oruro, relations of production in the frontier zone seemed less "capitalist," either because workers were sent to haciendas to work by their village leaders who then collected their wages, or because they were held in virtual servitude by Hispanic landowners. Yet, ironically, the Andean migrants were also more acculturated, albeit in different ways, than those in Oruro.

The conclusion summarizes the book's main findings, emphasizing how class divisions, kin networks, and access to land, as well as Andean and Spanish conceptions of gender and approaches to labor, all interacted to create the diversity of the work force and of indigenous society in general.

· 1 ·

Societies in Transition

Iberians and Andeans

THE EARLY MODERN period in Spain was a time of mercantile activity and the beginnings of industrial manufacturing that tentatively challenged older economic patterns based on sheep raising and manorial agriculture. The southern Andean region was also undergoing change. Beginning at least as early as the time of Aymara rule and accelerating under the Inca state, increased economic differentiation began to undermine a social system that relied on cooperation and sharing among extended kin groups. Each society had its own myths that buttressed its social structure, and in both cultures these myths began to change as established theories were adjusted or alternatives put forward to accommodate new economic and social relations.

To begin to untangle the ways in which colonial institutions were affected by the meeting of Andean and Iberian institutions and ideas, and the conflict between them, this chapter examines the history of the Andean region and of Spain, stressing the changes that were occurring in attitudes toward property, labor, and production before the invasion of the New World. This comparison reveals the cultural and material distance that might be expected between two societies with different modes of production and cultural traditions. However, it also shows points of congruence. Growing social stratification in Upper Peru had prepared the ground for the penetration of mercantile capitalism, while aspects of Andean economic organization resembled estatementary rural Spanish society. The chapter also focuses on Spanish and Andean ideologies of gender, since beliefs about the nature of men and women are shaped by material and social conditions, as they themselves structure economic activity.

Social Change and Ideological Adjustment in the Andes

A striking aspect of Andean thought is how it could be stretched and adjusted to include what might appear to be extremely different social arrangements under the same principles. Key examples of this elasticity are the concepts of *reciprocity* and *redistribution*, and the variety of situations to which they apparently were applied. While reciprocity might refer to equal exchanges of labor, glaringly unequal relationships could also be described as reciprocal, and redistribution might mean receiving a portion of one's own crop as a gift. Of course, it was not simply a question of phrasing drastically altered economic relations as forms of cooperative effort, or calling expropriation *generosity*, because words certainly had to be backed up by material rewards and, ultimately, by force of arms as well. But, in proper combination with the judicious use of resources and military strength, accepted principles of Andean social organization proved remarkably resilient throughout the pre-Columbian period and were even employed by perceptive colonial *encomenderos* to smooth their dealings with the native elite.[1]

Ecological Complementarity and Andean Social Structure

To understand how all this worked, one must begin with geography, because many of the principles that governed human relationships in the pre-Columbian Andes were related to a system designed to maximize the benefits wrung from a variegated and extremely harsh environment. In this system, the principles of reciprocity and redistribution bound together highland and lowland residents and enabled the delivery of food and other products from diverse geographical regions without recourse to formal markets or a medium of exchange.

The rugged southern Andean region is comprised of a series of micro-environments at different altitudes, and the climatic extremes, treacherous mountain passes, and bleak high-altitude plains must have posed a serious challenge to European newcomers accustomed to living primarily in one ecological zone. Even in the late twentieth century, a visitor traveling to Oruro by bus, not on foot or horseback, from Bolivia's capital city of La Paz is impressed by the city's desolate location. Leaving the natural hollow that shelters La Paz, one's vehicle first climbs to the flat, exposed *altiplano*, or high plateau, a tableland with altitudes between 3,800 and 4,000 meters above sea level. Having leveled off, the bus then continues for several hours through a dry landscape of beiges and tans occasionally punctuated by adobe settlements and salt lakes. The high plateau shimmers under a blistering sun in the daytime and freezes as soon as the sun goes down in the evening. Especially at night, visitors arriving in Oruro who are not accustomed to Bolivian geography can feel that they have found a much appreciated refuge in a vast and strange universe.

In fact, like most places on the high plateau, Oruro is not very far from regions with dramatically different environments. After spending the night in Oruro, one can set out again the next morning and have lunch in a broad valley with springlike temperatures or even in lush lowlands with high humidity and tropical vegetation.

The altiplano on which Oruro is located is a vast tableland extending for almost 800 kilometers between the eastern and western ranges of the Andes Mountains that divide on the Peruvian side of Lake Titicaca (see map 1). On the western side of the high plateau, the sheer Cordillera Occidental forms a formidable barrier to the Pacific coast, although a number of mountain passes allow access to the sea. In the east, the Cordillera Oriental is less forbidding and is broken by numerous valleys. Some of these, such as the Cochabamba Valley and those surrounding the modern cities of Sucre and Tarija, are relatively broad. With altitudes between about 2,000 and 2,800

MAP 1. Bolivia

meters above sea level, they have soil and climatic conditions suitable for growing grains and temperate-zone fruits and vegetables. Other valleys, such as the *yungas* northeast of La Paz, are so steep that in a journey of less than 80 kilometers from the capital, bus passengers first ascend to a high point of 4,725 meters above sea level and then, with knuckles white from clutching arm rests or fellow passengers, almost literally dive through clouds and mist into a world of tropical humidity with altitudes as low as 1,000 meters.

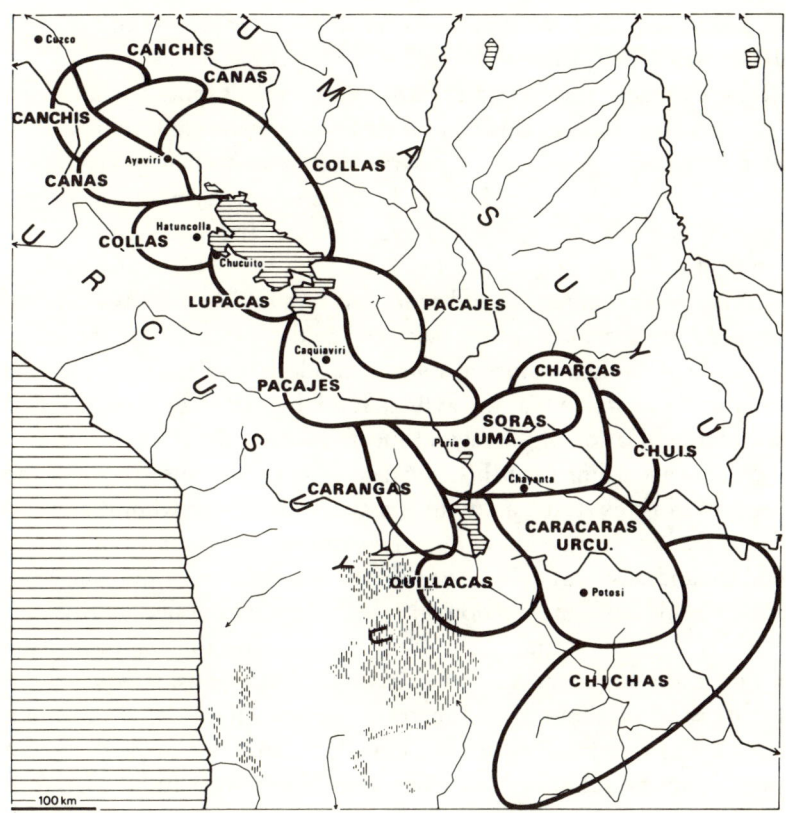

MAP 2. The Aymara Kingdoms

Source: Therese Bouysse-Cassagne, "L'espace aymara: Urco et Uma," *Annales E.S.C.,* 5–6 (1978): 1059.

From approximately 1200 A.D., this spectacularly diverse environment was home to a number of Aymara-speaking social and political groups. There were at least twelve distinct Aymara territories (see map 2) that were well fortified militarily and ruled by regional kings or nobles.[2] Like other Andean ethnic groups, the Aymara made the best of the varied geography by cultivating agricutual lands at different altitudes to provide the staples of their diet. In this system, most communities had their primary settlements on the sides of highland valleys or on the altiplano. Through access to the high plateau, or *puna*, and lands at slightly lower altitudes (3,000–4,000 meters above sea level), sometimes called *suni*, people were able to raise herds of alpacas and llamas and also grow various types of root crops and potatoes. Indeed, this combination of camelids and tubers, coupled with the technology to preserve both, was sufficient to guarantee subsistence; but even before the time of the Aymara kingdoms, lands in lower valleys provided vegetables, maize, coca leaf, cotton, tropical fruits, and chilies for highland polities.[3]

The most basic social and economic unit in the Andes was the extended family, which in turn belonged to the larger group known as the *ayllu*. Although historical sources, modern scholars, and Andeans themselves all agree that the ayllu is fundamental to the political and social organization of the region, the meaning of the word varies considerably according one's historical context and perspective.[4] For the purposes of this study, an ayllu is a group of people who in a broad sense are kin because they trace their origins to one spiritual or legendary ancestor. An ayllu also has a territorial dimension, since the group holds lands in common, although they are not necessarily contiguous. Finally, membership implies certain responsibilities to the group and a willingness to participate in rituals considered essential for its spiritual renewal and material reproduction.[5] It was through their ayllus that families obtained products grown in areas that were more than several hours' walk from their homes. Ayllu-held lands in distant regions were farmed by agricultural colonists (termed both *mitimaes* and *llacturuna*) who supplied the central communities in the highlands with products from tropical and temperate environments. For instance, the Quillaca-Asanaques, an Aymara kingdom occupying territory on the altiplano just south of Oruro, had mitimaes in temperate valleys of Cochabamba, Yamparaez, and Pilaya y Paspaya.[6]

Above the ayllu level, Aymara society had a dual structure that divided human communities and even the Andean geography into complementary halves. Each kingdom, as well as each village or settlement, was composed of two moieties, or *parcialidades*: a superior one called *hanansaya* and one of inferior status known as *hurinsaya*.[7] Each kingdom had two leaders, known as *kurakas*, or *mallkus*, one for each parcialidad, and on the district and village levels there were usually also leaders for both hurinsaya and hanansaya.[8] In addition to the parcilidades into which every town was divided, within the entire Aymara territory there was a social-geographical division that roughly paralleled the physical separation of the Andes into two separate ranges. The kingdoms (or portions of kingdoms) located along the western side of the altiplano, near the Cordillera Occidental, were referred to as *urcosuyu*, while those on the eastern side of the high plateau were known as *umasuyu*.[9]

Archaeologists and ethnohistorians studying the period before Inca rule on the north coast of Peru and in Ecuador have found evidence of considerable economic specialization in these regions; conceivably, there were full-time merchants and various objects were used as currency.[10] However, most scholars believe that in the southern Andes goods that families could not produce for themselves were not distributed through a market in which there was a medium of exchange, or even through a barter system.[11] Rather, the economy of most groups evidently operated according to the Andean principles of reciprocity and redistribution.

Webs of reciprocal obligations bound together members of the same ayllu, but one's degree of consanguinity and social position determined the nature of these obligations. Some reciprocity existed among equals, or near equals, as when two brothers and their families helped a third to clear land before planting. But the Andean ideology of reciprocity managed to incorporate many relationships that were both more distant and considerably less equal, including those between kurakas and commoners. Kurakas were responsible for the physical and spiritual well-being of the people of their communities. Their obligations included annual ceremonies to reaffirm the rights of families to plots of community land that were conceived of as under the kuraka's control.[12] Leaders were also responsible for distributing communal surpluses in times of shortage or other crises. In return, the ayllu members *reciprocated* by tilling the lands of their kurakas and religious leaders and by taking turns or shifts (*mit'as*) working at various tasks either for the leaders or for the group as a whole.[13]

The system of colonization of different ecological niches must be understood within this context. Work performed by mitimaes in the lowland farming areas, in the ideology of reciprocity, was considered to be part of their mutual responsibilities to the entire group. Even if they were absent for many years, or left permanently, mitimaes apparently retained their rights and privileges in their home communities. We know, for instance, that among the Chupaychu in Huanuco in the central highlands of Peru, at least some mitimaes even kept their homes and lands while they worked in the salt lakes or cotton fields.[14]

Goods produced in these agricultural colonies could be exchanged without markets because of the other ideal of Andean social organization: redistribution. Kurakas were responsible not only for allocating lands to villagers but also for periodically redistributing some of the community's wealth. In fact, the kuraka's generosity was essential to maintaining good relations with the people who produced his wealth—who were, after all, his kin. For instance, a leader was expected to provide workers with relatively lavish food and drink when they planted his fields.[15] It was also through the principle of redistribution that members of the community and other kurakas and leaders received goods produced by mitimaes. The kuraka had the prerogative of redistributing goods that had been produced for the community by the colonists, just as he used some of the food that community members grew for him when he feasted them at harvest time.[16]

The Mobilization of Labor and the Creation of Social Inequality

As has been suggested, in a society without money or a means of exchange, labor was all-important, since only by working or by mobilizing the labor of others could one acquire the necessities of survival. The more ties of obligation one had to other ayllu members—that is, to kin—the more labor one could count on, therefore a greater likelihood of prosperity. This type of reciprocal cooperation among relative equals, known as *ayni*, was essential to reproducing life as people knew it. But, since one could not do without the labor of one's relatives, one was always in their debt. Karen Spalding points out that this dependent relationship was bound to engender resentment and competition—an ambivalence reflected in Andean language. For instance, the Quechua word meaning "to take revenge on," *aynicapunacuni*, has as its root *ayni*, which means equivalence or an equal exchange of labor.[17]

Labor for kurakas was in a different category, since the specialized functions of leaders exempted them from common ayni obligations. Furthermore, as far as is known, there was no tribute in kind in the Andes. Rather, leaders acquired wealth by mobilizing labor to cultivate land, to colonize new areas, or to undertake projects such as irrigation systems that increased productivity.[18] Although there were different types of workers and various means of raising a labor force, the community as a whole commonly worked in a leader's fields at planting and harvest times. On these occasions, not only did the kuraka provide food and drink but also there was generally a festive atmosphere, with music and religious acts to ensure the fruitfulness of future harvests.[19] If labor help in the form of ayni was essential simply for the ordinary family to sustain itself, the work of the mass of the people, even if disguised by reciprocal gestures, enabled major kurakas to accumulate considerable material wealth.

An inspection of the province of Chucuito in 1567 by the royal official Garci Diez de San Miquel gives us some idea of the income received by the most important Aymara lords and how they acquired the labor power of their subjects. The leaders of the Qari and Kusi dynasties were kurakas of all the Lupaqa, an Aymara kingdom on the western side of Lake Titicaca. Consequently, they received resources from five Lupaqa communities in addition to Chucuito. However, the people of Chucuito *alone* annually did the following for their leaders: produced seventeen pieces of fine cloth (wool provided by the kurakas was spun and woven by the women of their ayllus); planted and harvested 150 *tupus* of land (a tupu was the amount of land considered necessary to sustain a domestic unit); and provided 107 *indios de servicio*, who were mostly mitimaes working for the kurakas in other ecological zones but also included twelve domestic servants.[20]

In addition to the mitimaes from Chucuito, two other Lupaqa communities provided these leaders with workers known as *yanas*, or *yanaconas*. Early colonial chroniclers described yanas as a servile (perhaps slave) sector of Inca society that came into being when a group rebelled against the Inca state and was pressed into service. Their status was assumed to be hereditary; unlike others in Andean society, even mitimaes, yanas neither belonged to ayllus nor had any of the rights or responsibilities of membership in an extended kin group. However, John Murra argues that yanaconas probably had more varied origins and status than most colonial observers believed. We now know that yanaconas existed before the Inca period; Murra suggests that the emergence of the group, at least among the Lupaqa, may have been related to an increased division of labor in agriculture and grazing activities. Furthermore, at least in some instances, only certain children of yanas assumed their parents' status, and instead of being from a subjugated minority, they often came from the same ethnic groups as the people they served.[21]

Whatever the origins of the yanaconas, and they may have been numerous, their existence and the fact that some rulers had access to the production of fifty or a hundred times more land than the ordinary family clearly indicates the development of class differentiation within Aymara society. On the village level, however, differences between kurakas and their subjects were probably much less pronounced, and the personal nature of the redistributive relationship no doubt minimized people's sense of exploitation. However, with the hegemony of the Inca state, inequality reached deeper into community life.

Imperial Rule and Ideological Reinterpretation

The Inca were one of a number of Quechua-speaking groups in the southern Andes in the fifteenth century. About 1440, under Emperor Pachacuti, they began expanding from their home base in the area of Cuzco and through a combination of military skill and administrative genius managed to incorporate under their power a region extending from present-day Ecuador in the north to northern Chile and Argentina in the south.[22] Part of the brilliance of Inca political organization was the ability to accept the diversity of the local Andean cultures and, instead of attempting to impose homogeneity, to build on and expand local and regional institutions, and thus to create a state of great geographical extension. While constructing roads and political centers to unify the empire, the Incas wisely (or through necessity) left much of the administration to local leaders.[23]

Another accomplishment was ideological: the conquerors from Cuzco managed to take the traditional language of reciprocity and redistribution and to stretch and extend these concepts until they took on new meaning. Reciprocity and redistribution were activities linking kin, and the Inca specifically took the idiom of kinship, the organizing principle of the ayllus, and used it to help them build and control an empire. Inca ideology fashioned a new "family" that linked all Andean peoples but gave imperial leaders a special relationship with the rest of the "relatives." They were considered to be children of the sun and the moon, which in turn had been created by the god Viracocha.[24] Previously autonomous kin groups were now expected to function as administrative units of the Inca state, and that role was reinforced by the construction of a shared history. The only problem with this approach, as Irene Silverblatt points out, was that by associating the state with older kinship structures, the Incas constantly reminded conquered groups of their original loyalties and the independence they had lost.[25]

As regional societies were subdued by the Incas, conquered groups must have fearfully anticipated the demands and sacrifices that their new rulers would exact from them. Certainly Inca domination did mean that a portion of each community's labor power was no longer used locally, but was siphoned off either for the state itself or for the benefit of individual Inca rulers. But, as in any society with a considerable degree of social differentiation, the burden of the new demands was not shared equally but was passed on by local and regional leaders to commoners. In fact, as we shall see, rulers were often willing to cooperate with the Incas because of the largesse displayed by imperial lords in their dealings with them.

Furthermore, perhaps the exploitation of conquered people was disguised to some extent, if not mitigated, because the Incas tailored Andean concepts to fit their objectives. In this new interpretation, the

Inca, as the descendant of the sun, was described as having ultimate control over all worldly property. Thus, when territory was conquered, the Inca determined which lands should be worked by the local people for the benefit of the state and the gods, and which portions would be granted to local lords and ayllus. In this way, lands that had originally belonged to the community through the kuraka were now returned to them through the generosity of the invaders. Labor service for the empire became a reciprocation for the Incas' redistribution of territory obtained through conquest.[26]

Aymara-speaking groups responded in different ways to the Inca invasions. In the area of Lake Titicaca, there was fierce military resistance, while the leaders of kingdoms further south apparently accepted Inca authority more willingly in return for certain concessions. In granting these concessions and phrasing them in terms of traditional Andean generosity, the Inca state was able to win the support of a large sector of the Aymara elite that was to prove crucial in their continued campaigns. For instance, the kurakas of the Charcas, Caracaras, Chuis, and Chichas were not only feted by the Inca leaders and showered with gifts, they were made officers in the Inca armies and their soldiers were given the responsibility of pushing the Inca frontier to the north.[27]

Other Aymara groups were not given military duties, but their leaders nonetheless received honors and material rewards sufficient to make them support the Inca program with various types of "humanitarian" aid. Colque, the primary mallku, or kuraka, of the Quillaca-Asanaques of Paria at the time of Inca domination, was given the honorary title of "Inca Colque," and his heir, Guarache, received lands for his personal benefit in Cochabamba.[28] In return, the Quillaca-Asanaques supplied mitimaes and workers for many Inca projects. Quillaca and Asanaque commoners tended royal herds of llamas and worked in Cuzco as masons, stonecutters, and weavers. The group also supplied mitimaes for Inca coca fields in the Yungas.[29]

The use of mitimaes is one example of how Andean institutions were expanded by the Incas until they were barely recognizable. Now members of different ethnic groups were sent as mitimaes and *mit'ayoc* (who were rotated annually) into various regions, not to grow food for their own people but to produce a surplus that could be used by the state. Mitimaes were also used for political and military purposes, to settle areas that were sparsely populated, or to create nuclei of colonists loyal to the Inca empire in regions where the indigenous inhabitants offered resistance. Perhaps the most extensive example of using mitimaes to farm state lands was in the Cochabamba Valley, where the Inca Huayna Capac (1493–1527) was said to have settled 14,000 colonists from many different ethnic groups. Among these temporary and permanent settlers were people from highland areas extending from Cuzco to Chile.[30]

Gender Ideology and the Inca State

Related to the process of class formation and differential access to resources were changes in gender relations under the Incas. As explained by Irene Silverblatt, on whose work this description draws heavily, in the pre-Inca Andes, gender was a very important organizational principle shaping religious conceptions and socioeconomic patterns. Men and women conceived of themselves as the descendants of ancestors of the same sex through whom they often inherited political and economic power. This gender parallelism also extended to religious cults: men often, but not exclusively, worshipped male gods, while women frequently propitiated female ones.[31]

Mirroring this division of the spiritual world was a more prosaic division of labor on the household level. The essential tasks for survival were considered the responsibility of both male and female family members, and all had to protect the welfare of the group. Although the assignment of tasks by sex was not so rigid that it could not be deviated from, in the southern Andes women generally wove cloth, herded animals, and sowed fields after men had prepared the ground with hoes and planting sticks. In addition to agricultural activities, men worked in construction and did military service.[32]

Under the Incas, gender ideology was altered to reflect changing gender relations, much as concepts of redistribution and reciprocity had changed to bolster the ruling group's power. In the Andes, as in other societies elsewhere in the world, a shift from kin-based organization to the class divisions of state organization apparently entailed a deterioration in the status of women.[33] But in constructing their new discourse on gender, the Incas continued to rely on the vocabulary of kinship, maintaining that all men were related to the Inca who was the son of the sun, while all women were kin of the *coya*, or queen, who was the daughter of the moon. Women were priestesses for the moon and other female dieties, and in some instances enjoyed political power equivalent to that of men of their class. But, as Silverblatt points out, while this system seemed to connect all people to divinity, "some humans were closer kin to the gods than others."[34] It was the elite women of Cuzco, followed by regional noblewomen, who enjoyed religious and political power and had the wealth to practice traditional Andean generosity toward the women they ruled. Furthermore, in the Inca system, the male hierarchy descending from the sun was considered superior to the apparently equivalent female hierarchy. The Inca was the ruler of all people; the coya had authority only over women.[35]

Male political power and authority over women was demonstrated by imperial use of women as tribute and rewards. Among conquered groups, the most physically perfect girls between the ages of ten and twelve were selected to be segregated from their communities and to live as virgins until imperial authorities decided their fates. Some were given in marriage to imperial or local leaders; others remained chaste and officiated at holy places; some were even sacrificed to the gods. The *acllas*, as they were called, have been compared to yanaconas because they were separated from their ayllus to serve the Inca state. Like yanaconas, the acllas have also been associated with a growing division of labor because they frequently worked as weavers.[36]

However, Silverblatt maintains that to look only at this economic function of the acllas is to ignore important evidence about Inca attitudes toward gender. First of all, only young girls were separated from their families and given as gifts to important rulers or designated as full-time religious functionaries. Young men were not given to noblewomen, no matter how important, as rewards for their allegiance to the empire, nor were there cases of men's sexual expression being controlled by the state.[37] Furthermore, the Incas used the idiom of gender complementarity to disguise conquest and submission. The Incas' conquest of another ethnic group was to be viewed as a harmonious marriage, with the victors taking women of the dominated group as concubines or wives.[38]

It is difficult to know how much or which parts of the Inca version of Andean ideology was accepted by the conquered peoples. We do know that while some regional leaders revolted against Inca domination, others apparently loyally supported the empire. The perceptions, or even the actions, of peasants, who on a local level produced the surplus for the state, are more obscure. It is possible that the ideology of reciprocity and redistribution might have been approaching its practical limits for accommodating economic and social change. Perhaps class differences and private access to property were becoming too great to be subsumed under these accepted principles, and society was near an economic and ideological breaking point that would have required a new legitimating philosophy. Likewise, if actual material and political inequality between men and women became too glaring, ideas of parallelism and complementarity might have been abandoned. But, of course, society could not develop undisturbed because in 1532 the Inca empire was invaded by the Spaniards.

Developments after the invasion give some indication of local societies' attitudes toward the Inca state. That more than a few ethnic groups were willing to make alliances with the Europeans at least indicates that they were not so wedded to the Inca vision that they would not abandon it if it seemed wise to do so. Furthermore, the large number of mitimaes who sought to sever their connections with their highland communities or the imperial capital also suggests that the language of reciprocity could not successfully disguise the fact that there were advantages to autonomy for the lowland dwellers, and that highland residents may have needed the agricultural colonists more than the mitimaes needed their distant kin.[39]

Spanish Economy and Society in the Fifteenth and Sixteenth Centuries

Like the Inca empire, at the end of the fifteenth century the Spanish Catholic monarchy had recently brought vast new territories under its control when it captured Andalusia from Islamic Spaniards, who had held it for almost 800 years. The final defeat of the Moors in 1492 was bolstered by an appropriate belief system, just as Inca cosmology explained the group's supremacy and attempted to convince its new subjects of its legitimacy. Unlike the Inca, however, who largely addressed their ideology to newly conquered groups, the Catholic Iberians' call for a racially and religiously pure Spain was used to mobilize Christians for the last battle to drive out the infidel. Its message was that military force was entirely justified if used against an ethnic minority who rejected the true religion.

The connection between this intolerance and militarism and the approach of the Spanish conquistadores to the Americas is clear and eventually became the substance of British propaganda against their colonialist competitors. However, the conquering Iberians perceived native Americans not only through a prism of religious orthodoxy and chauvinism. Other models of social and economic organization, models that emphasized personal freedom and market forces, also shaped colonists' thoughts and actions in the New World. The existence of such divergent ideological approaches suggests that material and cultural life in Spain itself was in a state of flux during this period. In fact, there are indications of change and conflict in almost every aspect of Spanish life, from attitudes toward confessional and ethnic minorities to discussions about the proper social roles for women and conflicts about the use of land and the mobilization of labor.

Back to the Future: Religious Orthodoxy and Underdevelopment in Spain

Many aspects of the xenophobia and ethnocentrism attributed to early modern Spain were of relatively recent origin. The fifteenth century was a period of growing religious orthodoxy: not only did it see the defeat of the kingdom of Granada, but also in the 1480s the Inquisition began to attack converted Jews (known as New Christians or *conversos*) who were believed to still practice Judaism.[40] Official policy hardened further in the sixteenth century when Spain's King Charles V, the Holy Roman emperor, became the primary defender of Catholicism against German princes who had become Lutherans and were attempting to secede from the empire.[41]

Although from the eighth century on the Christians had sporadically pursued the reconquest of Spain from the Moslems, this did not mean that the Iberian peninsula was in a constant state of war—in fact, periods of fighting alternated with periods of peaceful coexistence, or *convivencia*. While there was always tension, and different ethnic groups tended to live in relatively segregated neighborhoods and were of different classes, there was nonetheless a long tradition of diversity in Spanish society. The historical experience of interaction and even intermarriage with people from different cultures influenced the philosophical and moral positions that some Catholic Spaniards adopted regarding natives of the Americas.[42] Others, for whom moral considerations were not primary, because of the diversity of the Iberian peninsula could still picture themselves as part of a multiracial society in the Americas, albeit one in which their supremacy was assumed.

In addition to increasing xenophobia and intolerance, the official attack on Jews and New Christians had profound economic repercussions in Iberia. Heavily involved in commerce and various types of investment, conversos took large amounts of capital out of the country when they fled in the wake of the Inquisition.[43] Official anti-Semitism also retarded the development of capitalism among Old Christians, who became wary of engaging in trade because it was considered a Jewish occupation. According to Jaime Vicens Vives, this emphasis placed on "purity of the blood" reinforced, at least superficially, the values of *hidalguía*, which presumably included an aversion to manual labor and all forms of trade.[44] In fact, many nobles had long been engaged in various types of commerce, and many "hereditary" titles had actually been purchased, in some cases by New Christians.[45]

If bourgeois activities were at least theoretically eschewed by the nobility, the status attached to possession of large estates was reinforced. The Castilian landscape at the turn of the fifteenth century was dominated by huge landholdings. While exact statistics on ownership are difficult to verify, land concentration had certainly increased among the nobility, the clergy, and military orders as a result of the distribution of lands seized from the Moors. Other large holdings had been gradually consolidated through encroachment on common lands and the possessions of vulnerable peasants.[46]

Yet, despite the importance of landownership, agriculture languished. Royal policy favored sheep raising and gave the organization of herders, known as the Mesta, pasturage privileges that resulted in the destruction of much farmland.[47] Although there was an increase in land under cultivation at the beginning of the sixteenth century, production was insufficient during the bad harvests of 1502–1509, and grains had to be imported. Government efforts to prevent famine by establishing maximum prices for wheat further impoverished peasant producers and made them less able to expand cultivation or modernize agricultural techniques.[48] To make matters worse, although some of the fine merino wool produced on Iberian ranches was sold to textile producers in Spain, particularly Catalonia, the Mesta gained crown support for more lucrative exports of raw wool to Flanders, France, Italy, and England. By the end of the fifteenth century, domestic textiles were being eclipsed by finer and less expensive imported cloth, and Spain was reduced to being primarily an exporter of raw wool.[49]

Politically, since 1479 Castile had been officially joined to the kingdom of Aragon, a process begun by the marriage of Ferdinand and Isabella ten years earlier; however, the unity was perhaps less real than that in the huge area incorporated into the Inca empire. Economically, the kingdom of Aragon, and especially Catalonia, remained oriented toward trade in the Mediterranean; Castile's commerce was in the Atlantic. While the Incas had ordered the construction of a royal road to link new outposts of their far-flung empire with Cuzco, extremely poor communications were the rule in Spain. Restrictive Castilian commercial policies exacerbated the isolation: in some instances products from Aragon faced the same tariffs and marketing barriers in Castile as did foreign goods.[50]

Alternative Perspectives: Protoliberalism and Attitudes Toward Labor

Yet, within the Spain of rural property and aristocratic aspirations there were people who offered an alternative view of society. Spain had slowed socioeconomic change, not stopped it, and the work of Spanish Renaissance thinkers shows clearly that modern economic thought was challenging older feudal conceptions of society. As a group, I refer to the writers who countered feudal conceptions of society as protoliberals—*proto* because, while they espoused liberal positions such as the freedom of the individual and the inviolability of private property, they predated more complete philosophical formulations of liberalism; indeed, they articulated their positions before capitalism, with which liberalism is generally associated, was well established in Spain.[51] Nonetheless, the very fact of a debate about the organization of economic life indicates that despite the apparent revalorization of noble ideals and traditional sources of wealth, capitalist relations of production were developing in the Iberian peninsula.

Much of this protoliberal writing on political economy in sixteenth-century Spain deals with labor, since many analysts of Spain's situation had concluded that more productive use of human resources was the key to increased prosperity. According to José Antonio Maravall, in the Middle Ages work was considered to be a moral duty but not a means of social improvement. Furthermore, in the medieval period it was generally believed that if the common people had a comfortable existence they would only become derelict in their duties and succumb to various vices.[52] In the sixteenth century, while aristocratic ideology still maintained that noble status would be degraded by manual labor, influential writers, such as Juan Luis Vives, were extolling the virtues of labor as a means of counteracting antisocial tendencies and developing individual potential.[53] Others emphasized that a comfortable standard of living was necessary for workers to do their work well and that honest labor could be a means of changing one's station in life as one acquired greater wealth.[54]

Along with the exaltation of labor went virulent attacks on idleness. Some of these probably reflected an increased demand for labor,[55] a still fragmented labor market, and bad communications: there might be an excess of workers in one region and a shortage in another. The roads of one area could be clogged with vagabonds and beggars who, authorities feared, might turn to banditry, while in another zone a scarcity of workers might have a detrimental effect on production. Particularly, a shortage of skilled artisans was aggravated by the expulsion of the Jews and the flight of the conversos. In fact, in the early sixteenth century the royal government made efforts to attract foreign artisans.⁵⁶ But, unlike earlier periods when writers had generally viewed idleness as the *cause* of poverty, many now agreed with Sancho de Moncada, a professor of religion at the University of Toledo, that people were often idle because "no hay en que ganar de comer" (there is no way to earn their bread).⁵⁷

As Sánchez-Albornoz notes, this shift in thinking about labor reflected a changed conception of the nature of human beings and of social organization. In the older corporate, or estatementary conception, some people or social groups were considered superior to others, but not as a matter of chance, opportunity, or personal volition. Rather, it was the natural order of things as organized by the creator. Servitude, even slavery, was morally acceptable because it was believed that the lowest orders could and should serve the good of society at large.⁵⁸

By the sixteenth century, another current of thought had become common in Spain, this one emphasizing the freedom of human beings to direct their own lives.⁵⁹ For thinkers of this school, human freedom was closely related to the idea of the market in which commodities were exchanged according to the free operation of the law of supply and demand. Martín de Azpilcueta, a sixteenth-century legal scholar from the University of Salamanca, was among the first to discuss labor as a commodity that could be sold, like all other commodities, according to market demand.⁶⁰ Those who subscribed to this theory opposed any form of monopoly or combination, such as guilds, that would prevent prices from finding what was considered to be their true level. This type of thinking was widespread enough that in 1551 the Cortes of Madrid proposed the prohibition of organizations of artisans because they tended to make products more expensive.⁶¹

By the second half of the sixteenth century, wage labor was the rule in urban areas and was common even in the countryside in Castile.⁶² Although the reasons are complex, the following factors contributed to this change. The elimination of legal serfdom in the fifteenth century (1481 in Castile, 1486 in Catalonia) lifted one barrier to the mobility of the work force and allowed some part of the population to seek employment in cities. At the same time, many nobles were only too happy to dispense with the feudal dues they had previously exacted (in many cases purely nominal) and instead to charge much higher rents for the use of their land.⁶³ With the new rents, many tenants found themselves ruined after a few years of bad harvests and possibly were forced to turn to other means of subsistence.⁶⁴ Furthermore, communal lands, especially those near cities, were gradually encroached upon as urban bureaucrats, merchants, and nobles bought up agricultural land. As a result, fewer and fewer of the rural poor had access to land and were forced to sell their labor.⁶⁵ The first half of the sixteenth century also saw a modest increase in manufacturing, partly as a result of the influx of silver from the Americas and partly because of the opening of new markets in the colonies. Although this fortuitous situation did not last long, it conceivably contributed to a greater demand for labor and to making wage labor the most convenient and inexpensive type.⁶⁶

Humanism and Attitudes Toward Gender

Related to and interacting with current notions about economics, work, and the social good was the Spanish ideology of sexuality and gender. While ideas about women, like those on economics, were liberalized somewhat by the influence of humanism, a contervailing tendency was the attempt by a patriarchal society to control women in a period of social change, viewing them as a cause of disorder.⁶⁷

Liberalized ideas about gender differences by no means meant that Spanish thought held women to be the equal of men. On the contrary, the most important Spanish humanist writing about women attributed to them at best a "weak goodness" instead of the "strong evil" earlier theorists believed they embodied.⁶⁸ This author was Juan Luis Vives, who in 1523 wrote *De Institutione Foeminae Christianae* (The instruction of a Christian woman), on proper female conduct and education. Vives, whose ideas on labor have already been referred to, was born in Valencia in 1492 but spent much of his life abroad. He studied at the University of Paris, attended lectures given by Erasmus in Louvain, and himself taught at Oxford.⁶⁹ So Vives's book is the work of a worldly intellectual, not one that simply reflects Iberian customs. In fact, his *Instruction* was originally commissioned by Catherine of Aragon, daughter of Isabella and wife of Henry VIII, for her own daughter Mary.⁷⁰ The treatise was enormously successful, given the limited reading public in the period, and was published in approximately forty editions in six languages, including Spanish, during the sixteenth century.[71]

Unlike most of his predecessors, Vives maintained that many women had intellectual potential. But he also believed that a woman's most important attribute was her virtue, by which he specifically meant her chastity. Here Vives found a tension: women were assumed to be weak and more prone to moral failure than men, therefore likely to misuse or misunderstand any knowledge they acquired, thus endangering their virtue. Like other humanist thinkers, Vives traced this moral and intellectual weakness to Eve, who had been so easily misled by the devil.[72] Consequently, education for women had to be carefully structured not to misinform but to enhance goodness. Rigid as some of Vives's recommendations for women's education were, he differed from earlier, more conservative writers who held that women under no circumstances should be educated, since any learning at all would contribute to their maliciousness.[73]

What was appropriate educationally for women were readings that emphasized goodness, rather than those that introduced the feminine reader to issues of right and wrong.[74] Further, women were to be kept occupied with educational and domestic activities because idleness would only contribute to their voluptuous nature.[75] Finally, under no circumstances should women be teachers or writers. Vives argued that if they became instructors women would likely pass on incorrect information because they had misinterpreted what they had read.[76] Instead of writing to communicate, women should only practice their penmanship, and even this training should be accomplished by the repetition of moral or religious phrases that would improve their character.[77]

Other aspects of the *Instruction* were perhaps more in keeping with humanist writings on economics and labor. For instance, instead of blaming women for their wickedness and weakness, Vives insisted on a close connection between poverty and prostitution. This appreciation of the role of social conditions in forcing women into brothels became more common in general in the sixteenth century, with more convents taking on the role of rehabilitating "fallen women" and more charitable organizations providing dowries for poor young women who otherwise would not be able to marry.[78]

Of course, it is difficult to know to what extent the *Instruction* was followed, even by the elite who were able to educate their daughters according to Vives's prescription. It is known that there were remarkable women in early modern Spain whose intellectual endeavors went well beyond what the experts believed appropriate.[79] Nonetheless, it is safe to assume that most women had considerably less education than Vives thought permissible for their sex. Furthermore, not only books on comportment, or even poverty and lack of opportunity, limited the educational options and careers open to women; legal statutes regulated their activities in many spheres.

Although the laws governing women in Spain and in Spanish America are discussed in more detail in chapter 6, it is pertinent to mention a few legal restrictions at this point. In most situations, a woman needed either her father's or her husband's notarized permission before she could transact a legally binding agreement. Spanish women could not hold political office or be judges or lawyers. They were not to be judges because, according to the *Siete Partidas* (the thirteenth-century legal statute that dealt with women), it was inappropriate for women to decide cases in the presence of men.[80] Finally, under no circumstances were they to be priests or to preach, because Jesus had given the apostles, who were men, the right of absolution but had not given it to Mary because she was female.[81]

A variety of sources suggest, however, that in reality women were more active in various aspects of public life, including religion, than conduct books or official policy would indicate. Among these are Inquisition records describing investigations of those who held unorthodox views that the increasingly defensive Spanish church felt might be heretical. Those under suspicion held a variety of opinions ranging from opposition to audible prayer and self-flagellation to doubting that good works could achieve one's salvation. What is striking about accounts of inquisitorial trials is not merely that women participated in groups that challenged church orthodoxy, but indeed that they were among the spiritual and intellectual leaders of these movements.

For instance, Isabel de la Cruz was said to be the founder and spiritual leader of a group known as the Alumbrados, who believed in the interiorization of religion, rejected the conventional Catholic belief in eternal damnation for sinners, and believed that salvation came through grace alone, not through good works.[82] Another example was María Cazalla, who was suspect because she was thought to hold Erasmian views. In her trial, held between 1531 and 1534, she was questioned about a number of complicated religious issues and also about her position on conjugal love. Specifically, the inquisitors wanted to know if she had said that "in the act of conjugal union one can be closer to God than in prayer." While not directly answering the question, she did admit to having pleasure with her husband. María was also accused of preaching, which conceivably may have angered her inquisitors more than her specific beliefs.[83]

In fact, in both of these cases, and in a number of others, women are accused of assuming the roles of teachers, preachers, and counselors, occupations for which Vives specifically considered them unworthy. Their religious unorthodoxy would seem to confirm the dictum that women who instructed others would only mislead them. The coincidence is suggestive: perhaps Vives himself was actually responding to a growth in the number of women becoming active in public life by teaching or preaching and was attempting to stem the tide. While the two women just described seem quite capable of discussing church doctrine and Scripture, Mary Elizabeth Perry points out that many of the women processed by the Inquisition in Seville became spiritual leaders because of mystical experiences rather than scriptural exegesis. Although mysticism became an important religious movement in the sixteenth century for both men and women, Perry maintains that in some respects mysticism represented a "feminization of religion," since its emphasis on direct, emotional experience circumvented the church hierarchy from which women were excluded.[84]

Women's participation in economic affairs was apparently also quite varied, despite the fact that the only socially approved occupations for women were those believed to flow naturally from their feminine talents or to improve their biological function. For instance, Pedro de Valencia, a humanist jurist and theologian from Córdoba, opposed idleness in women just as he did in men; however, he urged women to work because those who did so gave birth to healthy children, while those who were idle did not.[85] Economic activities considered to be extensions of women's "natural" nurturing functions preparation, and certain agricultural activities.[86] Even prostitution, often viewed as a necessary social evil, was considered a natural profession for certain women (either the extremely disadvantaged or the very wanton, depending on one's perspective), while male prostitution was not even officially acknowledged but was subsumed under very severe laws against sodomy.[87]

However, recent research on the sixteenth century has shown that women were also involved in economic activities that were considered male prerogatives, often without the supposedly necessary permission of father or husband. Women bought, sold, and rented property and formed commercial companies, sometimes even with other women, that traded with the Indies. In some cases, women could even become guild members and take over their husbands' shops and tools when they died.[88] Although additional research will be required to establish how common were such business transactions for women, they appear to have been exceptions rather than the norm.

If the Inca cosmology seemed to disguise the lack of equality between men and women by emphasizing presumably parallel male and female politico-religious hierarchies, Spanish ideology operated from a different premise. While at least some women were active in economic and intellectual life, both prescriptive literature and legal statutes aimed at limiting, if not totally excluding, them from these spheres. Although economic changes and altered class relationships reflected the development of new liberal theories of human nature, these views were applied in a very limited fashion to women. Perhaps just as those who held a corporatist view fiercely defended caste prerogatives even as the lines between certain classes (nobility and bourgeoisie) were becoming blurred, both corporatists and liberals defended patriarchy and sought to control women in the face of social changes that were also affecting gender relations.

Toward Colonial Society

Given the complexity of the economic and cultural processes occurring both in the Andes and in Spain before the conquest, the results of the colonization of Upper Peru were bound to be varied. Bringing both corporatist and protoliberal conceptions of society with them, both corporatist and protoliberal conceptions of society with them, Spanish colonists confronted in the Andes an economic system without markets but in which the operating principles of reciprocity and redistribution permitted the development of considerable differences in wealth and power. In terms of gender: a society that espoused the complementarity of the sexes and women's political authority, while in practice it undermined female power, was to be ruled by one in which women may have actually had some power but were legally disenfranchised.

Although the contest between Spaniards and Andeans was an unequal one, the diversity in Iberian thought, ambivalence in colonial policy, and the incongruity between ideal goals and real accomplishments gave the colonized peoples room to maneuver. The chapters that follow examine the means by which the colonial state and private interests attempted to mobilize a labor force and the ways in which "laborers" tried to avoid exploitation as much as possible and turned the situation to their benefit when they could. However, since at the time of the invasion the Andeans were not one undifferentiated mass, who benefited and who suffered most was often related to pre-Columbian economic and social patterns as well as individual flexibility in confronting the new system.

· 2 ·

Colonial Economy and the Organization of Labor

> There are many Indians [in the mines] who work voluntarily just as in Spain there are many workers who sell their labor.
> —*Licenciado Castro y Padilla,*
> *Oruro, March 1, 1608*
>
> These Indians, thus distracted from their villages, support themselves on the haciendas of the Spaniards; . . . they rent part of the [estate's] lands and survive by paying the landowner with their personal service.
> —*Corregidor of Porco, June 26, 1677*

THESE TWO observations about the indigenous people of Upper Peru, separated by seventy years and referring to labor in different sectors of the economy, give some indication of the uneven development of relations of production in the Andes under colonialism. In 1608, Castro y Padilla compared Indian miners to Spanish workers who sold their labor; in 1677, another observer described a system whereby the Indians paid labor rent for the use of land on a hacienda. Chapter 1 outlined some of the material and ideological factors in Spain and the New World that contributed to the mixed nature of the colonial economy; the next two begin to examine the results of domination of one society by the other.

The present chapter explores the various approaches colonists in Upper Peru took to organizing labor as economic and political circumstances changed in both the Old World and the New. The debate about labor was still divided between corporatist and liberal views, pitting those who believed that coercion was the only realistic way to raise a work force against those who, for philosophical or practical reasons, supported the development of a free labor system. But between 1532 and the mid-seventeenth century, Spanish policy moved incrementally toward free labor as the commodification of the Upper Peruvian economy created conditions that made it necessary for people to work for money. Chapter 3 describes the demographic changes that contributed to the development of the economy: a drastic decline in the indigenous population and transformations that resulted from forced resettlement and migration.

The Caribbean Precedent and the Encomienda in Upper Peru

The Spanish first settled in Upper Peru on the altiplano or in mountain valleys because they discovered there important mineral deposits and a dense Indian population that could at least potentially serve as a work force and source of tribute. The city of La Plata was founded in 1538 by Gonzalo and Hernando Pizarro in a southern mountain valley about 2,700 meters above sea level. In the same year, a Spanish settlement was established at Porco, where local Indians were working silver mines.

In the Andes the Spaniards were confronted with a self-sufficient peasantry and an economy that operated without markets—so different from the growing landlessness and quasi-proletarianization of the Spanish countryside. While Spain's experiences with the Moors and the Jews sometimes served as precedents and points of reference for dealing with native Americans, the situation was clearly not entirely comparable either to that of Spain's Old Christians or ethnic minorities. Those concerned with moral questions were now forced to grapple with the broad issues of Christian doctrine, individual freedom, and contractual relations in a concrete situation in which corporatist justifications of force appeared more appropriate than a market-oriented liberal approach to labor.

When the first conquerors arrived in the Andes, they tended to draw on the experience of the earlier colonizers of the Caribbean and Mexico who had already considered some of these moral issues, even as they opted for and found ways to rationalize coercion. When the settlers of Hispaniola encountered the relatively simple agricultural economy of the Tainos and their notable lack of desire to mine gold for the newcomers, they adapted the *encomienda*, which had its roots in the Spanish Reconquista (the centuries-long crusade to drive Spanish Moslems out of the peninsula), to local conditions.[1] In a 1503 decree, Queen Isabella authorized the governor of Hispaniola, Nicolás de Ovando, to assign Indian workers to the settlers. In fact, this decree was a curious ideological compromise between "liberal" and corporatist thinking, even though its purpose was to authorize the use of force. Isabella emphasized that the Tainos were free people, not serfs, and therefore had to be paid for their labor. On the other hand, she admitted that given the absolute freedom she had mandated for the natives in earlier instructions, they had not been willing to work even for wages, nor had they voluntarily accepted Catholicism.[2]

Although the encomienda was supposedly different from slavery, in many instances it was scarcely distinguishable from it. Far from being paid labor, encomienda service was conceived as a form of tribute owed by the Indians to their encomenderos. And, as the population of Hispaniola died from epidemic disease and overwork, the means of obtaining workers became ever more barbaric. As early as 1505, King Ferdinand authorized military slaving expeditions to nearby Caribbean islands, particularly those without gold deposits.[3] These expeditions had a historical precedent in the Reconquista, when slavery had been condoned as part of a "just war"; in this case Indians who had resisted conversion or were thought to be cannibals could be legally enslaved.[4]

While it might seem that human freedom and idea of labor as a commodity were quickly brushed aside in a colonial setting, almost from the beginning many pointed out the immorality of the Spanish colonists' actions. As early as 1511, Father Antonio de Montesinos and other Dominicans in Santo Domingo attacked not only the abuses of the encomienda but also the system itself; a Cuban encomendero, Bartolomé de Las Casas, gave up his own grant and devoted the rest of his life to crusading against the institution.[5] However, those who opposed Indian slavery and the encomienda were unable to eliminate these practices in the Caribbean islands while there was still a significant indigenous population there, and both institutions were brought by the colonists to the Spanish American mainland.[6]

The complex, hierarchical societies that the Spaniards encountered in Central Mexico and the Andes in some ways facilitated the encomienda since, before the conquest, well-organized tributary labor systems had already existed. The initial approach of encomenderos in both regions was to leave the political system of the indigenous village in place as much as possible and to rely upon native authorities to extract a surplus in labor and products.

In colonial Peru, encomenderos apparently soon realized that amicable relations with the native rulers of their encomiendas were more profitable than hostile ones. Steve Stern and Karen Spalding show that early encomenderos in the Andes even attempted to duplicate Andean patterns of generosity—in effect, substituting themselves for the Inca—by inviting kurakas to dine in their homes and giving them gifts of lands or herds of animals.[7] If the Inca state had already given new meanings to Andean traditions, the largesse of encomenderos was now part of a system linking peasant communities to a world mercantile system that would ultimately extract levels of surplus never conceived of by the Incas.[8]

The Quillaca-Asanaques, natives of the region in which the city of Oruro was later founded, were apparently granted to an encomendero during the 1540s, even though by that time the royal government was beginning to take direct steps to curtail and eventually eliminate the institution. At the time of the conquest, the Quillaca-Asanaques were primarily settled on the high plateau around Lake Poopo but also had mitimaes in numerous other areas, including

Yamparaez, Cochabamba, and even San Lucas in Pilaya y Paspaya, the other region studied in this book. Some of these mitimaes predated the Inca empire, but (as mentioned in chapter 1) many had been relocated by the Inca state. Historians disagree somewhat about what happened to the Quillacas-Asanaques in the early colonial period. Waldemar de Espinoza maintains that while those in Paria were granted in encomienda to Lorenzo de Aldana, the Quillaca-Asanaques who remained in Cochabamba were distributed to other Spaniards. On the other hand, Alberto Crespo specifies that Aldana received not only the Indians of Paria and Toledo but also those of Tapacarí and Capinota (both in Cochabamba) in his repartimiento.[9]

Espinoza cites a 1548 document stating that the Quillaca-Asanaques were to send 100 *mitayos* to work in the mines of Potosí for Aldana and an unspecified additional number were designated for agricultural labor in the valley of La Plata. They were to provide Aldana with tribute calculated at 9,600 pesos, as long as no mines were discovered in the area of his encomienda.[10] However, in 1557 Indians discovered silver in Oruro, apparently making Aldana one of the wealthiest men in Peru.[11] Although no document has come to light that details Aldana's relationship with the native authorities of his encomienda, there is some evidence that he mediated domination and subordination with paternalism and redistribution. Don Juan Colque Guarache, the son of the mallku, or kuraka, at the time of the conquest, was educated at the Jesuit College of La Plata. Sons of the Andean elite often received Christian educations in the early colonial period, and Aldana probably paid for Don Juan's schooling. Furthermore, when he died Aldana left ranches containing 50,000 sheep to the Indians of his repartimiento.[12]

Pilaya y Paspaya, for various reasons, had no encomiendas. First of all, the land in Pilaya y Paspaya didn't become valuable until the late sixteenth and early seventeenth centuries, when the mining boom in Potosí created an attractive market for agricultural produce. And while it would have been possible to send Indians from Pilaya y Paspaya to work mines in Porco or Potosí at an earlier date, the nature of the indigenous population of the province discouraged their division into encomiendas. Only in the most northern section of the province were what the Spaniards considered "civilized" Indians, meaning agriculturalists who had been brought under the control of the Inca state. These residents were actually mitimaes from Paria and Porco (discussed in more detail in chapter 7).[13]

In the south and along the province's eastern frontier, the natives, known as Chiriguanos, proved to be formidable adversaries well into the colonial period.[14] The Chiriguanos combined slash-and-burn cultivation with hunting and gathering, both of which activities required migration over a large territory. Thus, having no permanent settlements, they were not accessible to the Spaniards, nor could they easily be forced to produce an agricultural surplus that could be siphoned off as tribute. All of these factors, plus the Chiriguanos' military resistance, had also prevented their domination by the Incas, so in this instance the Spaniards could not simply appropriate a system of exacting tribute developed by their predecessors.[15]

If relatively few encomenderos had acquired significant wealth in the first ten years or so of colonization, the potential for gain and the demands made on the native population of Upper Peru drastically increased when silver was discovered at Potosí. There, on the edge of the eastern range of the Andes to the southwest of La Plata, a veritable mountain of silver was discovered in 1545.

Even by Andean standards, Potosí's location was forbidding. The base of the Cerro Rico—literally, rich hill—was 4,200 meters above sea level. Europeans had trouble breathing at this altitude, and under normal circumstances, most would have looked for pleasanter places to live. But the desire for wealth has created boom towns in many uninviting environments, and it wasn't long before a city sprang up at the foot of the cone-shaped mountain. With silver came extravagance: a mint designed to look like El Escorial, an opera house, numerous music halls and churches. Once Potosí's potential became known, it was common practice for encomenderos to send their Indians there to work for them in the mines. In 1549, 5,000 Indians from seventy-two repartimientos worked in the city. They spent between seven months and three years at the mining site and paid an average tribute to their encomenderos of two and a half gold pesos a week.[16]

The Crisis of the Post-Conquest System and the End of the Encomienda

Among the many factors contributing to the gradual demise of the encomienda in the Andes was the very success of the silver industry, which made increasingly insupportable demands on the indigenous population through the encomienda. Potosí's fabulous mines were welcomed and encouraged by the Spanish government, since one-fifth of all silver minted was sent to Spain as a royal tax; thus royal support and word of mouth rapidly attracted more and more Spaniards to Upper Peru where they hoped to "make America." Once in the Andes, new arrivals demanded the same prerogatives as earlier colonists, including grants of native people who might work for them in the mines and in other profitable undertakings.

If the hierarchy of obligations placed on the Indian communities can be visualized as a pyramid, the encomendero, as indirect representative of the Spanish state, was at the peak and had to be satisfied first. The Indians of his repartimiento might supply him with a certain amount of silver from the mines, or pay a tribute in agricultural goods that the encomendero could then sell in the market, or both. For instance, in 1550 the community of Macha, which sent men to Potosí to work, had to provide its encomendero with 27,000 pesos' worth of gold or silver, 125 baskets of coca, and 1,200 *fanegas* of maize, to mention only the largest items.[17] Next, Indian commoners had to provide various goods and services for people lower down in the hierarchy. These included tribute, usually in goods but sometimes also in service, for the local priest; labor and provisions to maintain the *tambos*, or way stations for travelers; and various types of services for the kuraka himself. Finally, when all other demands had been met, community residents, who formed the base of the pyramid on which the weight of society rested, had to provide for their own subsistence.

By the 1560s, the pyramid was being undermined. The myth of reciprocity between encomendero and kuraka disintegrated as the former's demands increased. In turn, kurakas found it ever more difficult to maintain essential reciprocal relations with the people of their ayllus, as their role as agents for the Spanish became more apparent. Eventually, Indian commoners who, if not uncomplaining, had still generally not rebelled, began to show distinct signs of having been pushed past their limit. More and more villages or ayllus refused to follow orders. Finally, conspiracies to overthrow the colonial state were uncovered in the 1560s. Although paranoia may have led to exaggeration, correspondence between colonial officials detailed plans for coordinated rebellions from Quito to Tucumán that were supposed to link up with the neo-Incas who, since the 1530s, had challenged the colonial state from their jungle stronghold at Vilcabamba. It must have been particularly alarming to the Spanish that groups such as the Huanca of the Juaja Valley, previously loyal collaborators with the Europeans, actively participated in these plots.[18]

Also in 1565, an Andean religious revival known as Taki Onqoy was discovered in the southern sierra of Peru. Followers of this movement were possessed by Andean gods, or *huacas*, who exhorted people to reject Christanity and all aspects of European culture, including the Spanish language, clothing, and food. As a spiritual movement, Taki Onqoy condemned collaboration with the Spaniards and maintained that only through a return to the true gods could the Spanish be vanquished and a natural balance and harmony be restored.[19] While the importance of Taki Onqoy may have been blown out of proportion because of the different political and economic objectives of the Dominicans and the secular clergy involved in its discovery and extirpation, it was nonetheless another sign that the Andean population was being forced to a breaking point.[20]

Although in some ways these early anti-Spanish movements were more thoroughly outside the dominant culture than later oppositions to colonial rule, even in this period, only thirty years or so after the Inca defeat at Cajamarca, there are indications of the effects of Spanish culture on the rebels. The neo-Incas and the Huancas willingly adopted Spanish military technology and horses to pursue their campaigns, and neither group entirely rejected Christianity. Even the *taquiongos*, as followers of the huacas were called, had to make changes in Andean traditions in order to combat Spanish ones. For instance, they were forced to give up more narrow ethnic identities and rivalries among ayllus to form a unified front against the Europeans and their gods. Furthermore, the very act of rejecting Spanish intrusion went against Andean principles of ideological incorporation: vanquished ayllus generally worshipped the huacas of victorious groups that were assumed to be especially powerful.

Ominous as these signs of peasant resistance to increased exploitation were, alone they might not have been sufficient to cause a change in Spanish policy on labor. In fact, a number of political considerations and the petitions of various interest groups contributed to the realization that a general reform of the colonial system was necessary if it was to endure.

First of all, although the encomienda had filled an important political function in the interim between the conquest and the complete establishment of colonial control administered by representatives of the crown, the royal government became increasingly wary of the encomenderos, seeing in them a potential aristocratic class that might ultimately resist Spain's authority.[21] Even a reforming administrator like Juan de Matienzo, who acknowledged the encomenderos' contribution to the development of the colony, proposed that Indian communities should be more directly administered politically and judicially by government employees.[22]

Second, by the mid-sixteenth century the idea that Indians were free human beings who should work only voluntarily, and with appropriate remuneration, had gained considerable influence among clergymen and jurists. Las Casas's lobbying for abolition of the encomienda apparently was sympathetically received by both Charles V in the 1540s and by Philip II in 1555.[23] Even if royal motives were more cynical than those of Las Casas, the humanitarian argument was certainly useful to the royal government in its campaign against those who resisted changes in the encomienda.

Finally, the fact that the Indian population was declining rapidly, while the European population was growing, had important ramifications and influenced the official decision to curtail the institution. Not only was an encomienda more valuable when the encomendero's subjects were numerous, but also the royal government was beginning to perceive that overwork and abuse of the Indians by the encomenderos was contributing to high mortality rates.[24] Furthermore, as the number of Spaniards in the Andes who did not have encomiendas increased, they became an interest group that petitioned the king for their own privileges; without allotments of Indians, they could not hope to compete with those who had them. Because encomienda labor was unpaid, encomenderos could sell their products in the market at prices much below those of entrepreneurs who had to pay their workers. As Karen Spalding points out, far from having sympathy with the Indians, those without encomiendas were really protesting the fact that they did not have Indian communities to subsidize their own businesses.[25]

Although initial frontal attacks on the encomienda could not be sustained, by the 1570s the dismantling of the encomienda was well under way.[26] The royal government's efforts to guarantee that encomiendas were not perpetual began to have the desired effect, and increasing numbers of encomiendas reverted to crown control, especially after they had been held for two generations—the usual limit imposed by the government. By the 1570s, of sixty-seven grants in Upper Peru, twenty-three had become the domain of the royal government. These included the repartimiento held by Lorenzo de Aldana in Paria, which apparently escheated when he died.[27] Other measures restricted the powers of those who still held encomiendas. Although it was not always complied with, one of the most important was a royal decree of 1549 that forbade the exaction of personal labor service as tribute.[28]

Paid Forced Labor: The Repartimiento

As encomiendas came under royal jurisdiction and as more restrictions were placed on the use of the labor power of those Indians still held, colonial authorities considered alternate means of organizing labor that might better meet the needs of a more complex economy. Cognizant that indiscriminate exploitation of the native population by the settlers would not best serve colonial interests in the long run, priority for access to labor was now given to enterprises considered most important by the government. In the system that emerged, generically known as *repartimiento* labor, representatives of the state directly intervened to allocate workers to the colony's most lucrative activities, particularly silver mining. Although draft systems of labor

Colonial Economy and the Organization of Labor 47

certainly existed earlier in colonial Spanish America, the credit (or blame) for organizing repartimiento labor on a massive scale in the Andes goes to the Viceroy Francisco de Toledo (1569–1581), who initiated the *mita* for the Potosí mines.

King Philip II initially opposed the repartimiento system; he favored the use of free labor in the mines and other enterprises and hoped that Indians could be attracted to them solely through good treatment and fair wages. However, since the rich surface ores had declined in Potosí, making mine owners disinclined to pay attractive wages and making independent prospecting less appealing to workers, Viceroy de Toledo was highly dubious that workers would come to the center voluntarily. But since he conceived of a labor draft as one of a series of reforms designed to bring greater prosperity to the mining site, Toledo hoped that with the revival of the industry, benefits for workers would increase and coerced labor would not be necessary for long.[29]

To increase mining productivity, the viceroy encouraged technical experimentation that led to the perfection of a new method of refining silver in Potosí. This was the mercury amalgamation process, which extracted silver from ores that had been discarded because their quality was too low for simple smelting. For a number of years after the process was developed, refiners used it to treat tailings that had been thrown on slag heaps because of low silver content. In the long run, however, the greater productivity promised by the new technology could be achieved only by mining more ore. Since there was no technical innovation in mining to match that in refining, extracting more mineral was possible only by increasing the size of the work force.[30]

The viceroy understood that the difficulty of increasing the size of the labor pool for Potosí was directly related to the demographic situation in Upper Peru. Not only was the native population declining in absolute numbers; their dispersed settlements, well adapted to the Andean environment, made them relatively inaccessible for the Spaniards' purposes: evangelization, collecting tribute, and mobilizing labor. Consequently, Toledo's administration first undertook the massive task of moving huge numbers of people and resettling them in compact villages, or *reducciones*.[31]

These new communities were to be administered by a colonial official known as the *corregidor de indios* and were to have a native governing council, or *cabildo*, modeled on town councils in Spain. The corregidor, although he might work closely with other Spaniards in the area, was to be a direct representative of the government, while the council was conceived as a pro-Spanish alternative to traditional indigenous authorities.³² From the reducciones, groups of Indians could be distributed by government authorities for limited periods to employers who needed them, particularly miners and refiners in Potosí. By administering the system itself, the government not only made the decisions about which entrepreneurs were most worthy of receiving labor but also could (at least theoretically) regulate how much labor entrepreneurs could extract from the Indians and thus control abuses and, it was hoped, halt the decline in population. Finally, in the repartimiento, labor was not to be considered a means of fulfilling tribute requirements. On the contrary, in this new arrangement workers were to be paid wages and in turn to pay tribute in cash from what they earned.³³ Although Toledo's solution was far from the freely contracted wage labor envisioned by Spanish liberals and King Philip, the principle of remuneration removed it one step from slavery.

The Potosí *mita*—a word taken from *m'ita*, the Quechua word for turn or shift—was a rotating draft that each year drew on approximately one-seventh of the adult male Indian population of fifteen highland provinces in Peru and Upper Peru. Each worker was to remain for a year in Potosí and be paid for his labor. After his turn in the *villa imperial*, he could return to his village and theoretically was not to serve again for about seven years.³⁴ The combination of the new method of organizing labor and mercury amalgamation technology had the desired effect. Silver production in Potosí, which had fallen to less than 115,000 marks in 1572, accelerated in the decade after 1573 and reached an all-time high of 887,000 marks in 1592 (see figure 1).³⁵ With this mining bonanza in the late sixteenth century, Potosí's population almost literally exploded. By the early seventeenth century, the mining center had become one of the biggest cities in the world; in 1603 it was reported, perhaps with exaggeration, to have a population of 120,000 people.³⁶

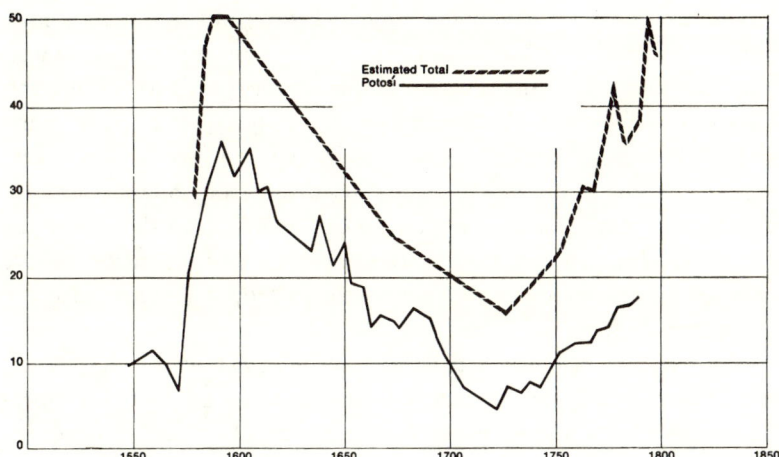

FIGURE 1. Estimated Total Peruvian and Potosí Silver Production, 1560–1800

Source: Brading and Cross, "Colonial Silver Mining," 569.

Regional Economic Development

In the major mining centers, particularly Potosí, and in some other important urban areas, there was evidently enough of a consumer market to stimulate specialized agricultural production and manufacturing within the viceroyalty.[37] A significant portion of this demand was created by indigenous people who were not entirely self-sufficient as peasants but worked at least part time for wages and purchased some of the food and goods they needed for survival. Some of these were forced (repartimiento) laborers who, although generally quite poor, still had to buy a few items for their subsistence. Moreover, many of the consumers in colonial cities were Indians who had voluntarily migrated to find employment and who formed a social sector that became increasingly more diverse and socially differentiated. In a circular fashion, the development of an internal economic circuit in the Andes created a demand for laborers who in turn increased the size of the internal market and further stimulated the economy.

As the viceroyalty's greatest mining center, Potosí alone required a wide variety of foods and goods for personal consumption and industrial use. Other silver towns, such as Oruro and some other nonmining cities, such as Lima, were secondary consumers of food and manufactured items. Spain's mercantilist strategy was to capture the bulk of the silver from the Upper Peruvian mines by exporting Spanish goods to these markets, as well as by the one-fifth tax on silver. Although some items were always imported from Spain—notably high-quality textiles, paper, certain spices, and African slaves—Spain was never able to perfect the system whereby manufactured goods, and even certain food products, from the metropolis were traded for raw materials from the Americas.

This failure was partly the result of inconsistent policies on the part of the Spanish government, which sometimes permitted competing industries to grow up in the Americas and at other times prohibited them.[38] And certainly some items were always too bulky or too perishable to be imported. More important, even when the system functioned properly, the Spanish fleets that were to visit the Indies once a year with products from Spain were inadequate to supply colonial markets. In fact, the convoys often were not on schedule; only twenty-nine arrived in Panama between 1600 and 1650.[39] This irregularity was often exploited by wholesale merchants who took advantage of conditions of scarcity to raise prices, and these higher prices became an incentive to produce similar items within the colonies.[40] Further, Spain's failure to establish a commercial monopoly in the American colonies also reflected Iberia's general economic problems—to be discussed in more detail later—that became more pronounced in the seventeenth century. Consequently, the growth of Upper Peru's silver industry, in addition to sending quantities of the precious metal to Europe, also had a significant impact on regional economic development.

Among the most important commercial commodities produced within the viceroyalty were basic grains, particularly wheat and maize. By the 1580s, agriculture in the Cochabamba Valley in central Bolivia was highly commercialized, and the area rapidly became the bread basket of Upper Peru.[41] In 1603 it was estimated that Potosí consumed 91,000 fanegas of wheat a year—most of it presumably from Cochabamba. In the second decade of the seventeenth century,

Vázquez de Espinosa claimed that Cochabamba exported a million pesos' worth of grain a year, sending it to Oruro and La Paz as well as to Potosí.[42]

Other comestibles, coca leaf, and wine, were also in demand in urban centers. In Potosí in 1603, approximately 20,000 fanegas of *chuño* (a type of freeze-dried potato) and 40,000 fanegas of potatoes were sold each year at a value of 120,000 pesos, respectively.[43] Staples of the Andean diet, potatoes and chuño were grown by Indians, but appear to have been marketed in cities by Spaniards who either bought them directly from the producers or who received these products in tribute and then sold them in urban markets.[44]

Coca leaf, grown in the tropical *yungas* valleys near La Paz and in similar areas near Cuzco, has always had important spiritual and social functions in Andean culture. Producing a mildly narcotic effect when combined with ash and chewed, it was used before the conquest. Although the issue is debated, coca use may have increased in the Indian population during the colonial period because it attenuated the fatigue and hunger caused by hard labor at high altitudes and because it was no longer an exclusive prerogative of the Inca nobility.[45] Tribute was frequently paid in coca, but by the late 1500s, there were also increasing numbers of Spaniards engaged in direct production of the lucrative crop.[46]

The most important grape-growing region was the area around Ica and Pisco on the Peruvian coast, which produced about 70 percent of Peru's wine in the 1620s.[47] However, after Viceroy de Toledo's "pacification" of the Chiriguanos in the 1570s, Pilaya y Paspaya also became an important wine-producing area. Although complete production figures for the province are not available, we know that the province's most prosperous hacendado, Antonio López de Quiroga, sent an average of 1,700 *botijas* of wine a year to Potosí between 1672 and 1680, and between 1681 and 1689 the annual total reached 3,150 botijas.[48]

Secondary among Pilaya y Paspaya's exports, but not insignificant commercially, were cattle by-products. These included jerked beef, tallow, lubricants and oils, and leather. Although ranchers in the province raised their own livestock, from which goods were made, they also bought cattle from other producers in Tucuman and Buenos Aires each year. López de Quiroga, for instance, purchased 1,000–2,000 head from these areas annually.[49]

This trade with areas in what is now Argentina tied Pilaya y Paspaya into one of the major long-distance trade routes in the viceroyalty: that between livestock-raising regions of Cordobá and Santa Fe and the Upper Peruvian mines. Throughout the sixteenth century, camelids raised by Indian communities on the altiplano had been the primary work animals for the mines and for trade, although the financial drain of tribute payments and the increasing involvement of Spaniards in the commercial aspects of the native livestock business diminished the benefit accruing to native communities.[50] By the early seventeenth century, however, mules from Cordobá began to replace the indigenous llamas as the most important beasts of burden in the area. By 1630 Cordobá was exporting an average of 12,000 mules a year to Upper Peru.[51]

By far the most important manufactured items produced in South America were woolen and cotton cloth. Up until the second half of the sixteenth century, textiles were produced in Peru through a distorted version of the Inca system of requiring tribute in textiles. The result was a kind of colonial "putting out" system in which village kurakas had the women of their communities spin the thread and weave the pieces of cloth that had to be supplied each year in tribute. These were then sold by the encomendero or crown official in Potosí or in another urban market.[52]

In the second half of the sixteenth century, however, the growth of urban areas and an increased demand for textiles among workers living in cities, contributed to the development of a new "industrialized" system of textile production. In workshops known as *obrajes*, which sometimes employed several hundred workers, the European technology of the day was introduced. This included hydraulically powered fulling mills, spinning wheels, mechanical looms, and carding machines.[53]

The impetus to develop obrajes actually came from the weakness of the Spanish textile industry, which was barely able to supply domestic needs and was totally incapable of meeting the growing demand from the American colonies for low-quality cloth. These shortages, combined with the inflation caused by the influx of American silver, caused the price of fabric to skyrocket within the peninsula. In an attempt to lower prices in Spain, in 1548 the government took an extraordinary step for a mercantile, colonial nation: it prohibited the American colonies to purchase textiles from Spain.[54] Shortly thereafter, the Spanish government granted requests from the colonies to increase local production, and technical experts began arriving in the Americas to install the latest European equipment there.[55] Although the royal policy toward colonial textiles later changed and attempts were made to roll back the American industry, these had relatively little effect, and obrajes multiplied and production grew until the late eighteenth century.[56]

The greatest center of textile production in obrajes was located in the area of Quito in present-day Ecuador, but there were also factories in La Paz, Paria, and Cuzco. Some obrajes were owned by indigenous communities who either ran them themselves or rented them. In either case, a portion of the proceeds were used to pay the group's tribute. Many factories, however, were the property either of individual Spaniards or creoles, and a certain number belonged to religious institutions.

The Emergence of Free Labor and Efforts to End the Repartimiento

By the early seventeenth century, there had been a shift in many sectors of the economy from indigenous production of commodities for tribute to direct control of production by colonists. This change meant that Andeans increasingly primarily contributed their labor to the process. Some workers for certain enterprises were provided through the repartimiento; however, there were now reasons other than direct coercion for people to sell their labor. Some were the direct result of a more mercantilized economy. Others, such as Viceroy de Toledo's tribute reform, were designed to artificially create market conditions that would force people to work for wages.

Toledo's new tax schedule not only adjusted the amounts that communities were to pay as compensation for demographic changes that had occurred since previous assessments, but also specified that the major portion of tribute was now to be paid in money.[57] The decision to demand a substantial amount of native tribute in cash was probably taken with considerable care. Toledo and his advisers surely realized that this requirement would have the effect of forcing Indians to enter the market in one way or another to earn the money. Writing about Toledo's tribute policy fifty years later, a commentator said specifically that making Indians pay a portion of the tax in cash was "so that in the use of [money] the Indians would be forced out of their brutality and would participate in trade with the Spaniards and have more communication with them."[58] Of course, communities might meet their tax payments by selling a portion of whatever agricultural surplus they produced. However, tax requirements often forced people to sell their labor power as well.

Somewhat ironically, the mita itself also caused people to work for wages when they weren't doing their forced stints in Potosí. This was because although workers were paid for mita service (generally at a rate of four reales a day), they frequently did not earn enough to cover their expenses while they were in Potosí and consequently were obliged to sell their few possessions.[59] Eventually, many were too impoverished to return home and either stayed on in the mining center itself or looked for work elsewhere in an attempt to recoup their losses. For instance, in 1596 Father Antonio de Ayans estimated that 6,000 men, women, and children from the province of Chucuito were living in Potosí because they had been too poor to leave when the men's turns of work were completed.[60] Still others left home precisely to avoid being sent to do their service by local kurakas; they went to work on haciendas where they might earn money for their tribute and either avoid the mita altogether or make some financial arrangement whereby they were exempted from service.[61]

Also, during the seventeenth century some Indian communities in Upper Peru lost land they needed for their subsistence, as Spanish estate owners paid officially assessed fees (*composiciones*), to legalize their haciendas' boundaries or bought crown lands that may have rightfully belonged to indigenous groups. A 1620 report to the president of the Audiencia of Charcas on social and economic conditions in provinces subject to the mita noted:

Spaniards who have come from Spain in such great numbers recently have helped themselves to lands either through purchase or by other means, some fair and some unfair. Many times the lands they acquire actually belong to the Indians.[62]

Loss of their lands often meant that Indian families had to migrate simply to find means of subsistence and to earn money for their tribute.[63]

The combination of fiscal obligations and economic exigency that weighed on the Indian population had fortuitous (but sometimes expensive) results for the owners of estates, mines, and other businesses. During the first half of the seventeenth century, as the economy expanded, Indian migrants became the backbone of the work force for enterprises in areas that did not have repartimiento laborers. Relations of production in these businesses varied according to region and economic activity; nowhere did immigrants simply switch from being peasants and forced laborers to being wage earners. Rather, once they left their home communities, there was variation in how freely they decided to sell their labor and the type of remuneration received. For instance, in Pilaya y Paspaya permanent agricultural workers commonly received land in usufruct as payment for their labor, while more temporary migrants were often sent to the province by kurakas to earn the money for their communities' tribute and never personally received any wages at all. (See chapter 7.)

In urban areas, wages were more common and labor contracts (*conciertos*) sometimes formalized agreements between workers and employers, an indication that at least in some quarters Indians were seen as freely contracting parties. Some of the contracts, however, mentioned only payment in kind, while others specified payment of some cash as well as food and clothing.[64] Mine workers in Oruro generally received wages that were higher than those paid to forced workers in Potosí, but they also customarily helped themselves to a small share of ore as well. (See chapter 4.)

The development of the economy created a competition for labor between colonists who received official repartimientos (particularly mining entrepreneurs in Potosí) and those who did not. The recipients of forced labor were constantly demanding that the government ferret out absent workers and return them to their home communities, from which they could be assigned to corvée labor. Producers operating without repartimiento labor either petitioned for mitayos, who would be an assured and less expensive work force, or maintained that at least they should be allowed to keep the workers they had. The conflict was similar to that between encomenderos and nonencomenderos. And just as the official tide had turned against the encomienda, the royal government now attempted to guarantee that entrepreneurs could receive workers through a system less oppressive than the repartimiento.

A royal decree (*cédula real*) sent to Peru in 1601 by Philip III abolished involuntary servitude and attempted to replace the repartimiento with a somewhat more egalitarian system whereby not only Indians but also mulattoes, mestizos, and poor Spaniards were obliged to report to central locations in towns to hire themselves to whom they wished. The decree further stated that Indians were to be paid wages "in their hands" (that is, no representative such as a kuraka was to receive the payment). Sánchez-Albornoz characterizes this new "voluntary" system as an attempt by royal authorities to create a labor market.[65] The one notable exception to these guidelines for less coercive labor practices was the mita of Potosí, which the king condoned on the basis of the paramount importance of the Potosí mines.[66]

Even though the 1601 decree required the "lower classes" to present themselves as laborers (while exempting the Potosí mita), the Peruvian viceroy, Luis de Velasco, found it impossible to enforce the legislation. Those who opposed it had an articulate defender in Father Miguel de Agia, a Franciscan priest, whose treatise attacking the cédula essentially repeated a familiar organicist argument: because the Indians would not work voluntarily, they had to be forced to do so, both for their own good and for that of the realm.[67] Just as observers in fifteenth- and sixteenth-century Spain condemned the indolence of the peasant masses, in colonial Peru there was no shortage of officials and entrepreneurs complaining about the Indians' disinclination to work. For instance, in the 1570s, a judge (*oidor*) of the Audiencia of Charcas commented,

[The Indians] content themselves with what is required for a week and will work only long enough to obtain what they can eat and drink in a week. They are enemies of work, friends of idleness and drinking and idolatry.[68]

For the time being, the corporatist approach won out. The cédula of 1601 was never enacted and in fact was superseded by another in 1609 that reestablished the repartimiento system of the 1580s.[69] Nonetheless, since relations of production were in the process of change, the debate about personal service and forced labor was destined to continue throughout the seventeenth century, with some even going so far as to advocate eliminating the Potosí mita.[70]

Decline in Silver Production and Economic Stagnation

Perhaps the decline in colonial siver output and its repercussions in the Americas and Europe have received more scholarly attention than any other issues in seventeenth-century Latin American history. In the case of Spain's other great silver-producing colony, New Spain (Mexico), scholars have questioned whether there truly was a decline in silver production and a resulting economic depression. They contend that evidence for the alleged drop in mining output is largely based on reports of the amounts of silver arriving in Spain, not on what was actually produced in Mexico. They maintain that there was no fall in production: instead, more silver was either sent to the Philippines or stayed in the colony for investment there. Domestic investment in Mexico led to a period of economic diversification and expansion much like that posited by dependency theorists for the depression of the 1930s in certain Latin American countries.[71]

Unlike Mexico, where many argue that production levels remained constant during most of the 1600s, treasury accounts and records of mercury consumption in Upper Peru prove fairly conclusively that there really was a prolonged downturn in mining after 1650.[72] (See figure 1, above.) As main causes of the industry's declining fortunes, researchers point to the exhaustion of the rich surface ores that could be mined relatively easily, the increased expense of deeper excavation, the lack of an inexpensive refining process for the plentiful silver sulphide ores (*negrillos*), the decline in the number of forced laborers in Potosí, and the high cost of free laborers in general.[73] Miners and officials in Oruro also cited these factors as causes of their economic woes after the first decades of the century.[74]

There is also debate about the nature of economic decline in Spain during the seventeenth century, but there the question is not between economic prosperity or depression: most agree that it was the latter. Instead, some historians question whether there ever had been a rise from which a decline could be measured, or if Spain's failure to modernize economically and proceed with the transition to capitalism, coupled with growing dependence on other European countries, had relegated it to chronic economic weakness long before the drop in the amount of silver coming from America.[75]

In any event, whether the decline in the flow of bullion from America caused a depression in a potentially buoyant economy or was the coup de grace to an already crippled one, the fact that less precious metal was arriving in the Iberian peninsula had serious repercussions in Spain that ultimately affected other European countries as well. Philip III (1598–1621), Philip IV (1621–1665), and Charles II (1665–1700) emptied the national treasury to finance wars against rebellious portions of the Holy Roman Empire. As secessionist Protestants in the Netherlands and in Germany challenged Spain's religious orthodoxy as well as its political hegemony, Spain, with the shortsightedness characteristic of most imperial powers, was determined to defend its territory and ideology, whatever the cost. From 1649 to 1654 alone, the royal government spent 66,865,000 ducats on military operations.[76] The empire's financial need led the royal government to adopt many dire measures—among them, seizing private shipments of silver from the Indies, levying extraordinary tax assessments in the colonies, selling appointments of all types to the highest bidder.[77] Consequently, a reduction in income from America further weakened Spain's armies, which were already showing signs of caving in, and contributed to more bloody and costly defeats.[78]

For quite some time—although how long has been debated—Spain's industries had been less advanced than those in the Low Countries, England, and France and were incapable of supplying domestic and colonial markets.[79] In addition, rising prices in Spain during the sixteenth century tended to make Spanish manufactures more expensive than imported ones, forcing the government to permit the sale of cheaper foreign goods in Spain itself as well as in the colonies.[80] Thus, when less silver arrived from the Americas, the impact was felt not only in Spain but in all those regions for which Spain was an important market.

Finally, scholars disagree about the impact of declining silver production on the Peruvian viceroyalty itself. Kenneth Andrien argues that instead of creating an overall depression, the lower profitability of the mining industry encouraged those with capital to diversify their investments, and that the weakness of the export sector even contributed to more balanced internal development.[81] Other historians demonstrate, however, that the prolonged drop in silver negatively affected other sectors of the viceregal economy and that markets for food and textiles shrunk drastically.[82] Of course, what happened, as Andrien maintains, probably varied according to region, period, and productive activity. Silver mines did not entirely stop producing; there were still markets for local products; and even in the seventeenth century Upper Peruvian society seems to have been too mercantilized for a complete return to subsistence activities. It may have been, as Peter Bakewell suggests, that while the mining downturn ruined small entrepreneurs, those with more capital and business sense were able to profit during the depressed period, often at the expense of those who failed.[83] Nonetheless, it would be incorrect to overlook the distinct signs of malaise, if not collapse, in many sectors of Upper Peruvian society.

First, the region's main mining towns suffered massive losses of population. By 1683 Oruro's total Indian population had fallen to 8,616 people and, although earlier figures are not available, by the late eighteenth century the population of the villa imperial of Potosí was reduced to about 22,000 people.[84] In the case of Oruro, while less labor was needed in the worst years of the depression, immigration to the center never stopped entirely. However, with fewer people living in urban areas, the demand for food and manufactures from regional production centers undoubtedly slackened.

A study of Cochabamba in the eighteenth century, when the impact of the decline in mining was still being felt, indicates that with lessened demand for the province's maize and wheat in Potosí, the region indeed stagnated economically. Large grain growers shifted from direct production for the market to various types of speculative activities and to renting out their land in small parcels to Indian and mestizo peasants. Over the course of the century, the once prosperous center of commercial agriculture became an area dominated by subsistence farming.[85] Carlos Sempat Assadourian indicates a similar development in areas of rural Chile that previously sent grain and beef products to markets in Lima. He remarks that those who had formerly been involved in this trade tended to withdraw to their haciendas, where they hoped to supply all their needs with minimal expenditures—an approach that Chevalier maintained was also common in Mexico in the same period.[86]

While there are some indications of economic decline in Pilaya y Paspaya during the seventeenth century, including a slowed rate of Indians migrating to the area to work on the province's estates (discussed in chapter 7), the decline of the silver industry appears to have had a less extreme impact there than in Cochabamba. Data on prices and quantities of wine sold are not complete enough to determine whether the hacendados' income declined over the century, but extant statistics do indicate that wine prices remained quite stable for a century after 1676.[87] Pilaya y Paspaya's landowners in the seventeenth and early eighteenth centuries do not seem to have moved away from producing for a market and toward collecting rent on small parcels of land, as happened in Cochabamba in the later eighteenth century. There is no indication that growing grapes became the domain of peasant renters during this period of economic decline, nor that the region substantially reverted to subsistence agriculture. One reason for this difference between Pilaya y Paspaya and Cochabamba may be that, while Cochabamba suffered from the reduced demand for grains in Potosí in the seventeenth and eighteenth centuries—the demand could be met by regions that were closer to the mining center than Cochabamba was—there was no wine-producing region closer to Potosí than Pilaya y Paspaya.

Irreversible Change

By the seventeenth century, despite economic downturn, socioeconomic change had advanced too far in Upper Peru for a decline in the region's mines to cause a reversal of the trends toward mercantilization and the commodification of labor. Certainly there were marginal sectors of the indigenous population that had no contact with the market. Others were figuratively, and sometimes literally, dragged kicking and screaming into the market through the mita, other types of forced labor, and tribute payments. But there was also a larger group who, in one way or another, were now forced to combine remunerated labor with community agriculture. Miguel de Agia was only partially correct when he contrasted the Indians' lack of materialism and disinclination to work with the Spaniards' acquisitiveness and capitalist mentality. Wage labor was a relatively recent phenomenon within Spain itself (one reason why colonists were so ready to revert to coercive solutions), while not only humanitarians or unrealistic Spanish liberals, but even landowners in Pilaya y Paspaya and mine owners in Oruro, could testify that Andean people would indeed, under certain conditions, work because of economic factors instead of physical force.

Economic change and demographic change were closely related in the Andes. Epidemic disease, overwork, and physical abuse resulted in population declines that left lands empty for Spanish settlers, made encomiendas less valuable, created shortages of workers in some places, and ultimately threatened to decimate the labor power upon which the whole system depended. But, if in Spain one problem in the development of wage labor had been the lack of mobility of the work force, the Andean practice of cultivating lands in different ecological zones may have facilitated the other type of demographic change in colonial Upper Peru: the migration of large numbers of peasants from ayllu-held lands and their reappearance in other contexts as renters, laborers, artisans, servants, and petty merchants. The next chapter examines patterns of population decline and migratory trends for Upper Peru as a whole as a backdrop for understanding the origins of the labor forces in Oruro and Pilaya y Paspaya.

· 3 ·

Indian Population and Migration in Upper Peru in the Sixteenth and Seventeenth Centuries

IN 1590 the Jesuit provincial in Lima wrote to the general of the Company of Jesus describing a horrible pestilence that had engulfed all of western South America, from Cartagena to southern Chile. He reported that those afflicted were covered from head to toe with horrible pustules that made them virtually unrecognizable. Frequently victims had eruptions even in their mouths and throats, which caused difficulty in eating and even breathing. The sores apparently gave off a disgusting odor, and those who approached the stricken often had to hold their noses, an affront the suffering may have been too sick even to notice. In addition to these and other gruesome details, the provincial also remarked that this dreadful illness seemed primarily to strike the native population, leaving Spaniards and those of Spanish descent largely unaffected.[1]

Indian Population and Migration

Six years later another observer, Father Antonio de Ayans, commented on a different phenomenon affecting the Indian population. Discussing the province of Chucuito, he said that villages that ten years earlier had contained 2,000–3,000 people now had only 150 to 200. Ayans claimed that in the town of Juli twenty years before there had been 16,000–17,000 communicants, but in 1596 there was almost no one left to confess and the few who remained were women and old people. Although he acknowledged the effects of disease on the natives of Chucuito, he thought the depopulation was primarily the result of people abandoning their homes to avoid being sent as forced workers to the Potosí mines.[2]

Each of these observers pinpointed an important cause of demographic, and ultimately cultural, change in Upper Peru during the colonial period. While epidemic illness had an absolute impact on the native population, colonial policy and the introduction of a market economy caused dispersal, resettlement, and social disruption. First, government-forced migration created residential pools from which workers could be rounded up and sent to the Potosí mita. Then flight from these communities, of the type described by Ayans, often caused people to sell their labor to mine owners or hacendados because away from their communities they usually lacked enough land for their subsistence. However, this did not always mean that migrant workers were totally without resources and ready to accept any terms employers offered. In fact, despite the need to work for money, some immigrants seem to have pursued their own survival strategies, which could include returning to their home communities and using wage labor as a means of ensuring the social reproduction of their ayllus. This chapter takes a detailed look at the demographic restructuring of Upper Peru in the sixteenth and seventeenth centuries and how population decline and immigration interacted to create the types of work force that developed in Pilaya y Paspaya and Oruro.

Illness and Death

A complete history of the impact of epidemic diseases on the native population of Upper Peru has not yet been undertaken. However, following N. D. Cook's demographic history of the area that is now Peru between 1520 and 1620, one may surmise that, at least in broad outline, Upper Peru followed a similar pattern. According to Cook, although influenza, smallpox, measles, plague, and other illnesses took their toll in all parts of the Andes, the effects were most devastating in the lowlands because in coastal areas and valleys settlement tended to be dense. Intermontane valleys were generally narrow and heavily inhabited, while on the coast people were of necessity concentrated in cramped river valleys. Under these conditions, disease could spread easily and mortality was likely to be greatest. The high-altitude flatlands, where the population was actually more numerous than in the lowlands, were never as densely settled. Cook estimates that whereas the total indigenous population of Peru was approximately 9 million at the time of the conquest, between 1520 and 1570 it dropped to just over 1 million, and by 1620 it was about 600,000.[3]

It is difficult to estimate the decline in Indian population of Upper Peru from the period of initial contact to the seventeenth century; little is known about the pre-conquest population and many colonial censuses were of dubious quality. However, the region apparently suffered from many of the same waves of disease that struck Peru and other areas in the Andes. The smallpox epidemic of 1525, which arrived in parts of the Inca empire even before the Spaniards themselves,[4] may also have decimated the population of Upper Peru, since Inca authorities, soldiers, and other people certainly must have been in contact with the residents of the area south of Lake Titicaca. Again, there is no documentary evidence that the measles epidemic that caused devastating mortality in Central America in 1530–1531 reached the Andes at all.[5] However, a major pestilence, which had raged in New Spain in 1545, spread throughout the entire Andean region the next year.[6] This disease, characterized by high fever, a rash, and bleeding from the nose, has been difficult for modern scholars to identify; among the diagnoses are plague and typhus.[7] In 1560–1561, another unidentified epidemic struck Potosí (and presumably other parts of Upper Peru) during the dry season. Its numerous victims usually died within twenty-four hours of falling ill and exhibited a variety of symptoms, including swelling of the feet and stomach, high fever, and blisters.[8]

Again in 1588–1589 there was a general epidemic all over the Andes, the malady that the Jesuit provincial in Lima described in the next year. Scholars now believe that this pestilence may actually have been several diseases, including smallpox and influenza, that struck different areas at different times. It took its toll in Upper Peru. One contemporary account stated, "There were days when more than ten thousand Indians and some Spaniards sickened in Potosí."[9] In 1615 a diphtheria epidemic ravaged the provinces of Upper Peru.[10] In 1619 and again in 1630, it was measles.[11] There seems to have been a moderate respite between 1630 and 1690, when all of Upper Peru again suffered from a measles epidemic.[12] Finally, one of the last and worst pandemics in the Andean region occurred between 1719 and 1722. All areas of Upper Peru were apparently affected by this wave of illness, which probably involved more than one disease.[13]

While reports of these maladies are shocking, little is known about their relative impact in high-altitude and lowland areas, nor about overall population decline in Upper Peru. Sánchez-Albornoz attempts a general estimate for ten provinces of Upper Peru for which census figures are available, comparing totals from 1561, 1575 and 1683. (See map 3.) The provinces of Yamparaes, Tomina, Porco, Chayanta, Tarija, Sicasica, Cochabamba, Mizque, Carangas, and Paria included mountainous terrain as well as temperate and even subtropical valleys. In these areas, at least in the valleys, mortality might be expected to be high. Using the rate of population decline between 1561 and 1575 as an indication of the rate of the drop between the conquest and 1561, Sánchez-Albornoz estimates that the native population of at least that section of Upper Peru was reduced by about 60 percent between the conquest and 1683. It was probably not until after the 1719–1722 epidemic that the Indian population of the zone finally began to recover, so the total decline in the area may have been 75 percent.[14]

Coerced Resettlement: Reducciones and Their Abandonment

Though the impact of forced migrations of Indians following the resettlement program of the Viceroy Francisco de Toledo in the 1570s was not as devastating to the area's demographic structure as the epidemics, they had serious cultural and economic consequences. It has been estimated that as a result of population concentration more than

MAP 3. Provinces of Upper Peru

Source: Jeffrey A. Cole, *The Potosi Mita: 1573–1700* (Stanford University Press, 1985).

1 million people were removed from their homes and forced to live in newly created reducciones.[15] Furthermore, in the mid-1560s, only a few years before the reducción policy was introduced, new administrative districts, or *corregimientos*, had been created to replace the encomiendas. Although the corregimientos were roughly the same as ex-

isting native political units, they still sometimes divided highland communal centers from lowland zones of colonization.[16] For instance, the corregimiento of Omasuyos was created on the puna on the eastern shore of Lake Titicaca, while slightly further east and in a lower altitude the district of Larecaja was established. This political division had the effect of limiting the access of the highland people to the lowland maize-producing regions upon which they depended.[17]

Sometimes the reducciones were founded on the sites of actual pre-Hispanic villages, although people from several previous communities might be settled in them. In other cases they were situated in new locations altogether. In general, the colonial government considered about 500 adult men, or 2,500 to 3,000 people, to be the optimum size for these settlements because that was thought to be the number of people a single priest could easily catechize.[18] This meant a significantly reduced number of villages in any given territory. For instance, in the province of Pacajes, the 1,228 adult male Indians in the repartimiento of Callapa had resided in nine villages before the resettlement program, whereas afterward they lived in three. In Caquiaviri, also in Pacajes, for some reason, the 500-man rule was not followed and 1,500 adult men were reduced from twenty-three towns to a single town.[19] This pattern was repeated throughout much of Upper Peru. In the provinces of Carangas, Paria, Porco, Chayanta, Cochabamba, and Tarija, a total of 901 towns were reduced to forty-four. The average total population per town before the reduction was 143 people, and afterward it was 2,920.[20]

While each village was supposed to be allotted sufficient land nearby for its subsistence, the amount most groups actually had access to was probably considerably reduced after resettlement, because the government reasoned that since the Indian population had fallen due to epidemic diseases, communities needed less territory.[21] In addition, since the reducciones were generally located either on the altiplano or on high-altitude valley sides, highland groups were often separated from colonies they had traditionally maintained in valleys. This meant that in addition to having less land than before, many groups also apparently lost the labor of some of their mitimaes in different ecological niches. On the other hand, with the creation of new towns and new *corregimientos* (the district under the jurisdiction of a corregidor), mitimaes sometimes found themselves subject to colonial fiscal and labor demands in both the highland zone that was their original home and the lowland area in which they lived. For instance, mitimaes from Omasuyos who lived in Larecaja continued to pay tribute to their kurakas on the puna and to serve in the mita of Potosí with contingents from Omasuyos. Yet, in addition, they were subject to agricultural mitas in the valleys they lived in and also had to pay tribute to local officials and to take turns serving the parish priest.[22] Under these circumstances, many indigenous colonists made efforts to dissociate themselves from the communities on the altiplano that claimed them as members.

Many of Toledo's reducciones endured and are today the sites of towns or indigenous communities; others, however, began to be abandoned by their populations shortly after their creation.[23] Many people simply returned to home communities which they had been forced to leave. But, with access to lowland zones now more limited, both temporary and permanent migration to valley areas became alternate means of acquiring needed agricultural products.[24] In fact, it appears that in many cases this type of migration was actually a group strategy in which highland kurakas played important roles. Kurakas from both Pacajes and Chucuito, having lost the labor of their mitimaes, bought haciendas in lowland areas and sent people from their communities there as migrant workers.[25] Migration to haciendas owned by Spaniards was also organized by community leaders both as a means of acquiring essential valley products and of raising the money to pay the groups' tribute. Temporary labor on haciendas as a community strategy, discussed in more detail in chapter 7, was common in the province of Pilaya y Paspaya.

Perhaps the most important factor contributing to the desertion of the reducciones was the mita for the Potosí mines, since mitayos were drawn from the new settlements, whereas the valley zones, to which many people fled, were not subject to the labor draft. Just as mitimaes chose to disconnect themselves from their puna ayllus of origin to avoid the draft, so highland residents could escape it by leaving their homes and hiding their ties to their communities.

To fully understand the mita's role in causing people to leave their villages, one must remember that the labor draft was more than

TABLE 3.1 Estimated Monthly Living Costs for a Mitayo in Potosí, 1596

Expenses	Cost in Pesos
Half *fanega* of *chuño*	10
One alpaca	4
Fish, chilies, salt	2
Firewood, straw	4
Coca	5
Chicha	1
TOTAL	26

Source: Antonio de Ayans, "Breve relación de los agravios que reciben los indios que ay desde cerca del Cuzco hasta Potosí," in *Pareceres en asuntos de indios*, ed. Rubén Vargas Ugarte (Lima: 1951), p. 38.

just an onerous burden for the individuals involved: the mita actually functioned as a conduit for transferring the Indian communities' surplus to the Potosí mining industry. Actually, ever since the discovery of the mountain of silver at Potosí, miners had been able to attract a sizable work force to the site without the assistance of a state-controlled labor draft.[26] What the mita did for the entrepreneurs of Potosí was to guarantee that the labor force was inexpensive. Wages paid to forced workers were generally below subsistence level, and the difference between what workers were paid and what they required for survival was made up by their villages. In other words, the Indian communities actually subsidized the silver industry.[27]

In 1596 Father Antonio de Ayans wrote of the high prices in Potosí and calculated that a mitayo required approximately twenty-six pesos a month simply to feed himself (see table 3.1).[28] Mitayos earned on the average two and a half pesos a week, or ten pesos a month—clearly a gaping deficit between their salaries and necessary expenditures. They attempted to make up, or at least reduce, this deficit in various ways. First of all, workers always brought food and provisions from their homes when they came to Potosí. Records of contingents of mitayos dispatched from the province of Chucuito during the seventeenth century indicate that each man took with him a number of llamas loaded with such things as chuño and chilies to eat during the journey and during his stay in Potosí. Caciques who were responsible for delivering the workers from their communities generally were able to bring the most animals with them, sometimes as many as two dozen, while common mitayos often had only two or three.[29]

Second, relatives, particularly wives, were indispensable to the mitayos during their shifts in Potosí, because, in fact, it was the couple, or the family, that was the productive unit during the mita. Men often could not complete their tasks in the mines without their wives' help. A kuraka from Pacajes explained: "The work is so formidable every week, day and night, that [the women] continually help by carrying metal on their backs." Women and children frequently found additional employment outside the mines to help the family survive. The same kuraka claimed that mitayos were forced to "sell or indenture their wives and daughters in private homes and in *chicherias*."[30] The fact that men are said to be "selling" their wives instead of their wives selling their own labor is a significant point.

Considering the drain on the human and economic resources of the Indian communities, it is not surprising that many people ultimately chose to leave. Nor was it accidental that among the first reducciones to be abandoned were those closest to Potosí. By 1590 the towns of Puna, Chaqui, Yura, Visisa, and Caiza, between two and twelve leagues (or up to sixty kilometers) from Potosí, were so depleted of adult male Indians that they no longer sent contingents to the mita.[31] In addition to being convenient pools from which mitayos were drawn, these towns' accessibility probably also meant that taxes could be easily collected in them and that their populations might be called upon to provide various other goods and services to Spaniards who were flooding the area.

Patterns of Dispersal and Conflict over Labor

Of those who left their communities, an unknown number took refuge in marginal areas of Upper Peru that were beyond the effective political control of the Spanish.[32] The majority did not venture quite so far afield, however, and if they managed to avoid the mita, they

Indian Population and Migration

were still integrated into the regional economy in other ways. Indians gravitated to valley haciendas, or *chacras*, in zones that were not subject to the mita. Smaller mining centers in Upper Peru also drew migrant Indians who hoped to become mine workers and possibly to benefit from some independent prospecting. Still others took up residence in Indian communities other than their own, where, if they did not enjoy all the rights of original residents, presumably also did not suffer all the burdens, including the mita.[33]

These migrations caused a major redistribution of the Indian population of the zone. Nicolás Sánchez-Albornoz and Nathan Wachtel have compared census figures from 1573 (the *visita* of the Viceroy Francisco de Toledo) and 1683 (the *numeración* of Viceroy de la Palata) for portions of the Andean region. Sánchez-Albornoz concentrates on ten provinces in the southern and eastern portions of Upper Peru—Yamparaes, Tomina, Porco, Chayanta, Tarija, Sicasica, Cochabamba, Mizque, Carangas, and Paria—which contain substantial valley zones, while Wachtel examines population change in eight central and northern provinces on the altiplano on both sides of Lake Titicaca—Carangas, Paria, Pacajes, Chucuito, Omasuyos, Asillo, Paucarcolla, and Cavana. Two provinces that appear in the findings of both scholars, Paria and Canrangas, are highland ones. The results from both studies, given in table 3.2, indicate the effects of population decline and migration over a wide area of Upper Peru.

The primary census category in both counts was the adult male Indian, or tributary, since adult men were subject to tribute assessments. Theoretically, all men between eighteen and fifty years of age fell into this category no matter where they lived, although in reality some may have escaped taxes by migrating beyond the reach of the tax collector or their community leaders who were given the responsibility of delivering the tribute. Table 3.2 compares the number of tributaries to the number of *originarios* (Indians who were living in the reducciones to which they had been assigned by Viceroy Francisco de Toledo). Being an originario, or original resident, did not necessarily have anything to do with where one's ancestors had lived before the Spanish invasion or even before the 1570s.

Looking first at the totals for all sixteen provinces, we see that while the number of originarios declined by 68 percent, the number

TABLE 3.2 Variation in Originario Population and Tributary Population in Sixteen Provinces of Upper Peru, 1573–1683

	1573	1683		% of Variation	
	Tributary Population (Adult Males)	Tributary Population (Adult Males)	Originarios	Tributary Population (Adult Males)	Originarios
Provinces studied by Sánchez-Albornoz					
Yamparaes	1,861	1,224	455	−34	−76
Tomina	531	509	260	−4	−51
Porco	3,733	4,543	3,094	+21	−17
Chayanta	5,759	7,997	4,440	+39	−23
Tarija	833	1,323	659	+59	−21
Sicasica	3,445	3,442	901	0	−74
Cochabamba	3,180	1,794	319	−44	−90
Mizque	1,308	805	192	−38	−83
Carangas	6,254	2,580	2,251	−58	−63
Paria	7,717	2,779	2,287	−64	−70
Provinces studied by Wachtel					
Pacajes	9,282	3,647	2,499	−61	−78
Chucuito	17,963	7,259	4,538	−60	−75
Omasuyos	8,223	4,978	1,362	−39	−83
Paucarcolla	5,495	2,528	1,242	−54	−77
Azangaro, Asillo	6,669	3,432	1,848	−49	−72
Cavana	8,065	4,570	2,257	−43	−72
TOTAL	90,318	53,410	28,604	−41	−68

Sources: Sánchez-Albornoz, *Indios y tributos*, pp. 28–31; Wachtel, "Hommes d'eau," pp. 1154–55.

of all adult Indian men dropped by only 41 percent. (Toledo's census makes no distinction between tributaries, or adult men, and originarios, since every man gathered in the new reducciones was assumed to be in his proper place, and therefore an originario.) The variation is explained by the fact that when an originario left his place of origin, he often reappeared somewhere else and was still counted in censuses. Likewise, in many cases, when a man left his home community, his place was taken by another migrant from somewhere else, because community leaders generally tried to rent vacant lands to raise revenue for tribute payments and other expenses. So, while absolute population decline cannot be minimized, it still was not as great as the reduction of the originario group seems to indicate.[34]

Comparison of the two regions shows that the ten provinces studied by Sánchez-Albornoz (in the south and eastern areas of Upper Peru) had fewer adult male Indians in Toledo's time (1573) than the eight used in Wachtel's research.[35] Yet the northern and central zones experienced greater decline in adult men between 1573 and 1683 (54 percent); in the eastern and southern provinces, the drop was only 22 percent. This was because a number of these eastern and southern provinces received migrants from the northern altiplano region, since the influx of indigenous people was greatest in valley regions where Spaniards were developing agricultural estates or in highland zones where there were silver mines.[36] Altiplano provinces that were subject to the mita of Potosí, where the traditional grazing economy was in decline, and where Spaniards had not developed significant agricultural enterprises, attracted the fewest migrants.

The variations in population change according to ecological region may also be seen in table 3.2. In Cochabamba, a province comprised primarily of temperate valleys, both adult men and originarios declined between 1570 and 1680, although the number of originarios declined much more drastically. Both mortality and flight probably contributed to the loss of originarios, since epidemics must have been virulent in the valleys, while five villages in the highland portions of the province had to send mitayos to Potosí each year—thus spurring emigration.[37]

Also, Cochabamba's reducciones may have been particularly vulnerable internally, since they were more artificial and less ethnically cohesive than those in other regions of Upper Peru. This had its origins in Inca policy that had uprooted many mitimaes and local ethnic groups from the valley and replaced them with a patchwork of forced immigrants, many of whom then returned to their home communities after the Spanish victory.[38] The *pueblos reales*, as Cochabamba's reducciones were called, were actually conglomerations of remaining mitimaes and people from local ethnic groups. They were probably even more likely than many others to be abandoned; in fact, one of them, Tiquipaya, had virtually no men of tribute-paying age by 1617.[39] Since Cochabamba was an area of commercial agriculture, particularly grain production, it wasn't difficult for Indians seeking to avoid the mita to find work on haciendas. This replacement of the original residents by immigrants explains why the originario population could fall by 90 percent while the adult male population fell by only 44 percent.

Paria, Pacajes, and Chucuito, three provinces on the altiplano, also saw major declines in both categories between 1573 and 1683, and the greatest drops in total adult male population of all the provinces studied. All three provinces sent men annually to Potosí and were impoverished by this continual drain on the resources of their communities.[40] Furthermore, they were probably also affected by the general decline in the traditional grazing industry on the high plateau (see chapter 2). These factors undoubtedly contributed to the flight of original residents. That the decline in the originario group was still somewhat greater than that for all adult men in these three provinces probably indicates that people from other areas settled in villages abandoned by originarios. In addition, both Paria and Chucuito had silver mines, so it is also possible that the flight of original residents was compensated by the arrival of immigrants who came to work in the mines.

Of all provinces listed in the table, Tarija showed the greatest growth in the number of adult male Indians between 1573 and 1683, while the decline in the originario population was also quite low. A distant valley frontier zone in which originarios were not required to do mita service, like Pilaya y Paspaya, Tarija received many short- and long-term migrants who came to work on agricultural properties and in some cases may even have become small landowners themselves. It was a region where work was available but also one in which a fugitive from the mita might lose himself in the diverse population, which included acculturated Chiriguanos as well as free blacks and mulattoes. (See chapter 7.)

The flight of people from their communities made it difficult for the colonial government to collect taxes and ensure that entrepreneurs in Potosí received the proper number of mitayos each year. The

Indian Population and Migration

departure of originarios also increased the burdens on kurakas who had to bring the contingents of workers to the mining center. In 1625 Diego Chambilla, a *capitán de la mita* from the community of Pomata in Chucuito, claimed he had gone with a Spaniard to the valleys of Upper Peru to try to reclaim originarios from his village. He reported that the task was impossible because owners of chacras (*chacareros*), eager to hold onto the Indians living on their lands, had threatened to kill them.[41]

Chambilla's reception would seem to be clear evidence that the estate owners were determined to keep the fugitives on their estates. As early as 1599, a judge from the Audiencia of Charcas had written to the king explaining the position of the chacareros:

> In this province there are more than one thousand chacras . . . on which more than 3,000 men, both Spaniards and Indians are occupied. Rather than deprive [the owners of their workers], the government should encourage them, because with these Indians the chacras raise food for a multitude of people, such as those in the city of Potosí, the mining center of Porco, and those in provinces that are sterile and do not produce food.[42]

In the late sixteenth and early seventeenth centuries, men and their families who left their villages and worked on Spanish estates were generally called *yanaconas*, the pre-Hispanic name for those in servile capacities who were no longer associated with their ayllus. Initially after the conquest, the term yanacona was applied to Indians who attached themselves to individual Spaniards as personal servants and retainers, often accompanying conquistadores on military missions into unexplored territory.[43] By the time of Viceroy Francisco de Toledo, the number of yanaconas had multiplied significantly, and they were found working in a number of contexts, including on agricultural properties where they were usually given parcels of land in usufruct.[44]

While in some instances Indians apparently voluntarily chose *yanaconaje* on haciendas, the experience of Diego Chambilla and other evidence indicates that this was not always the case, or at least that once having decided to be a yanacona, one could find it very difficult to change one's mind. Thierry Saignes cites the testimony of a *juez reducidor* (official responsible for returning people to their reducciones) who was sent to various frontier zones, including Pilaya y Paspaya, to retrieve Indians from Chucuito. The official claimed to have brought back "more than 250 young males and females who had been held in the valleys and chacras by force and against their wishes. Some had been spirited away and deceived by the owners of the chacras and others sold as if they were slaves."[45]

The situation presented a series of problems, both ethical and practical, which colonial administrators and jurists, beginning with Viceroy Toledo, tried to resolve. Ethically, the institution of yanaconaje flew in the face of Spanish philosophical principles favoring freely contracted and remunerated labor. In practical terms, every Indian working on an estate as a yanacona was one less laborer who would serve in the mita draft for the viceroyalty's most valuable mines. In 1574 Viceroy Francisco de Toledo himself set forth regulations designed to curtail the multiplication of yanaconas without depriving estate owners of their work force. In these "Ordenanzas de yanaconas de Charcas," Toledo attempted to deal with the fact that many of these Indians were actually new arrivals on the estates where they were working, were not descended from any traditional servile group, and should be allowed, under certain limited circumstances, to leave. He issued a series of guidelines, the most pertinent of which I quote below.[46]

> #7 Yanaconas who have been residing on chacras for four years or more must remain there, and no one can make them leave against their will; nor can they go anywhere else without just cause and express permission to do so from the Audiencia of Charcas, or its president, to whom they must first apply for permission. If permission is granted, it will only be to return to their communities.

> #8 Indians who have been living on chacras less than four years may return to their villages, if they wish to, within two months of the publication of the *Ordenanzas* . . . and own-

Indian Population and Migration 77

ers of the chacras will not receive any new Indians, except for vagrants whom they will obtain with the help of the local *corregidor*.

The ordinances of Viceroy Toledo also stipulated how yanaconas were to provide their subsistence and earn the money for their tribute. They indicate again the government's view that these Indians should in some situations be considered free contracting parties: yanaconas were to be allowed to sell their labor and market their produce without the control of the landowner.

> #11 Owners of chacras will give yanaconas land to plant . . . and oxen, plows, and plowshares with which to work. They will also give [yanaconas] time to work in their fields before they work on the lands of their masters, so that they can feed and clothe themselves and their families. [Landowners] will allow yanaconas to go and sell their produce when the owners send their own produce to the city or to Potosí. [This will not be done] in any other manner. [Owners] will not contract with the yanaconas themselves, under penalty of a fifty-peso fine . . .

> #14 Yanaconas, if they are married, from the age of eighteen years until that of fifty, will pay one *peso ensayado* every year in tribute to His Majesty. In addition to the time allowed to them to work in their fields, [chacareros] will give yanaconas ten days a year to hire themselves out in order to earn the peso which they must pay in tribute. The landowners themselves may hire the yanaconas on these days, paying them the same wage that they would receive from another.

While these two provisions imply a certain freedom of action for yanaconas, especially with respect to marketing their goods without coercion, Toledo's only direct comment on the yanaconas' freedom under the Spanish legal code sounds more like cynical formalism than a genuine attempt to deal with an ethical or moral problem:

#13 Since the yanaconas are free, in sales of chacras no mention, verbal or written, will be made of them under penalty of a fine of 1,000 pesos and the notary's loss of his position.

This last regulation obviously suggests that yanaconas were often transferred like slaves when property changed hands, even if they did not appear in notarial records. In fact, many Indian workers complained of this abuse in Pilaya y Paspaya well into the eighteenth century (see chapter 7).

Toledo's ordinances were part of the viceroy's overall administrative reorganization of Peru, but other aspects of his program (mercury amalgamation, the mita, the reducciones) actually increased the flight of Indians from their villages and therefore the number of yanaconas. After his administration, succeeding viceroys attempted to maintain the Toledan status quo: that is, to prevent the creation of new yanaconas while accepting as legitimate those yanaconas and their descendants who had been recognized by Toledo. But since yanaconas were exempt from the obligation to serve in the mita, and since agricultural production greatly increased under the stimulus of the Potosí market, there was more reason for Indians to want to "yanaconize" themselves and more reason for hacendados to welcome their arrival.

When King Philip III issued the 1601 royal decree that sought to abolish personal servitude in the viceroyalty of Peru (see chapter 2), he specified that yanaconas living on chacras be informed that they were free to leave and could contract independently with employers. In 1604 the cabildo of the city of La Plata responded to the decree. Its members wrote: "Once outside of the chacras where they are currently enrolled, under no circumstances will [yanaconas] want to work, because they are lazy and the enemies of work . . . and without their presence on the chacras there will be no food for this land."[47]

In the next decade, the marques de Montesclaros, who was viceroy of Peru from 1607 to 1615, also made an attempt to resolve the yanacona problem. He sent a *visitador* to inspect the chacras in the jurisdiction of La Plata to determine how many Indians were working as yanaconas who were actually from indigenous reducciones subject to the mita. His emissary, Francisco de Alfaro, found 920 chacras in the area. On these properties there were almost 7,000 men from villages that were obligated to send workers to Potosí and had no claim to be descendants of the yanaconas living on the estates in the time of Toledo. The next viceroy, the principe de Esquilache, attempted to force all Indians to return to their villages and even offered some minimal relief from their communal obligations by reducing the number of workers each *congregación* had to send to Potosí. Failing in his efforts, he apparently despaired of resolving the problem and in 1620 wrote to King Philip III about the thousands of illegal yanaconas Alfaro had found. He said, "We don't dare to return them [to their villages] because at that point Potosí will perish of hunger."[48]

The conflict between the Potosí interests and the landowners is particularly interesting because while each group maintained that without coercion they would not have a work force, the reality appears to be otherwise. As explained, the mita was an *inexpensive* work force, not the only form of labor available to the mine owners. Laborers were also apparently willing to work on the region's agricultural estates; they did not have to be brought by force, only prevented from leaving. This suggests that indigenous people in the Andes were not simply lazy and unwilling to sell their labor, but rather that landowners either wanted to pay less than was necessary to attract and keep a work force, or that people abandoned their employment once they had earned enough to meet certain pressing necessities, or both. Each possibility is related to the native population's continuing access to the means of production in the form of peasant agriculture. The separation of the work force from the land would take centuries in the Andes; it is not entirely complete even today (see chapter 4). We shall return frequently to this issue in examining the development of noncoerced labor in Pilaya y Paspaya and Oruro.

Forasteros and Yanaconas

Migrants to urban areas were also sometimes known as yanaconas, and frequently served in convents or other religious institutions. In the early years in Potosí, before the introduction of the mercury amalgamation process, yanaconas were the masters of the *guairas*, or small kilns used for smelting metal at the mining site.[49] At the time of his 1573 inspection, Francisco de Toledo found yanaconas in Potosí involved in many commercial and craft activities as well as working as miners.[50] By the seventeenth century, yanaconas in cities such as Oruro worked at various occupations, especially crafts, many of which required considerable skill (see chapter 5).

In the seventeenth century, and sometimes earlier, the term *forastero*, meaning outsider or stranger, also began to be used for Indians who had left their communities. Forasteros were often found living in circumstances similar to yanaconas: in mining camps, in cities, and on haciendas or chacras. In fact, in all these settings both types of migrants commonly coexisted. People who had taken the places of absent originarios in indigenous communities were generally referred to as forasteros as well. Both types of migrants were Indians who had left their reducciones (or descendants of those who had left); however, there were certain differences between a forastero and a yanacona.

Forasteros in the seventeenth century generally came from reducciones created during Toledo's administration and most often could state their origins: the town they came from and frequently the ayllu and parcialidad (or moiety) as well.[51] They could often identify their roots so specifically that scholars suspect that they may have been functioning as mitimaes or llacturunas (temporary or seasonal colonists) and that, in fact, migration was a communal rather than an individual effort.[52] In a study of the community of Sipesipe in Cochabamba in 1645, Sánchez-Albornoz suggests that about twenty-nine forastero couples out of 166 in the community were likely connected to one of these Andean migratory groups. It was also feasible that an Indian considered a llactaruna in his village of origin might have been judged a forastero in the valley where he settled; as ties between a highland village and its colony became more attenuated, an individual's identification might have changed.[53]

The forastero may also have sought to maintain his link with his community of origin to avoid permanent immigrant status. Children and even the grandchildren of forasteros were considered outsiders, apparently not becoming originarios of the communities in which they lived even if the family had lived there for several generations.[54] In the case of yanaconas, the emphasis was different. Although many were also refugees from Toledan communities, they commonly claimed to have no knowledge of their ancestors, or to come from families of yanaconas based in major colonial cities.⁵⁵ Sánchez-Albornoz, however, comments that perhaps the term *yanacona* appeared suitable to hacendados because of its connotation of perpetual servitude. On the other hand, the term *forastero* was used more in Indian communities where the community wanted to reinforce the immigrants' status as outsiders, therefore denying them the rights and privileges that accrued to originarios.⁵⁶

By the mid-seventeenth century, forasteros outnumbered yanaconas among Indian migrants to the region. In 1645 the viceroy, the marques de Mancera, ordered a count of Indian men in Upper Peru to determine the size of the tributary population and to test the possibility, by including the Indian population of provinces that were previously unaffected, of sending more men to serve in the Potosí mita. The records from this enumeration are almost certainly incomplete and therefore unreliable for measuring the size of the Indian population in this period or for comparison with earlier and later censuses. It is not even certain that all towns in the designated provinces were counted. Furthermore, the existing summary of the census results may not incorporate all the areas counted. Nonetheless, the totals for the male Indian population in the bishoprics of Cuzco, La Paz, and Chuquisaca (table 3.3) give a general idea of the numbers of migrants and their offspring in the Indian population in 1645.⁵⁷

The summary demonstrates that while almost 22 percent of the men counted were forasteros, only 14 percent were yanaconas. These yanaconas were primarily concentrated in the cities of Cuzco, La Paz, and the province of Porco, where they probably mostly lived in the mining center with the same name. However, some agricultural zones, notably Pilaya y Paspaya, Omasuyos, and Sicasica, also had fairly high percentages of yanaconas.

Of the three major areas represented in the table, La Paz had the highest percentages of both forasteros and yanaconas, and only 51 percent of the Indian men in the zone were originarios. However, a misleading figure for the city of Potosí tends to inflate the number of originarios in Chuquisaca. Presumably the 9,000 originarios in the villa imperial (Potosí) were either mitayos who had come from the sixteen provinces of Upper Peru subject to the draft, or former mi-

TABLE 3.3 Categories of Male Indians in Upper Peru in 1646

	Originarios	(%)	Forasteros	(%)	Yanaconas	(%)	Total
Cuzco							
City of Cuzco	0	—	412	(14)	2,497	(86)	2,909
Quispicanches	2,235	(78)	449	(16)	162	(6)	2,846
Canas y Canches	3,219	(78)	797	(19)	128	(3)	4,144
Azángaro	2,478	(80)	484	(16)	130	(4)	3,092
Cabana	2,137	(63)	1,105	(32)	172	(5)	3,413
Paucarcolla	1,775	(58)	1,085	(36)	178	(6)	3,038
Chucuito	3,194	(71)	925	(21)	365	(8)	4,484
SUBTOTAL	15,038	(63)	5,257	(22)	3,632	(15)	23,927
La Paz							
City of La Paz	0	—	132	(15)	718	(85)	850
Larecaja	3,883	(58)	1,916	(28)	951	(14)	6,650
Omasuyos	963	(41)	890	(38)	508	(21)	2,361
Pacajes	2,546	(74)	571	(17)	301	(9)	3,418
Sicasica	1,286	(35)	1,664	(46)	672	(19)	3,622
SUBTOTAL	8,878	(51)	5,173	(30)	3,150	(19)	17,001
Chuquisaca							
Potosí	9,000	(89)	0	—	1,065	(11)	10,065
Paria	1,987	(86)	307	(13)	16	(1)	2,310
Porco	3,547	(67)	433	(8)	1,349	(25)	5,329
Carangas	1,391	(91)	91	(6)	40	(3)	1,522
Cochabamba	1,047	(24)	2,946	(68)	318	(8)	4,311
Mizque, S. Cruz	1,662	(91)	169	(9)	0	—	1,831
Tomina	995	(75)	179	(14)	152	(11)	1,326
Chichas	1,667	(82)	224	(11)	152	(7)	2,043
Pilaya y Paspaya	280	(24)	667	(58)	212	(18)	1,159
SUBTOTAL	21,576	(72)	5,016	(17)	3,304	(11)	29,896
TOTAL	45,292	(64)	15,446	(22)	10,086	(14)	70,824

Source: Sánchez-Albornoz, "Migraciones internas en el Alto Peru," 15–16. Based on summary of census by Phelipe de Bolívar (1646) published in Silvio Zavala, *El servicio personal de los indios en el Perú* 2:109.

tayos who had stayed on in the city after their shifts had ended.[58] Therefore, although they were in Potosí at the time of the census, it is inaccurate to count them as originarios of the city or even of Chuquisaca, since their origin was unknown.

Two of the three provinces with the highest percentages of forasteros, Cochabamba and Pilaya y Paspaya, were valley areas that produced commercial crops for urban markets. In these zones most of the forasteros probably worked on agricultural estates, although in both provinces some forasteros lived in Indian communities.[59] The province with the third highest percentage of forasteros, Sicasica, was primarily a highland zone, but its extreme eastern portion was made up of hot jungle valleys, or yungas. Some of the forasteros in Sicasica may have lived in Indian reducciones. Others, however, probably took refuge in the yungas, where a migrant might find work on a Spanish-owned chacra or hacienda that sent agricultural products to La Paz and to other cities. In Paucarcolla, in the bishopric of Cuzco (the province with the fifth highest percentage of forasteros), immigrants probably rented land from Indian communities but also found work on the ranches that Spaniards were developing in the area.

By 1646 a clear pattern of Indian migration had been established: 36 percent of the men counted in that year's census were migrants and their descendants (forasteros and yanaconas) and were primarily concentrated in valley agricultural zones, although a significant proportion had also gravitated toward urban areas. By 1683, when the census was conducted at the request of the duque de la Palata, migrants and their descendants had risen to 54 percent, 47 percent being forasteros and 7 percent yanaconas. In that year as well, immigrants were concentrated primarily in frontier valleys and in highland urban areas.[60]

Conclusion

Researchers generally interpret the development of this sizable immigrant population in the seventeenth century in two, not necessarily contradictory, ways. The first sees the migrations as reflecting the drastic restructuring of indigenous society in Upper Peru that had occurred since the Spanish invasion of the previous century. Not only had the native population been absolutely reduced by the waves of epidemic diseases, but also resettlement in compact communities and forced labor in Potosí had caused people to leave their ayllus. Moreover, leaving home was frequently associated with reliance on wage labor. As one writer explained, "Other [forasteros] place themselves at the service of Spaniards and . . . have no land to cultivate and eat from their labor."[61] Migration and selling one's labor might be seen as the first steps in a process of acculturation by which class eventually took precedence over ethnic identity. With this change in culture and consciousness there would also eventually be an increase in racial and ethnic mixing, since choices about marrying and forming families would be shaped more by class situation than community membership. This transformation would be a prolonged and uneven process, one that still continues today, but, at least in some cases, it could be argued that it was well under way in the late seventeenth century.

The second view of the migrations is that sometimes they actually minimized the disruptions caused by colonialism. Adapting to and utilizing the market economy allowed some individuals, families, and communities to find substitutes for the ecological zones to which they had lost access and therefore helped them to sustain communal relations. Likewise, participating in the market, whether as a worker or as a landowner (as some kurakas did), could conceivably foster the continuation of certain reciprocal relationships based on an exchange of goods and services.

The following chapters explore the extent to which either of these scenarios describes the experiences of migrants in Oruro and Pilaya y Paspaya in the seventeenth and early eighteenth centuries. They look at reliance on remunerated labor and degree of acculturation, and attempt to distinguish between individually adopted economic and social strategies and those that were communally based. They also examine how women's participation in the market differed from or complemented that of indigenous men. While some Andean communal projects continued under colonialism, more than a hundred years of colonization by a mercantile capitalist power clearly brought about social differentiation in the native population. Any understanding of how native society changed rests on an appreciation of these new class divisions that now overlay and interacted with ethnic identity.

· 4 ·

A Colonial Andean Mining Center

Oruro, 1607–1720

IN 1607 Felipe de Godoy, secretary of the Audiencia of Charcas, made an inspection the new mining center of San Felipe de Austria, popularly called Oruro. In his report he observed,

> Many [Indians] go to Oruro because Indians always go where there is the most to be gained. . . . In Oruro the profit is great from the metals the Indians carry to their homes. Besides this, they are right next to their villages and their houses to which they can go every day. The necessities for their survival also cost one-third to one-half less than they do in Potosí.[1]

In this passage, Godoy appears to desribing an intermediary stage between agricultural self-sufficiency and wage labor; the workers needed to buy some portion of their necessities, but they were also near their homes where it seems likely that they had land. In fact, his description sounds remarkably modern; in many parts of Latin America today, because laborers and their families produce at least some portion of their subsistence through peasant agriculture, employers can pay wages below those required for the family's reproduction.

However, rather than seeing them as exploited semiproletarians, Godoy clearly thought the Indians who came to work in Oruro's mines were fortunate, especially when compared to mitayos in Potosí. Furthermore, unlike many of his contemporaries, rather than emphasizing the workers' lack of acquisitiveness and their laziness, Godoy paints a picture of so many fledgling capitalists, always going "where there is the most to be gained." Godoy then explains another reason why going to Oruro was desirable: "When I arrived in that city," he wrote, "I found the *cerro* [hill] of San Cristobal full of stands occupied by Spaniards who assisted in redeeming the metals that [the Indians] stole."[2] Workers seem to have made a substantial portion of their mining income through independent prospecting, or by "stealing" metals, even though they were also paid a wage.

Was this just the biased point of view of a member of the elite who wanted the royal government to lower production costs for Oruro entrepreneurs by assigning allotments of forced laborers to the mines? Certainly Godoy's opinions reflected the attitudes of his class, but his comments point to a significant contradiction in the colonial economic system. Essentially, in early seventeenth-century Oruro the workers' connection with the means of production in the form of land had mixed results. On the one hand, it may have allowed owners of mines and mills to pay low wages, although entrepreneurs insisted this wasn't always the case. On the other hand, the Indians' access to land forced employers to permit "ore sharing" in order to attract enough workers. Because this raised their costs, it potentially undermined the owners' control of the industry. To put the paradox another way: while the government was determined (for practical and principled reasons) not to extend the mita to Oruro, the forces of capitalist production had not yet evolved to the point where employers could impose a strict wage labor system, either. This anomaly not only gave workers some leverage in their dealings with employers, it also curiously permitted the continuation of Andean cultural patterns in the most industrialized sector of the colonial economy.

Obviously, wages and other forms of compensation, as well as the degree to which workers could use labor in Oruro to sustain communal life, changed over the seventeenth century, most particularly in response to the productivity of the mines. But labor in Oruro also has to be understood in the context of the Upper Peruvian mining industry as a whole, especially the mita for the Potosí mines. Extraeconomic coercion made mita labor very cheap; it was migrant Indians, often fleeing the mita, who made up Oruro's work force. Because there was free and forced labor within the same industry, owners constantly strove to reduce all wages to the lowest level. Entrepreneurs did not merely want to pay a simple wage and eliminate ore sharing; they wanted to pay as little as their counterparts in Potosí did. So, if workers in Oruro had some advantages because of access to land, they also had to struggle against being forced to the poverty level of mitayos.[3]

This chapter examines how the silver industry in Oruro changed in the century after Godoy's 1607 visit and the effects of these changes on labor. How did mine owners mobilize a work force and lower their costs? To what extent were they able to impose a wage-labor regime and curtail the workers' practice of "stealing" metal as part of their compensation? Was it ever possible to pay their workers as little as mitayos? What sector of the population was totally dependent on wage labor, and how dependent were those who had other means of subsistence? This question of dependence on paid labor is closely related to the issue of acculturation and whether a shift occurred from consciousness based on ethnicity to one that incorporated both ethnic and class identity.

Oruro and the Development of Its Mines

The Villa de San Felipe de Austria was officially founded in 1606, several months after the judges of the Audiencia of Charcas sent Manuel de Castro y Padilla to supervise the planning of the city. It was to be constructed according to the Spanish model and to be called a *villa*, in recognition of the importance of the area's silver deposits and the many Spaniards already settled there despite the harsh environment.

Located on an incline, Oruro's central plaza is 3,703 meters (12,148 feet) above sea level. The city is surrounded by a vast desert, complete with shifting sand dunes to the north and east. The area is extremely windy, and in winter (July to October) when gusts are the worst, twisting columns of sand and dust rise over the altiplano. Dust darkens the sky, floods in under doors and through windows, and covers all vegetation. Shrubs and trees in the city's center need special care just to survive. The sandstorms would be worse if it were not for a series of hills that form a protective crescent around the city and block the wind to some extent. In these hills are the silver mines that first brought people to the area. Mitigating the climate's inhospitality to some extent is the blazing midday sun. Oruro's average temperature is about 50 degrees Farenheit, but that figure disguises the huge difference between day, when it may reach 70 or 80 degrees, and night when the temperature can drop to well below freezing.[4]

The city that Felipe de Godoy visited in 1607 had a checkerboard layout around a main square, in accord with crown specifications for colonial settlements. According to José de Mesa and Teresa Gisbert, Oruro's designers followed this model so intently that they razed existing buildings that could not easily be incorporated into it. The end result was a grid pattern of seven blocks by eight blocks with the cathedral and buildings used by the cabildo (town council) in the central plaza. In the northern part of the city, adjacent to the Spanish town and extending parallel with it from the folds of the surrounding hills was the Indian town, or *ranchería de indios*. This was apparently planned as a separate neighborhood, or *barrio*, when the city was designed, and the ranchería's streets were grouped around the Church of San Miguel which was on the plaza with the same name.[5]

A unique feature of the urban organization of Oruro was what would now be called industrial suburbs that were considered part of the city. (See map 4.) Since water was in short supply and was necessary not only for personal use but also for the process of refining metal, silver grinding mills had been set up near Oruro on the Paria River in Las Sepulturas and on the Sorasora River.

In his report Godoy estimated that 6,000 Indians lived in the city and surrounding mills (*ingenios*), but it is not certain whether he means Indian men or the entire population.[6] Mesa and Gisbert were also uncertain as to Godoy's meaning on this point, but tentatively decided that he referred to Indian men only and placed the total Indian population of the city at about 18,000.[7] Added to this number were 258 Spanish men involved in mining and refining metals, plus 520 others—merchants, officials, etcetera. Assuming that they were heads of households with at least three others in the family, the city's total population was about 20,000, excluding the 127 men listed as lacking gainful employment.[8]

Felipe de Godoy made his trip to Oruro at a time of political conflict in the viceroyalty concerning the mining economy and the profitability of the Potosí mines. Viceroy conde de Monterrey had died in February 1606, and until the arrival of his successor, the marques de Montesclaros, in December 1607, the audiencias of Lima and Charcas competed for control of the region. In this conflict each audiencia supported a different group of mining interests in Upper Peru: Lima championed the cabildo of Potosí and seconded its resistance to giving aid (in the form of mitayos, mercury, or special subsidies) to any other mining center, including Oruro. The oidores in Lima argued that despite some decline in the ore mined in Potosí, the center was still one of the Spanish empire's greatest sources of wealth, and that any concessions granted to other sites would only drain resources from Potosí, where they could be put to better use. On the other hand, the members of the Audiencia of Charcas, who had founded San Felipe de Austria, favored the Oruro interests and advocated active government support for developing these rich new mines.[9]

However, if officials in Charcas supported Oruro and perhaps were even involved in mining ventures there, the audiencia's president, Licenciado Alonso Maldonado de Torres, was a vigorous advocate of the Potosí *azogueros*.[10] It was he who sent Felipe de Godoy to Oruro to report on mining conditions and to investigate rumors that Potosí was losing its best professional miners, skilled workers, and even its mitayos to Oruro because of the greater productivity of its newly discovered mines and high wages offered to laborers. Consequently, he may have been surprised when, instead of suggesting means of counteracting Oruro's presumed negative impact on Potosí, Godoy minimized these problems and proposed measures to aid Oruro's development.[11]

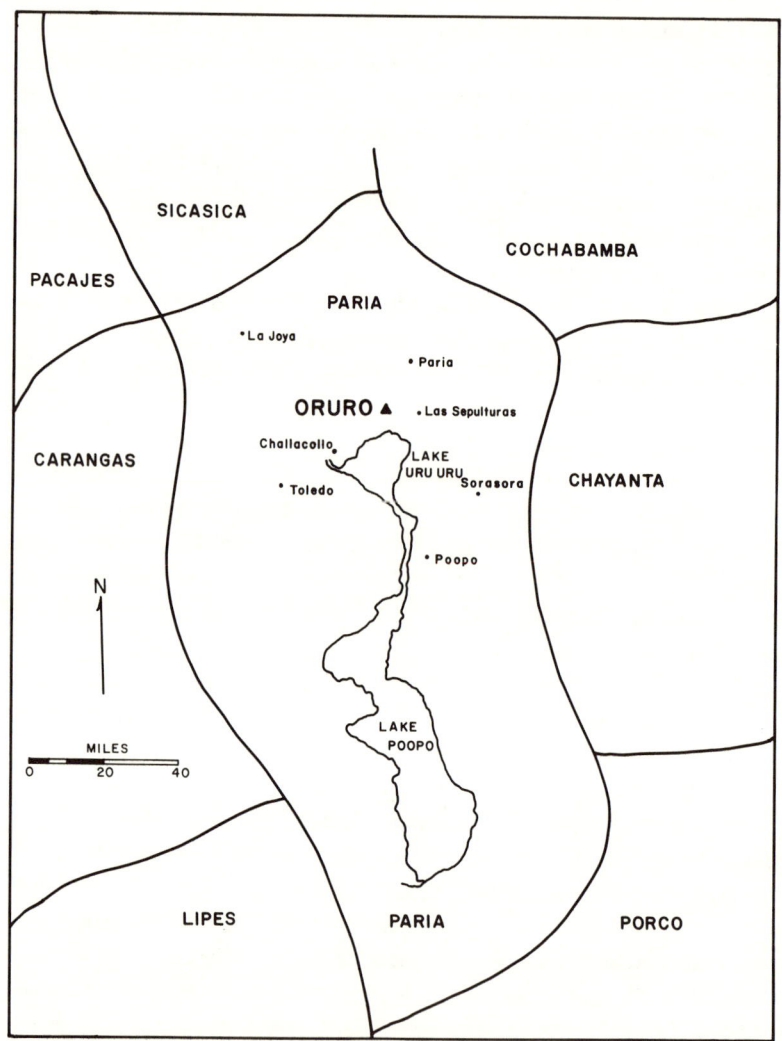

MAP 4. Oruro and Environs

During Godoy's 1607 visit, mining was under way in four of the hills surrounding the city: Pie de Gallo, La Flamenca, La Colorada, and San Cristobal. Mines, which according to law could be no more than eighty *varas* long, or approximately eighty meters,[12] were reached by tunnels (*socavones*), that crossed the major veins of metal. Although one person might own several mines, most owners were smallholders and frequently went bankrupt. There were 258 mine owners in 1607, but only 100 had enough capital to work their mines continuously. Most major undertakings, such as opening tunnels and cleaning mines for the first time so they could be worked, were done in partnerships because of the expense: few individuals had the money for these projects.[13]

Two of Oruro's earliest mine owners, Francisco and Diego de Medrano, had discovered the most important vein in the cerro of San Cristobal. Diego de Medrano, one of the town's most important entrepreneurs, had represented the industry in dealings with the viceroy and the Audiencia of Charcas; yet in the early years in Oruro his financial situation was quite precarious. After having registered mines in San Cristobal, the de Medranos had no money to pay workers to clean them. They allowed Indians, or anyone else, to take slag and ore from their mines and process it, simply to clear the mines so that they could be worked. They were also forced to rent several mines because they had no money to exploit them. In 1606, one Alonso Alvarez de Nava Revolledo arrived in Oruro and with 4,000 pesos formed a partnership with the de Medranos, who had obtained another short-term loan from a relative. Together they were able to begin mining full-time.[14]

Godoy reported that while the mineral content of ore mined in Oruro was generally high—three pesos per hundred pounds (or *quintal*)—output varied considerably.[15] For instance, in La Flamenca in veins in which the mineral was soft and easy to excavate, a team of one pickman (*barretero*) and one *apiri*, who hauled the ore out of the mine, could mine three quintales of ore in a day. In other mines, two barreteros and an apiri might only remove five or six quintales in a week.[16] After the mineral was mined, some very high-quality ores could be smelted in simple ovens. Most, however, had to be processed (ground and refined) in one of the ingenios on the rivers outside of town.[17] These mills depended on water: they ground more metal when there was rain and sometimes had to suspend operations during a drought. For instance, the ingenio of Juan Cabrera de Cárdenas on the Paria River, one of the most productive mills in the area, could grind between 160 and 180 quintales of metal in twenty-four hours during the rainy season. In the dry season (August to November), it ground only eighty quintales in that period.[18] In 1607 ten functioning ingenios were run by water, and one used horse power. Another eleven mills were either under construction or had been allocated construction sites.

A mill consisted of one or more heads (*cabezas*), which were mechanisms made up of a hydraulic wheel, an axis, and a number of hammers of iron or bronze in the shape of truncated pyramids called *mazos*, that pulverized the ore. (In 1607 only one ingenio in the Oruro area had more than one head, and only one of those was grinding.) After ore was ground, it was refined with mercury. Although the process varied according to the quality and type of metal, the basic procedure was to first combine the crushed and sifted metal with salt and mercury. This mixture was then tended for several days by Indian workers called *repasiris* who kneaded it with their feet. Next, impurities were rinsed away and the remaining silver and mercury were pressed through a fine screen that separated most of the mercury from the silver. The silver finally was placed in clay molds and smelted for eight to ten hours until the remaining mercury vaporized.[19]

At least six of the mine owners in Oruro in 1607 also owned ingenios, and only two men, who were partners, together owned two mills. Since building an ingenio required considerable capital, many mine owners paid an independent mercury grinder, or azoguero, to grind and refine their ore.[20]

Getting mercury in Oruro was frequently difficult. Before the royal treasury office, or *caja real*, was established in the city in May 1607, refiners bought quicksilver from private merchants who charged more than the official rate fixed by the royal mercury monopoly. These merchants also bought the refined blocks of silver (*piñas*) from the *ingenieros* and miners. Sellers in Oruro also lost in this transaction because they were forced to accept two reales less per mark of silver than the merchants received when they resold the ore in Potosí.[21] But, according to Godoy, things did not improve after the treasury office began to sell mercury and to buy ore: the amount of silver produced in Oruro declined because the mercury made available to the city was strictly limited. Viceroy de Montesclaros continued the policy of not allotting sufficient mercury to Oruro when he took office at the end of the year.[22]

Labor

Besides the scarcity and expense of mercury, the other major complaint of Oruro's entrepreneurs was the high cost of labor. They frequently asked the audiencia, the viceroy, and the king to send contingents of mitayos to the site. These petitions continued until midcentury, even though it should have been obvious by about 1608 that the colonial government had no intention of aiding Oruro with forced labor. But even after it was evident that no incentives were to be given, whether in the form of mita, inexpensive mercury, or even a reduction in the sales tax (*alcabala*) on goods used in mining production, Potosí's azogueros continued to be alarmed by what they perceived as Oruro's competitive advantage. For while in Oruro they grumbled about the high wages they had to pay, their counterparts in Potosí accused them of luring away their best workers.

According to Godoy, when the first Spaniards began to work mines in Oruro, they contracted laborers from among the Indians who were passing through and paid them four *reales* a day, the same wage as mitayos in Potosí earned. In some cases, as noted, instead of paying wages, mine owners simply allowed Indians to carry off ore fragments and slag to clean the mines and get them ready for exploitation. After forming a partnership with the de Medrano brothers, Alonso Alvarez de Nava Revolledo went to Pacajes to look for workers. He came back with thirty-seven Indians whom he paid a peso a day. This arrangement worked so well that he recruited more workers on a second trip. After this, none of the workers in Oruro would work for four reales a day. So the peso-a-day wage for an apiri, or five pesos a week, became generalized, while barreteros earned eight pesos a week. In addition, Indians often received rations of bread, wine, and coca, which served to "entertain and pet them," as Godoy put it.[23]

Word spread rapidly of the favorable working conditions in Oruro, and no further recruitment was necessary; the Indians came looking for work. So rich were the ores mined in the first years of the silver bonanza in Oruro that it was even common for Indians to refuse to work in mines that were not considered first-rate, because from the better veins they could get the most valuable pieces of ore (*corpas*) for themselves. Godoy commented that this attitude was especially characteristic of the Indians who were the most skilled and hispanicized.[24]

But if free workers in Oruro seemed to be favored when compared to mitayos because of their wages and the corpas that they insisted was their right, they had another advantage as well: they were paid by the day, not by the task.[25] Indians who rented themselves out, called *mingados*, received the same salary no matter how much ore they mined, while mitayos received a daily wage contingent upon the completion of certain tasks, usually a fixed number of sacks of ore that they had to bring out of the mines each day. The free workers would refuse to work if any such production quotas were imposed on them, and consequently Godoy estimated that if free apiris mined five or six quintales of ore in a week, mitayos could be forced to deliver at least seven or eight.[26]

Actually, there were some mitayos working in Oruro, both legally and illegally. One contingent had been transported to the city with the permission of the Audiencia of Charcas from the mines of the Salinas of García Mendoza, which were no longer productive. Because the people who had had these Indians assigned to them generally did not have mines in Oruro, they formed partnerships with those who did, one contributing the Indians and the other the mines. The mine owner supervised the work and paid all expenses until the silver was mined, and the profit was split fifty-fifty, which gives some indication of how valuable the mitayos were. There were 168 of these workers from García Mendoza in Oruro, but an unspecified number of mitayos were in the city illegally. These were Indians rented out by people from Potosí who no longer had (or had never had) productive mines or mills but still received contingents of mitayos.[27]

Although such arrangements existed, they were not the general rule. Even Maldonado de Torres, president of the Audiencia de Charcas, who supported the Potosí interests, claimed that most of the people who had gone to Oruro were the unemployed of Potosí, not mitayos, and that "for the tranquility of the Republic it was convenient that they had left."[28] Oruro mine owners did not find it quite so "convenient," since most spent more on wages (to say nothing of

TABLE 4.1 Mining and Refining Expenses for Two Weeks, Oruro, 1607

	Cost in Pesos/Reales	% of Total Cost
Labor expenses		
2 barreteros	32 p	23
1 apiri	10 p	7
1 palliri	1 p	1
Grinding ore (4 reales/quintal)	22 p, 4 r	16
2 workers to mix ore with mercury	6 r	0
Repasiris	6 p	4
2 workers to pour metal in molds	4 p	3
Carrying ore to ingenio (4 reales/quintal)	22 p, 4 r	16
Other expenses		
Candles	4 p	3
Salt for refining	14 p	10
12 lbs. iron	15 p	10
Refining (4 pesos/bar)	4 p	3
Charcoal for smelting	2 p, 4 r	2
Depreciation of smelter	4 r	0
Duplicating the bars[a]	2 p	1
Hood[a]	1 p	1

Source: Godoy, "Relación," p. 447.

Note: Wages for technicians, cleaning and repairing galleries, and the price of mercury are not included.

a. Purpose not clearly identified in manuscript.

profit they lost when their workers helped themselves to ore) than on any other production expense. Godoy itemized the typical expenses of a mine owner who did not own an ingenio (see table 4.1).

The sums listed in the table for the barreteros, the apiri, those who sorted the ore for quality (*palliri*), grinders of ore, those who mixed the ore with mercury (*repasiris*), the Indians who put the metal in the molds, are all clearly labor expenses. Carrying the metal to the ingenio also obviously involved labor, but since it was probably carried by llama or mule, it is difficult to determine what proportion of the total was for labor and what was rent for the animals. If we estimate that half of the cost of transport to the ingenio was a labor expense, then more than 62 percent of the costs itemized are for labor, even excluding the ore taken away by the workers.

Although owners viewed the workers' practice of carrying away mineral as a necessary evil, the mines were constantly policed to minimize the amount of metal taken. In 1607, many Spanish or creole professional miners were hired by Oruro's mine owners primarily to explore for veins of mineral and supervise mining operations. They were also in charge of overseeing the workers. Godoy noted that a large number of supervisors was needed to minimize surreptitious ore sharing. Two were necessary for every mine: one to stay in the mine and another to accompany the workers carrying the metal. Two more were needed to guard the area where the ore was collected at the mouth of the mine. All of this cost the mine owners money, and despite extensive policing, stolen ore was still openly sold inside the mines. Had workers in Oruro been subject to a task system, like mitayos in Potosí, possibly less ore would have been stolen, because the requirement of producing a certain amount each day would have left less time for independent mining.[29]

The mine owners were further hampered by the "weekend miners" who went into the hills on Saturdays and Sundays and worked other people's mines. Those who led these expeditions were Spaniards described by Godoy as "unmarried men without professions" and "unattached vagabonds."[30] These prospectors generally hired Indian assistants, whom they paid three pesos a day. Thus, an Indian worker might make six pesos in a weekend, which was more than he could earn in an entire week as an apiri. Although Godoy does not specifically say this, an Indian who went on a weekend expedition might not need to work the rest of the week, being able to return to his village if he chose. This system of weekend exploitation was known as "doubling"; as Godoy comments sardonically, "in this land things are never called by their true names."[31] When Diego de Portugal became corregidor of Oruro in 1607, he attacked the problem of illegal weekend exploitation by driving many of the unemployed, said to be involved in "doubling," out of town.

Godoy's outline of the occupational structure among Spaniards in Oruro is given in table 4.2 which also includes commercial enterprises. In fact, some businesses listed were probably stalls in the plaza run by Andean women who sold items usually consumed by Indians: coca and corn flour, for instance. The bakeries, Godoy is careful to tell us, were real bakeries, not household operations. The carpenters, tailors, shoemakers, and so forth, were Spaniards who employed "many skilled Indian workmen." This means that as early as 1607, in addition to working in the mines, Indians were already employed in many urban occupations, a phenomenon discussed in the next chapter.[32]

Many Indians were also employed in bringing foodstuffs to the city. Wheat, maize, and wine generally came from Cochabamba. Beef cattle were raised on ranches that were between five and fourteen leagues of Oruro, and sheep ranches were even closer at hand. Bacon was brought from Cochabamba, but ham and bacon from the province of Paria itself had an excellent reputation, as did the local cheese. While goods imported from Europe tended to cost about the same in Oruro as in Potosí, food grown and produced in Upper Peru was said to cost less because Oruro was closer to some agricultural zones.[33]

Mining Production and the Changing Conditions of Labor

While the comparatively low cost of food may have offset the high cost of labor to some extent, early observers believed that miners and azogueros in Oruro could continue to do well only as long as the ore mined was very rich and foretold disaster when the bonanza passed.[34] Silver production didn't decline drastically as soon as predicted, but nonetheless a drop began as early as 1626, and after 1649 the bottom fell out of the industry. Figure 2 shows the *quinto real* paid by the center for most years between 1611 and 1730. The quinto was the one-fifth tax paid on all silver assayed at the royal treasury and theoretically should have equaled 20 percent of that produced. While this was not the case, the quinto records are the best data

TABLE 4.2 Occupations and Enterprises of Spanish Men, Oruro, 1607

Types of Employment	Number
Spanish Religious	
Parish priests	3
Priests in Taipi-cala	1
Priests without congregations	8
Monks, Monastery of San Francisco	6
Monks, Monastery of San Agustín	3
Monks, Monastery of N.S. de las Mercedes	4
Monks, Monastery of Santo Domingo	4
SUBTOTAL	29
Administrative and Political Positions Filled by Spaniards	
Corregidor	1
Teniente de Corregidor	1
Alcaldes ordinarios	2
Alcaldes de la Hermandad	2
Ensayadores	2
Aguacil Mayor	1
Tenientes	4
Alfarez Real	1
Fiel Ejecutor	1
Corregidores de Cabildo	8
Procurador General	1
Letrados Abogados	7
Escribanos Públicos	2
Escribanos Reales	10
Receptores de Alcabalas	2
Procuradores	2
Officials of the Caja Real	2
SUBTOTAL	49

Types of Employment	Number
Spaniards in Mining and Related Activities	
Professional miners	84
Mule drivers who carried ore from the mines	6
Masters of making ingenios	2
Veedores del Cerro	2
Alcalde Mayor de Minas	1
Escribano de Minas	1
Others occupied in mining	277
SUBTOTAL	373
Unemployed Spanish Men	127
TOTAL	578
Commercial Enterprises	
Stores selling imported cloth	22
Stalls in the plaza selling imported cloth	5
Purveyors of meals	14
Stalls selling corn flour	6
Stalls selling coca, fish, corn, and other goods	15
Bodegas	29
Restaurants	4
Bakeries	10
Pastry shops	3
Dealers in second-hand clothing	2
TOTAL	110
Craftspeople	
Candle makers	3
Silversmiths	4
Sword makers	3
Carpenters	12
Barbers and surgeons	11
Blacksmiths	4
Drapers and hat makers	8
Tailors	16
Shoemakers	14
TOTAL	75

Source: Godoy, "Relación," pp. 453–55.

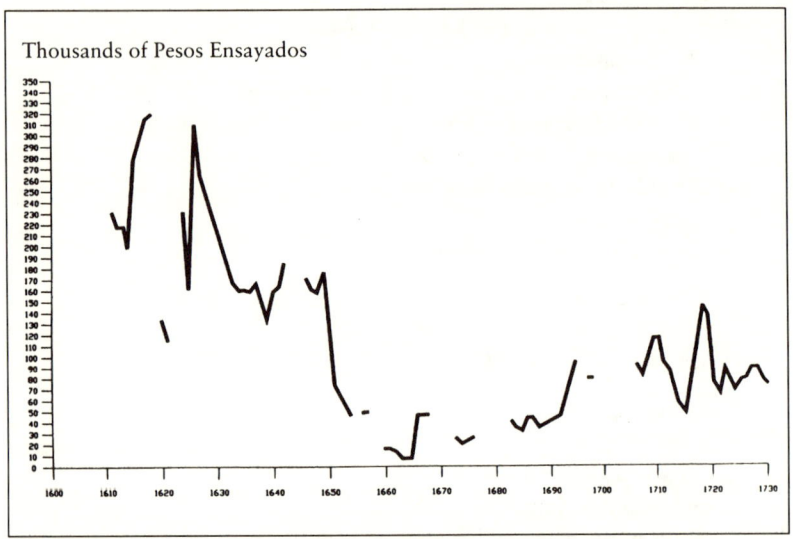

FIGURE 2. Quinto Real, Oruro, 1611–1730

Sources: AGN, XIII-8-2-4; 8-2-5, 8-2-6; 8-2-7; BMO, Libro Real de la Real Hacienda, March 9, 1611 to March 29, 1612; 1649; 1678; 1684; 1694; 1695; Libro Comun de 1639; Libro Real de Contador 1646; 1647; 1648–49; 1656–57; 1664–65; 1667–68; 1673; 1699; Libro de Tesorero 1637–38; 1638–39; 1640–41; AGI, Charcas, 37; 18; TePaske and Klein, *Royal Treasuries*, vol. 2, pp. 188–213; Bakewell, "Registered Silver," 101–03.

available from which to judge silver production in Oruro. Although Brading and Cross use mercury consumption to calculate an estimate of silver output in some colonial mining centers, this would be virtually impossible in the case of Oruro. In the early years, the city was given no official allotment of mercury, and even later when it did receive consignments, they were not sufficient and azogueros continued to purchase quicksilver from individual refiners and silver merchants in Potosí and from other treasury offices. In other words, the records of mercury distributed in the city are likely to be even more inaccurate than those for the quintos reales.[35]

Even though the quinto is the most reliable barometer of silver production in Oruro, a graph of the tax does not exactly reflect the site's fortunes. Certainly, some silver escaped being taxed: smuggling was always prevalent.[36] Furthermore, there is reason to believe that some of the quinto tax figures are fragmentary. I compared records of the royal fifth collected in archives in Buenos Aires, Sevilla, and Oruro itself with totals given by other researchers who have worked with the royal treasury records.[37] Yearly totals are listed in appendix 1. I arrived at annual figures for years with months missing by calculating monthly averages. Particularly in the 1660s, when quintos fell to an all-time low, entries for the tax are apt to be incomplete. Thus, figure 2 gives a good indication of Oruro's silver production but is not a literal representation. Chances are that output was always higher than tax records indicate.

Despite a prediction as early as 1609 by the president of the audiencia, Maldonado de Torres, that Oruro's mines were beginning a permanent decline,[38] after a few years of production drops (between 1611 and 1614), the city's quintos rose spectacularly to reach an all-time high of more than 320,000 *pesos ensayados* in 1618 (a peso ensayado was worth about 12.5 reales). In 1612, when the quintos were far from their peak, yet totaled a respectable 220,000 pesos ensayados, Oruro's ingenios were very busy and employed many workers. In that year all the owners on the Sorasora River, except one, Cristobal Niño, were the same as those who had owned ingenios, or were building them, in 1607. More than half of the mills now had two cabezas, and one had more than a hundred workers. The other ingenios on the river were estimated to have forty or more Indians working in them. In 1612 there were three ingenios in Paria, one with two cabezas and two with one. One of these mills, owned by Miguel Ortiz, employed sixty Indians. Las Sepulturas had twelve mills (one more than in 1607), and each was said to have a work force of fifty to seventy people.[39]

After falling to less than 120,000 pesos ensayados in 1621, the quintos from Oruro increased to more than 230,000 pesos ensayados three years later. With the exception of a drop in 1625, the royal fifth remained above 200,000 pesos ensayados per year until 1631. A 1626 letter from the audiencia to the king still described Oruro as the viceroyalty's second most important city economically and the third most populous.[40] This recovery in the 1620s after what looked like the beginnings of collapse at the end of the previous decade, was probably due to the development of an efficient method for refining *negrillo* ores, which until then had required a large amount of mercury in the amalgamation process. The new technique, developed by an Oruro azoguero, Antonio de Salinas Ruberto, was later adopted in the mining sites of Lipez, Chichas, and Berenguela.[41] One of Oruro's most important and most tenacious miners and azogueros, Antonio de Uriona, testified to the utility of de Salinas's invention. Despite the high wages he had to pay his workers, Uriona was able to increase his output and therefore the quintos reales. Naturally, the increase in the quintos implied an increase in his own earnings, even though in 1628 Uriona claimed to be paying his barreteros eleven and twelve pesos a week, and his apiris seven and eight.[42]

So when technology lowered the cost of processing metal, it seems that entrepreneurs were able to make a profit even if their wage bills were high. Abundant, rich ore near the surface also compensated for what mine owners considered exorbitant wages. But, as mines got deeper and required more complex installations for drainage, and as the negrillos, even with the new system of refining, produced less silver than before, miners complained of the high cost of labor and production began to decline. It is interesting, however, that in Potosí even in the worst years of the mining decline after 1660, the Cerro Rico's premier miner and refiner, Antonio López de Quiroga, was still able to expand his operations and make extraordinary profits—despite the fact that two-thirds of his workers were wage laborers who earned up to three times as much as mitayos. He did this by investing in technology, particularly by digging tunnels that provided access to clusters of mines and, if constructed correctly, drained flooded ones. Such undertakings were enormously expensive and probably beyond the reach of most Oruro entrepreneurs, even if they had been willing to accept the risks involved in constructing them.[43] Still, López de Quiroga's success demonstrates that given sufficient capital and the entrepreneurial nerve to invest it, mining could be very remunerative despite a decline in the quality of ore and the high cost of labor.

In Oruro, as relatively accessible high-quality ores diminished, Indian workers tried to move on to more recently discovered mines. But such possibilities were limited, and by the end of the century wage levels in Oruro fell. However, in the 1630s azogueros and royal officials complained not only of the high cost of labor but also of its scarcity. One of Oruro's most important miner-financiers, Joseph de Cuterillo, said he had to pay higher and higher wages to keep workers from leaving to seek other employment. Although he does not specify what he paid his barreteros and apiris, he claims to have paid three Hispanic professional miners twenty to twenty-four pesos a week. The royal treasurer of the city in 1631, Gaspar de Elosu Echevarría, rejected the suggestion that the difficulty of obtaining workers in Oruro was related to the continuing decline of the Indian population of Upper Peru. On the contrary, he said, there had never been more Indians since Peru was discovered; the difficulty was that the Indians had become like Spaniards and didn't want to work.[44] Clearly, new ideas emphasizing the dignity of labor at a just wage and its importance for the body politic had not penetrated the consciousness of this colonial official. Further, the validity of his explanation is questionable, since, as Felipe de Godoy had suggested, it may have been the *most* hispanicized Indians who were most actively involved in the labor market (see chapter 5).

In fact, the problem the Spaniards kept coming up against was how to get Indians to work like proletarians when they still had land. While in seventeenth-century Oruro one sector of the Indian population apparently depended entirely on wage labor (to be discussed later), they were a small minority. In most instances, the mine owners enjoyed certain advantages: Indians' access to land meant that workers didn't have to earn their entire subsistence from wages; they could be hired seasonally and dispensed with when not needed.

But the system also had its flaws: incentives often had to be relatively high to pry the peasants loose from their communities. Tirades about laziness reflected the entrepreneurs' frustration at not having access either to a totally immiserated work force that would accept wages as low as those paid mitayos or to coerced labor. Some studies of precapitalist societies in Europe contend that when economic conditions were favorable peasant families tended not to increase their labor but instead consumed more or simply enjoyed more leisure time.[45] For example, Chayanov holds that Russian peasants preferred to forgo the drudgery of additional agricultural labor once family consumption standards had been satisfied. In Upper Peru, however, it seems that workers sometimes continued to work even after they had earned enough to pay their tribute and buy the few things they didn't produce, *if* the reward was great enough. In Oruro, apparently, many were willing to put up with the drudgery of mine work if their corpas were hefty.

After about 1640 complaints about the shortage of workers stop appearing in documents, and there is reason to believe that Indian workers in many parts of the mining industry lost their jobs. The decline of the ingenios in Las Sepulturas demonstrates what happened. In that industrial suburb the slump began in about 1662, due to the drop in the amount of ore mined in Oruro. By 1672 only one ingenio was functioning. According to witnesses, the Indians who had lived in Las Sepulturas and worked in the ingenios had abandoned the area. The only functioning ingenio had eleven workers in 1672, while in 1612 it had had as many as seventy.[46]

Interestingly, reports about Las Sepulturas do not say that the Indians went back to their villages or their lands, but that they had moved into Oruro itself to live in the ranchería.[47] Perhaps Indians were able to find intermittent work there while waiting for the ingenios to start functioning again. They also probably did some illegal prospecting in other people's mines on weekends and scavenged in slag heaps for ore they could sell. The fact that Indian workers from Las Sepulturas moved to nearby Oruro suggests that they were totally dependent on paid labor and either had no lands to return to or could not easily rejoin their communities. Distance may have been a factor here, because workers in Oruro came from a wide geographical area, as discussed in chapter 5.

As rich ores became more difficult to mine and production declined, so did Oruro's population. A 1683 enumeration of adult Indian men found 1,560 in the city itself and 594 more living in ingenios in the suburbs. Assuming a typical family of parents and two children (as indicated by the 1683 census; see chapter 5), approximately 8,616 Indians lived in the city and its environs in 1683. This represents a decline in the indigenous population of 52 percent from Mesa and Gisbert's estimate for 1607.

Although Oruro's silver industry was in a severe slump (quintos for 1683 totaled only slightly over 46,000 pesos ensayados), it did not collapse absolutely and Oruro continued to produce silver.[48] Workers were therefore necessary, and Indians continued to immigrate to the city, although not as many as before. In 1683 there were at least fourteen functioning mills employing 315 workers. The largest of these, which belonged to Captain Agustín Buyan, employed forty Indians.[49] There were also numerous mines being exploited with Indian labor, and many Indians in the city worked in crafts or hired themselves out as casual laborers.

Evidently, the long decline in silver production finally had the effect on wages that mine owners had long desired. In 1639, the last year for which records are available from the seventeenth century, wages were still reported to be one peso a day for apiris.[50] The next record of wages paid in the city, from 1714, indicates that they had been reduced by half.[51] Although that amount is based on the books of only one mining firm, one can probably assume that all mine owners in the city paid their workers similar wages. Mine owners and azogueros paid as little as possible for labor and, as we have seen, when one entrepreneur paid more, the others were forced to do likewise.

Indeed, the drop in production in Oruro had depressed wages, at least nominally, to the same as those paid to mitayos in Potosí: four reales a day—but this was only a nominal change, because in Oruro workers were still paid by the day, not by the task, which meant that they worked fewer hours than mitayos for the same pay and the work was less arduous.[52] According to 1714 records, Oruro workers were also paid in advance, and the mine's administrator complained of Indians who accepted the money and then didn't show up for work. Laborers also continued to help themselves to ore when leaving the mines, and this may have compensated somewhat for the cut in wages.[53]

The Forced Distribution of Merchandise

So, while entrepreneurs did lower their costs to some extent by reducing wages, they were not able to impose the superexploitative regimens that were possible with forced workers. Nonetheless, an extraeconomic mechanism which served to artificially create a market may have had the effect of pushing workers to accept lower salaries. This was the *repartimiento de mercancías*, or forced distribution of goods, in which the corregidor was the linchpin of a system that benefited the crown and merchants in Lima, as well as owners of mines and estates. Corregidores, or local magistrates, bought their offices either from American authorities (before 1678) or from the government in Spain. Since corregidores earned low salaries, to recoup their losses and to profit from the investment, they customarily forced the Indian population of their jurisdictions to buy animals and manufactured goods at greatly inflated prices—sometimes double the wholesale cost. The officials usually acquired the products they distributed on credit from merchants in Lima. Most were items that people did not need or didn't need in such quantity, that they could have manufactured themselves, or that they generally could buy more cheaply elsewhere. To pay for the goods, which they received on credit, Indians were frequently forced to sell their labor in mines or on haciendas. Thus the repartimiento created not only a market for unwanted merchandise but also a labor force.[54]

The repartimiento reached its peak in Upper Peru in the eighteenth century. First, because the serious and prolonged decline in mining output after about 1680 caused a slump in overseas trade, and merchants in Lima tended to turn to internal commerce (provisioning corregidores) to take up the slack. Their situation was exacerbated after 1776, and their participation in the repartimiento probably increased, when Charcas was placed under the jurisdiction of the new viceroyalty of Río de la Plata, and Buenos Aires merchants gained dominance of the Upper Peruvian market. The royal government's decision to legalize the repartimiento in 1754 to limit its abuses and to collect the sales tax on these transactions, probably also contributed to an increase in the practice until about 1780.[55]

Although the heyday of the repartimiento was the second half of the eighteenth century, there were plenty of instances of forced distribution of goods in the seventeenth century as well. The system possibly became important earlier in Oruro than in other parts of the viceroyalty because of the midcentury slump in the mining industry. In any event, as early as 1656 the cabildo of the city wrote to the viceroy, the conde de Alba de Aliste, complaining about the local corregidor. They said that even though the sales tax, or alcabala, had been raised from 2 to 4 percent, the total amount collected from the

A Colonial Andean Mining Center

tax in each of the last four years was lower than before. Ignoring the possibility that the decline in sales taxes was related to the general economic situation, the members of the cabildo instead blamed the drop on the magistrate's involvement in commerce. They said he was monopolizing trade (and paying no sales tax) to the detriment of other merchants, through the forced distribution of goods to Indians in Oruro. How the Indians acquired the money to pay the corregidor for these goods is not explained, but most likely they had to find employment to meet this additional expense and, being in debt, may have had to to accept work at reduced wages.[56]

In 1658 Alonso de Ortega was again cited in the official review conducted after his term in office, or *juicio de residencia*, for repartimientos de mercancías, as are four other corregidores in 1664, 1675, 1680, and 1685.[57] The practice was therefore well established in Oruro in the seventeenth century, but not until 1722 do we find a good description of how the system functioned. In that year two miners in La Joya, a silver mining area within Oruro's jurisdiction, complained about repartimientos made by the corregidor's assistant, Francisco de Miranda. Their testimony ironically demonstrates that while the repartimientos made by Miranda might have originally forced the workers to work in the mines, when a corregidor undertook to collect what was owed him, it could have unpleasant consequences for the employers. In 1718 Miranda put one of the owners, Antonio de Elizondo, and three Indian workers in jail for cloth he had distributed to the Indians and for which he had not been paid. This was not the first time that Miranda had taken action against Indians employed by Antonio de Elizondo and Andres de Ocana, and a witness noted that almost all of the Indians in La Joya had debts with the corregidor's assistant.[58]

Trapiches: The Democratization of Production

If the repartimiento served in part to force people to work for cash when wages were low, workers in Oruro's mines had a means of compensating for the reduced remuneration. In 1720, due to a protest by the city's big miners, a common way of producing silver came to light that effectively by-passed Oruro's azogueros and depended upon what the mine owners viewed as outright theft.[59] Well established in Oruro at least since the 1680s, the practice consisted of grinding ore in small, human-powered mills called *trapiches*. After the metal was ground, if it was of high enough quality, it was simply smelted to produce silver, because rich ore did not require amalgamation with mercury. When the metal ground in these mills did need to be combined with quicksilver, amalgamation was performed in processing plants much smaller than those in the major ingenios. Not only did it cut the ingenio out of the production process, the trapiche system made it possible to produce a certain amount of silver that eluded the quinto, because if no mercury was obtained from the royal treasury, officials couldn't be sure that the producer paid taxes on it.[60] The use of trapiches probably became widespread in the late 1600s partly because the Peruvian viceroy, the conde de Monclova (1689–1705), had relaxed restrictions on the origins of commercially sold ores.[61] The fact that some of the ores ground in the trapiches did not need mercury refining also meant that miners explored for and exploited new mines that produced at least some ore that was rich enough to smelt.

Sometimes owners legally constructed trapiches close to their mines to grind the mineral they excavated. More often, trapiches were built by people who bought ore from Indian workers. The line between the corpa, or metal that workers carried out of the mines more or less legally, and what was considered theft, had always been a fine one. Now azogueros protested widespread stealing by laborers who sold the stolen metal to *rescatadores*, who either processed it themselves or had it processed by a *trapichero*. In addition to what was carried out by workers during their regular shifts, silver ground in trapiches may have been dug during weekend mining expeditions.

It is difficult to determine the relationship between the trapiches and the rise in quintos reales in the late seventeenth century, or how much of the silver produced in the trapiches was actually taxed. On the other hand, much of the exploration for new mines was probably conducted by small miners, Indians and others, and the possibility of finding rich ore to sell to rescatadores was an important incentive to further prospecting. Enrique Tandeter asserts that in the 1750s about 38 percent of the silver produced in Potosí came from trapiches,[62] but we have no way of verifying the proportion that was produced in this way in Oruro. Nonetheless, the trapiches no doubt contributed to the upturn in production at the end of the seventeenth century and helped to maintain production levels in the eighteenth.

In 1720 the azogueros and other big miners in Oruro suspended work in their mines and allowed them to become flooded, refusing to operate the winches necessary for drainage until the local government put a stop to the illegal procedure of refining in trapiches. They maintained that 600 Indians were involved in stealing ore, claiming that Indians were able to smell the richest minerals, which they then secreted on their bodies when they left the mines.[63]

That the miners and azogueros should be particularly disturbed about the trapiches in the 1720s is no coincidence. In 1719 a severe epidemic influenza struck the entire viceroyalty of Peru, including Oruro. Combined in some places with typhus or bubonic plague, the disease affected places as far distant as Huanuco in north-central Peru and the Paraguayan missions in the south. There were even reports that what appeared to be the same sickness had reached Buenos Aires. In Arequipa in 1719, one-third of the city's Spaniards and two-thirds of its Indians died. The illness struck Cuzco in April 1720, and estimates for deaths in the city alone were as high as 20,000 and close to 40,000 for the whole bishopric. The epidemic arrived in the area of Potosí in 1719 and lasted on Upper Peru's high plateau at least until the end of June 1720.[64]

The effects of the illness in Oruro were certainly grave, but it is difficult to evaluate the mortality rate because the results of a count of Indian tributaries taken after the epidemic in 1722 are almost certainly incomplete.[65] The year 1719 was rather good for the Oruro silver industry, with quintos totaling more than 140,000 pesos ensayados. But in the next two years production dropped, in part reflecting the effects of the epidemic. In 1720 the quintos fell to just under 81,000 pesos ensayados and in 1721 to less than 61,000. If in the worst days of Oruro's silver industry the supply of workers exceeded demand, causing a drop in wages, the epidemic created a labor shortage which the azogueros complained about in their 1720 protest.[66] It was precisely because of this shortage that they felt particularly vulnerable to the trapiche system. When workers were scarce, mine owners knew that the only way to attract Indians was by permitting them their corpas, and with laborers at a premium, the miners' power to control theft was limited. Now they handed the problem to the government, demanding that the cabildo and the corregidor take steps to eliminate the trapiches and force the Indians to work for a simple wage.[67]

The miners and refiners were quite right in assuming that they would never be able to convert these Indians into wage workers without government enforcement. At the end of the eighteenth century, when mine owners in Mexico eliminated the *partido*, the share of ore workers customarily took for themselves from the mines, there were work stoppages in some mines and sporadic violence. In many areas, industrial armies were necessary to enforce the proletarianization of the work force. In 1766 what Doris Ladd calls the first industrial strike in Mexico occurred in the mines of Real del Monte, north of Mexico City, when the management attempted to lower wages and reduce the share of ore that workers received for their labor. Ultimately, in some Mexican mines the old practice continued, while in other centers the only possible way to eliminate the partido was by raising wages.[68] Oruro's entrepreneurs, always jealous of the economic advantages of Potosí azogueros with their contingents of mitayos, were certainly not about to pay higher wages as the price of eliminating the corpa. And, although the authorities might help azogueros from time to time when abuses became particularly flagrant, a government whose policy had consistently been to deny Oruro miners contingents of mitayos was unlikely to provide the massive state repression required to enforce wage labor.

In fact, in 1717 Oruro's *justicia mayor de minas*, Joseph Rizo Valmazeda, had issued an order that made it illegal for anyone to buy metals from "any Indian, mestizo or mulatto who worked for a wage in the mines." The crime was punishable by severe penalties: for the first offense the fine for a Spaniard or mestizo was 100 pesos. A second offense brought double the fine and banishment from the city and its jurisdiction. An Indian, mulatto, or black caught buying ore from a mine worker would receive 100 lashes and a month in prison, as would anyone who sold him the ore.[69] In spite of stiff penalties, the practice had not stopped, and by 1720, if the azogueros weren't exactly losing control of the silver industry, they certainly felt that other people were profiting at their expense.

Who these other people were is an interesting question. It seems that some portion of the trapicheros were mestizos or mulattos. Testimony given by several of these men notes that they could not sign their names because they were illiterate.[70] This would seem to indicate that even if they were Spaniards or creoles, they certainly did not come from the upper reaches of colonial society. Some were miners, but they generally owned only one mine; others rented mines. The trapicheros who also worked mines claimed that they only processed their own ore in their trapiches, but others had built mills with no pretense of mining metal themselves. The trapiche owners depended on local money lenders, who provided them with mercury and advanced them cash to pay the Indians for their ore. For instance, Juan Crisostomo Pintado, a trapichero, owed Juan de la Caba Cajero at least 6,000 pesos for mercury and loans.[71] In most cases, the money lenders also bought the refined silver from the trapicheros at prices below official rates and took it themselves to the royal treasury to pay the taxes.[72]

Thus, in the late seventeenth century there developed an industrial-commercial cycle in Oruro that apparently circumvented the azogueros and miners who had made the major investments in the silver industry and instead benefited the money lenders, the purchasers of stolen ores, trapicheros, and Indian mine workers. But, while the azogueros might demand the destruction of all unlicensed trapiches and fulminate about the theft of their richest metals, they knew they had to proceed with caution. The corpa had attracted workers in the first place, and in 1720, when there was a labor shortage due to the epidemic, eliminating it was realistically out of the question. In the end, Oruro's major industrialists contented themselves with a government investigation of the situation, the razing of several trapiches, and a prohibition against licensing new ones. No action was taken against the Indians who were the source of the mineral processed. The problem persisted and was resolved extremely gradually in Upper Peru. Enrique Tandeter notes that it wasn't until the beginning of the nineteenth century that azogueros in Potosí managed to impose as customary a fifty-fifty split with the *kajchas* who worked in other people's mines on weekends and then had the ore they excavated ground by trapicheros.[73]

Conclusion

Over the course of a century, relations of production changed little in Oruro's mines. Workers still helped themselves to ore and, although entrepreneurs called on the local government to control the situation, it can be argued that at least in the short run this wasn't even what the entrepreneurs wanted. To eliminate the corpa, they might have had to increase wages considerably, as was done in some Mexican mines in the eighteenth century. Since most mine owners were chronically short of cash and relied on *aviadores* who bought silver from producers and loaned them money for operating expenses, they would hardly be willing to pay wages that would cover the cost of the workers' reproduction. The only other alternative was some form of coerced labor to shift the burden of a portion of the workers' subsistence to their communities; the colonial government, for both practical and philosophical reasons, refused to organize such a draft for Oruro.

But even if relations of production had not changed radically since the early days, nonetheless there had been a gradual shift in favor of the entrepreneurs and to the detriment of the workers. First of all, since the repartimiento de mercancías forced Indians to accept employment regardless of the terms, debts to the corregidor generally worked to the mine owners' advantage. Second, sometime after 1640 the azogueros apparently succeeded in lowering wages to four reales a day. Even if they were not able to eliminate ore sharing and advance payment of wages, or to impose a task system—innovations that would have made labor in Oruro as cheap as forced labor in Potosí—they still reduced their wage bills. And the fact that during the mining depression some workers hung on in Oruro even though they lost their jobs suggests that they had no alternative but to make a living by whatever means they could. Finally, even after the epidemic of 1719–1720, when azogueros argued that workers had the upper hand, the owners still managed to exploit the new veins found by workers who were looking for rich ore to sell to trapicheros. In this context, the corpa their workers took might be considered a type of incentive pay for exploration. Furthermore, since the trapicheros and rescatadores were very dependent on credit, some of Oruro's more solvent miners were involved themselves as moneylenders.[74] In any event, once the indigenous population recovered from the effects of the last major epidemic to affect Upper Peru, the bargaining power of the labor force declined and the situation shifted back to favor the owners.

The change in the situation of Oruro workers raises interesting questions: did it affect their connections with peasant agriculture and their ayllus, and if so, did it make it more difficult to use migration and paid labor as part of an Andean survival strategy? Had the group of Indian laborers who stayed in Oruro after being laid off in Las Sepulturas in the early 1670s really become proletarians? Had they lost their lands or contact with their communities? If so, did erosion of kinship ties and reciprocal connections mean especial impoverishment, that these people had entered the class system on a lower rung than those who could use Andean support systems to enhance their positions within a mercantile society? These questions are explored in chapters 5 and 6.

· 5 ·

The Indian Labor Force of Oruro in 1683

In 1683 the viceroy of Peru, the duque de la Palata, ordered an enumeration of all the indigenous people in the area between Quito and Tucumán primarily to determine how many Indian men were liable for mita service and tribute payments. La Palata also wanted to identify those who had abandoned their reducciones hoping to avoid these obligations, shifting the burden of taxes and forced labor to fewer and fewer community residents. Once the total number of native men had been established (both originarios and forasteros), la Palata intended to ensure that, whether individuals lived in their native villages or not, they contributed their share of tribute and took their turns working in Potosí.[1]

Oruro, of course, was exactly the kind of place that la Palata wanted to have counted meticulously, since mining centers were known to be magnets for Indians leaving their villages. In fact, the corregidor of Oruro, Luis de Miranda, freely admitted in the report included with the census returns that all the Indians in the city were immigrants, "some subject to the mita of Potosí and others called yanaconas of the king, who are those who don't acknowledge caciques or governors and claim to be descendants of those who since their first origin were designated as such."[2]

Miranda's statement and the individual returns themselves show the situation to be more complicated than la Palata's simple formula: that those who had left their villages were no longer paying tribute or serving in the mita. The corregidor goes on to say that many of the Indians living in Oruro in 1683 were born there, and frequently their parents had been as well. On the other hand, the census indicates that many residents born in the city still could identify their "origins" and their ayllus. Furthermore, Miranda explained that many Indians working in the city were from nearby towns in the province of Paria, such as Toledo and Challacollo, and frequently came and went between Oruro and these *pueblos* every day. These commuters were closely watched by their *governadores*, who collected tribute.

The census returns, carefully examined, reveal the diverse circumstances of Oruro's indigenous workers and, most particularly, the economic and social differences between yanaconas and forasteros. They are useful for teasing out information about the range of dependence on paid labor among the town's workers and the extent to which urban Indians involved in mine work or craft production were developing a new identity through their participation in a market economy. A surprising finding is that, although they were cut off from communal agriculture and needed paid employment to survive, yanaconas were not evolving into a mining proletariat, but instead were concentrated in craft professions. On the other hand, forasteros, who generally did work in the mining industry, were not exclusively wage laborers, since most of them apparently maintained contacts with their ayllus, or even continued to live in their home villages. The census essentially bears out the conclusions of the previous chapter: the colonial economy was mercantilized, but labor was not entirely commodified and in many circumstances workers continued to operate according to Andean principles of ecological complementarity and communal reciprocity.

Conduct of the 1683 Census and Reliability of the Data

While la Palata's enumeration can be extremely useful for historical purposes, it is hardly demographically accurate by late twentieth-century standards because of problems with how the count was conducted throughout the viceroyalty as well as specific features of the Oruro enumeration.

One difficulty from the beginning was that rather than paying special agents to carry out the census, la Palata relied on corregidores and their assistants, a procedure ripe for abuse. Because local magistrates were interested parties, the viceroy sought to minimize fraud by ordering a separate ecclesiastical census to be conducted at the same time. He planned to compare the results of the two counts to uncover any discrepancies. If the prospect of two censuses wasn't enough to keep the corregidores honest, la Palata hoped that severe penalties for not reporting all Indians in their jurisdictions and rewards for finding the undocumented would ensure their rectitude. Various local officials claimed that these provisions may have resulted in overcounts in some places, as corregidores included transients or the missing in the census.[3]

Several other procedural problems may have contributed to the census's inaccuracy. First, although the count, like a modern national census, was supposed to be conducted in all parts of the viceroyalty simultaneously, this proved impossible. Many corregidores received their instructions late and wrote to Lima for clarification of sections they did not understand. Further, as soon as word got out that the enumeration would be used to impose mita obligations on those evading them, forasteros fled the sixteen provinces subject to the draft. Various colonial officials maintained that because of this flight an unspecified number of people were counted in two or more places: where they lived when the census was announced, in the nonmita provinces where they took refuge, possibly in their communities of origin, and even conceivably where they stopped briefly during their flight. However, Brian Evans and Nicolás Sánchez-Albornoz, who have studied the enumeration extensively, believe that irregularities are probably not as great as contemporaries' complaints would indicate and that official claims of gross overcounts may have been motivated by self-interest, since corregidores and kurakas were the ones who had to produce larger numbers of workers or greater amounts of tribute.[4]

But, if the accuracy of the number of tributary males is debatable, there clearly was an undercount of certain groups of females. In analyzing the returns for 23,000 individuals, Evans found that while there were quite equal numbers of adult men and women (fifteen to forty-nine years of age), females made up only 43 percent of the population below the age of fifteen.[5] The most likely explanation is that since the enumerators were most interested in tracking down male children, who would eventually pay tribute and serve in the mita, they were careless about recording girls.

Another problem with the data is that ages (when supplied) are only approximate. The returns show marked "bunching" at five- and ten-year digits. Ages were sometimes little more than estimates by the census takers, especially for the very young and the elderly. However, for Andean people of the period, age was closely associated with one's social role, so a person would be more likely to be identified as an "adult" or an "elder" than as being specifically twenty-seven or sixty-two years old, and therefore one might attach little importance to reporting one's exact years to the census taker.[6] Apparently colonial officials were satisfied with this approach; Evans observes that little or no effort was made to check reported ages against baptismal records.[7]

But despite these problems, and the variation in the quality of the data from province to province, out of thirteen provinces the results were only thrown out by the viceregal government in one and and corrections were only ordered in six communities out of 104. Sánchez-Albornoz concludes, "Taking into account the limitations of the period, the information appears to be of a minimally acceptable quality for the stated purposes."[8]

In the extant returns from Oruro, some entries are illegible due to the deterioration of the paper, and there may be missing folios as well.[9] As in the *padrones* (census returns) from other provinces and cities, female children appear to have been underregistered by the census takers. Furthermore, while the returns provide ages for all males and for female children, there are no ages at all given for adult women, and the count does not even list single women or widows. Indeed, this lack of interest in women is evident in almost every section of the census. Women's occupations are not given, although many were certainly gainfully employed, nor are women's birthplaces or ayllus included. As a result, a complete demographic analysis of the entire population is impossible, although some tentative generalizations can be made based on the information provided for men. Chapter 6, which deals exclusively with women and their families, attempts to compensate to some extent for what is missing from the census.

Information on nine characteristics was recorded for each of the 1,275 forastero men listed as individuals (that is, not listed as children of other respondents) in Oruro. Since the census takers (the corregidor and his assistants) were primarily interested in information on mita service and tribute payment, responses to questions on these subjects were recorded for almost all the men in the census. Age, marital status, and province of origin were also important for tax collection and the mita, so these categories tend to be remarkably complete. On the other hand, the information collected on birthplace, number of years of residence in Oruro, occupation, and number of children is less complete. For the 285 yanacona men in Oruro, the same information was registered except that, as a group, they were exempt from mita service, so that category is not present in their section of the enumeration. In addition, only a very few entries indicate how long a yanacona had lived in Oruro. (I analyzed returns only for Oruro, because those for Indians living in surrounding areas under Oruro's jurisdiction were incomplete.)

The 1683 Enumeration for Oruro

Since many of the ages given in the 1683 census were only approximate, I divided Oruro's male Indian population into three major age groups rather than attempting to discuss five-year or even ten-year cohorts. These groups are children (defined as up to fourteen years of age), economically active adults (between fifteen and forty-nine years old), and elders (fifty and older). I placed the upper limit of the eco-

TABLE 5.1 Indian Males in Oruro, 1683

	Age	N	(%)
Children	0–4 years	528	(41)
	5–9	422	
	10–14	185	
Economically active adults	15–19	193	(48)
	20–24	303	
	25–29	212	
	30–34	306	
	35–39	95	
	40–44	173	
	45–49	40	
Elders	50–54	134	(11)
	55–59	14	
	60–64	83	
	65 and older	57	
TOTAL		2,745	(100)

Source: AGN, XIII-17-1-4.

Note: The table reflects statistics for all male children and adults for whom age is given.

nomically active range at forty-nine years because, after that age, men theoretically no longer had to pay tribute and were certainly considered to be past their prime as workers.[10]

Active adults made up approximately 48 percent of the city's male population, boy children about 41 percent, and elderly men, about 11 percent (see table 5.1). This means that a high proportion of Oruro's male population was in the economically active age group. One might expect this in a mining center, which attracted able-bodied, adult male immigrants. This conclusion is borne out in a comparison of Oruro's 1683 census with demographic studies of rural communities based on counts from the same decade.

Using a parish census conducted in 1689, Magnus Mörner examines the demographic characteristics of an indigenous community in Cuzco, Huaquirca, that was made up almost entirely of orginarios. He concludes that the town had a severe shortage of adult men, which resulted in a low birth rate. He attributes the disequilibrium between the sexes to higher mortality rates among males due to forced labor in the mines of Huancavelica and possibly to the migration of single males.[11]

A study of Livitaca, another community in Cuzco, based on an enumeration from the same year, examines originarios and forasteros separately. Clara López-Beltrán finds that 47 percent of the male forastero population was between fifteen and fifty years old, virtually the same proportion as among forasteros in Oruro. In contrast, only 37 percent of the originario men in Livitaca were in that age range. López-Beltrán suggests that the reduced number of adult originario men in Livitaca is probably due to emigration, and that this loss to the community was somewhat compensated for by the arrival of forasteros.[12] The depletion of active adult male originarios in Huaquirca and Livitaca, as well as the fact that forasteros in the same age range were well represented in Livitaca, tend to confirm the hypothesis that individuals in their economically active years were the most common migrants and that it was no accident that a significant proportion of men in Oruro were between fifteen and fifty years of age.

Of men age twenty and older in Oruro, 80 percent were married. This percentage is apparently lower than that calculated by Brian Evans from the 1683 returns for fifteen indigenous communities in the provinces of Sicasica, Larecaja, Chayanta, and Pacajes. Although he does not give a percentage for married men, he concludes that marriage after age twenty "was well nigh universal."[13] However, in Oruro many of the single men were in their early twenties and presumably could be expected to marry soon. In Oruro the vast majority of married men lived with their wives; there was no bachelor society of immigrants.

Table 5.2 shows that 1,261 married couples had 2,037 children, or an average of 1.6 children per couple, evidently not enough for the population to reproduce itself. However, as noted, female children were probably not registered as scrupulously as males, since they were not future tributaries.[14] The census, in fact, lists 1,312 male children and only 725 females. Since there is no reason why the pop-

TABLE 5.2 Indian Families in Oruro, 1683

No. of Children	No. of Families	(%)
0	259	(21)
1	401	(32)
2	342	(27)
3	141	(11)
4	81	(6)
5	23	(2)
6	8	(1)
7	6	—
TOTAL	1,261	(100)

Total no. of children = 2,037

Source: AGN, XIII-17-1-4.

ulation should not have included approximately the same number of children of both sexes, the number of children per couple may actually have been higher—perhaps closer to two, which would mean that the population was at least able to reproduce itself.

Considering the undercount of girls and the fact that the infant mortality rate was surely high, the number of children in individual nuclear families indicated relatively high fertility, especially when compared with rural Livitaca (table 5.2). While 21 percent of married couples had no children, another 9 percent had between four and seven offspring. Thirty-two percent (401 couples) had one child, 27 percent (342 couples) two, and 11 percent (141 couples) three children. Compared with Livitaca, these appear to be big families indeed. In that community, in 1689 a full 52 percent of married couples had no children at all, and only three couples (less than 2 percent) had three or more children.[15] This difference in the size of family groups between the rural community and Oruro is explained by the shortage of adult men under age fifty in Livitaca and the high number of married men in this age range employed in the mining center.

Table 5.3 shows the remarkable diversity of occupations among the Indian men in Oruro: 267 men were engaged in craft professions,

TABLE 5.3 Occupations of Male Forasteros and Yanaconas in Oruro, 1683

	No. of Forasteros	(%)	No. of Yanaconas	(%)	Total N	(%)
Mining and related work		(10)		(2)		(9)
Pickman	6		0		6	
Mine worker	44		1		45	
Metal carrier	39		0		39	
Refinery worker	33		2		35	
Fireman, refinery	9		3		12	
Miner's asst.	2		0		2	
SUBTOTAL	133		6		139	
Transport and trade		(13)		(24)		(15)
Traveler	151		65		216	
Muleteer	8		4		12	
SUBTOTAL	159		69		228	
Crafts		(14)		(30)		(17)
Silversmith	15		3		18	
Candlemaker	10		1		11	
Shoemaker	22		16		38	
Butcher	19		0		19	
Mason	13		2		15	
Tailor	28		20		48	
Baker	22		10		32	
Draper	8		7		15	
Barber	2		3		5	
Guitar maker	7		2		9	
Painter	3		8		11	
Carpenter	14		3		17	
Blacksmith	4		1		5	
Weaver	5		0		5	
Pastry chef	5		0		5	
Hat maker	2		6		8	
Potter	1		0		1	

TABLE 5.3 Occupations of Male Forasteros and Yanaconas in Oruro, 1683 (cont.)

	No. of Forasteros	(%)	No. of Yanaconas	(%)	Total N	(%)
Crafts (cont.)						
Adobe maker	1		0		1	
Cook	0		1		1	
Chair maker	0		2		2	
Dyer	0		1		1	
SUBTOTAL	181		86		267	
Administrative and religious work		(2)		(3)		(2)
Tribute collector	5		2		7	
Governor	3		1		4	
Cantor	6		4		10	
Sacristan	10		1		11	
Organist	1		0		1	
SUBTOTAL	25		8		33	
Other work		(1)		(4)		(1)
Farmer	4		0		4	
Herdsman	3		11		14	
Fisherman	1		0		1	
Textile worker	1		0		1	
SUBTOTAL	9		11		20	
Occupation not given	768	(60)	105	(37)	873	(56)
TOTAL	1,275	(100)	285	(100)	1,560	(100)

Source: AGN, XIII-17-1-4.

including forty-eight tailors, thirty-eight shoemakers, thirty-two bread bakers, nineteen butchers, and eighteen silversmiths. However, male Indian artisans also worked in more unusual fields: there were nine guitar makers and five pastry chefs, for instance. The city had eleven candlemakers, who were particularly important in Oruro, or any mining town, because candles were necessary to light the mines. There were many bakers in mining areas (colonial Potosí also had numerous bakeries), and the existence of thirty-two bakers in Oruro would seem to indicate that many families bought this staple instead of making it themselves. In 1631 the city's royal treasurer caustically complained to the king about the occupational expertise of the Indians in Oruro, saying it was difficult to get Indians to work in the mines because they became hispanicized and learned new skills precisely to avoid mine work.[16] Most of these Indians were probably assistants to Spaniards or mestizos in these professions, since other documents specify Spanish residents of Oruro who performed these crafts with the help of Indian workmen.[17] Likewise, the muleteers (*arrieros*) almost certainly worked for Spaniards who owned the mules; they transported silver from Oruro to Potosí or to Arica and returned with imported goods for the mining center.

Ann Wightman has located artisan guilds in seventeenth-century Cuzco that admitted Indian craftspeople. Karen Spalding also refers to Indians belonging to the same guilds as Spanish artisans in early colonial Lima, but says that by the eighteenth century they had their own organizations because of discrimination in the Spanish-creole guild structure.[18] I have not found any direct references to guilds in Oruro. However, in the census returns a few men were identified as masters (*maestros*) in certain crafts: a draper, a mason, a tailor, and a painter. Being a master might refer not only to one's expertise but also to one's position in the guild system. All four were mature men (the tailor was said to be seventy years old), which presumably would be necessary for a master in a trade. Another hint that at least some of Oruro's Indian workers were organized into guilds were a few other men in the census who were listed as *oficiales* (journeymen), another term associated with the guild system, and one young man of eighteen who was said to be "learning the trade of silversmith." Most of the craftsmen in the census, however, simply gave their professions without any suggestion of guild membership.

The single most common occupation given in the census is that of "traveler," meaning someone who brought provisions of one kind or another to the mines. The fact that 228 men were involved in this kind of work reflects the size of the urban market. In the arid zone in which the mining center was located, camelids and sheep were raised and some important crops, such as potatoes and quinoa were grown, while other foods had to be brought from lower altitudes. Travelers supplied corn, corn flour, wheat, coca, and wine to the markets in Oruro from surrounding areas such as Cochabamba and some closer river valleys. Since traditional Andean agriculture used different types of land at different altitudes, where a variety of crops and animals could be raised, even people who had land near Oruro may have needed to buy some products from other zones, if they did not have access to other ecological niches. One indicator that not all indigenous people had land or resources to supply all of their own needs is that men identifying themselves as butchers and travelers usually said that they were providing food for the "Indians of the mines," not for local Spanish and creole townspeople. Certainly the majority of people in Oruro were Indians, therefore logically constituting the bulk of the market for regionally produced goods. Furthermore, Indians who lived in cities certainly developed some new tastes in food, clothing, and entertainment. As an extreme example of changes in fashion, urban yanaconas were described in the 1660s by highland caciques as wearing silk stockings, capes, and shirts of the European style.[19] A cyclical process was set in motion: entering the market as workers contributed to Andean peoples' acculturation, which in turn further expanded the size of the internal market: satisfying the new habits of consumption required continued work for money.[20]

The puzzling thing about the occupations listed in the 1683 census is that very few men in Oruro (only 139 in all) said they worked in the city's mines and refining mills, while 60 percent of the forasteros and 37 percent of the yanaconas claimed no occupation at all. I believe that most of the men not giving occupations probably worked in the silver industry, but it was not recorded because their work was in some sense casual. Some may have worked for several different employers; others probably worked only part-time. For instance, in periods when production was high and there was increased demand for labor, men may have worked at less skilled mining tasks, such as sorting and hauling ore. When fewer workers were needed in times of drought, when there was insufficient water to power the mills, or during shortages of mercury, they may have worked in mines and mills when employment was available and supplemented their earnings by performing various services in Oruro. Finally, many may not have been totally dependent on wages, deriving their subsistence, or part of it, from agriculture.

Forasteros and Yanaconas

For a more accurate picture of Oruro's Indian population, we should look separately at the two major groups of Indians in the city: the yanaconas and the forasteros mentioned by Luis de Miranda in his introduction to the census. Miranda's comments reveal extreme skepticism about the yanaconas' credentials. Instead of viewing them as legitimate descendants of yanaconas from the time of Toledo, he seems to consider most of them as evading their responsibilities to the government and to their communities. At one point, he refers to "those Indians who pass for yanaconas."[21] The census itself frequently notes that a man is listed as a yanacona because he pretends not to know his village or origin, suggesting a feigned amnesia about ayllu and parcialidad. In any event, whether because of generations of being separated from Andean communal life, or due to more recent adoption of new social mores, in the 1683 census yanaconas show social and demographic characteristics distinct from those of the forasteros.

Perhaps most striking are the occupational differences between the two groups (see table 5.3, above). Higher percentages of yanacona males were involved in craft occupations (30 percent compared to 14 percent for forasteros), and more of the yanaconas worked in trade and transport (24 percent of the yanaconas compared with 12 percent of the forasteros). The large number of yanaconas working as artisans seems to be typical of the group in cities in Upper Peru. In Potosí in 1672, more than 62 percent of yanaconas who gave their occupations worked in crafts.[22] In 1663, Don Gabriel Fernández Guarache, kuraka of Jesús de Machaca, frustrated in his attempts to track down community members who owed him tribute, claimed that Indians learned trades specifically so they might call themselves yanaconas and avoid obligations to their communities. He echoed the remarks of Oruro's treasurer when he said, "They change their dress, use the

Spanish language and claim not to know their own. They apply themselves to other trades: the occupations of draper, tailor, carpenter, because with this malicious subterfuge they become free yanaconas."[23]

To understand the divergent migration patterns of yanaconas and forasteros in Oruro, we must first distinguish clearly between census information regarding place of birth and place of origin. For the forasteros, place of origin meant the town or community to which a family had been "reduced" in the 1570s during the administration of Viceroy Francisco de Toledo. In its place of origin, a family had rights to land and was responsible for paying tribute and performing mita service, on a rotating basis, for a year in Potosí. Since these "origins" had been established by the colonial government more than a century earlier, many families had moved in the intervening period, and thus the majority of forastero men in Oruro were originarios from one place but born in another.

The origins of yanaconas were somewhat different. As noted before, the enumeration ordered by the Viceroy de Toledo in 1573 lists only yanaconas living in cities. They are usually referred to as *yanconas de la real corona* (of the royal crown), or *del rey* (of the king) if they worked in nonreligious capacities, or *de la catedral* (of the cathedral) if assigned to a church institution. The *yanaconas del rey* generally paid their tribute to a captain who was responsible to the government for delivering the proper amount of taxes.

Since the time of Toledo, there had been a rapid, unofficial proliferation of yanacona men both on chacras and in cities. Unlike forasteros, however, those who became yanaconas tended to want to obliterate their true origins and this desire undoubtedly contributed to the high number of yanaconas in Oruro who claimed to be from major cities. This difference between the two groups might be attributed to the fact that in many cases forasteros still maintained (or hoped to maintain) some contact with their villages of origin and enjoyed some of the privileges of community membership; while yanaconas, in their efforts to escape the mita and to pay tributes generally lower than those paid by originarios, had more completely severed these connections.[24]

A full 40 percent of male forasteros in Oruro were born in the city (see table 5.4). If we look at what I call "Greater Oruro," which

TABLE 5.4 Birthplaces of Male Forasteros in Oruro, 1683

Province	N	(%)
Paria		
Oruro	515	(40)
Greater Oruro		(10)
Toledo	62	
Challacollo	5	
Sepulturas	23	
Sorasora	19	
Parish of Paria	18	
Other towns	29	
Pacajes	32	
Carangas	69	
Porco		(4)
City of Potosí	49	
Other towns	1	
Sicasica	23	
Chayanta	11	
Cochabamba	18	
Chucuito	21	
Omasuyos	17	
Quispicanches (Cuzco)	4	
Paucarcolla	1	
Yamparaez	2	
Azangaro	5	
Lampa	6	
Canas y Canches	13	
Larecaja	2	
Condesuyos	2	
Chumbivilcas	1	
Arica	1	
Lipez	1	
Birthplace not given	326	(26)
TOTAL	1,275	(100)

Source: AGN, XIII-17-1-4.

includes five nearby towns, several of which were centers for grinding and processing ore, we find that half of the forastero men counted in the census were born in or near the mining center. Furthermore, many of the men born in the city itself specifically said that they had lived in Oruro all their lives. Clearly, this means that much of the migration to the town was not recent, since these men's parents, or even grandparents, had first moved to Oruro. Although it cannot be confirmed, we might speculate that many immigrant families came to the city soon after the discovery of silver at the beginning of the seventeenth century, in the first rush to the mines. The presence of so many men born in the site also suggests a stable work force.

After Greater Oruro, the next largest number of forasteros listed in the census were born in the adjacent province of Carangas and the city of Potosí. Potosí, of course, was itself a mining center, and men who worked there were probably attracted to Oruro by higher wages. Following Potosí and Carangas, the provinces of Paria (excluding Greater Oruro) and Pacajes are the next most frequent birthplaces listed. Thus, it appears that men who had moved to Oruro, rather than being born there, were generally born in nearby provinces having more or less the same altitude and geographic conditions—mostly within the area of the Bolivian high plateau. The census lists some forasteros whose birthplaces were very distant, but they are a small minority.

In many cases we can determine how long forasteros had lived in Oruro. Out of 276 men not born in Oruro or its environs for whom the number of years of residence in Oruro is reported, 60 percent had lived in the city more than five years (see table 5.5). If we include men born in Oruro and environs, the percentage who had lived there more than five years increases to 85 percent. Thus, Oruro's forasteros were not a transient population, since only 119 men had lived there from one to five years, and only seven claimed residence of less than one year. We cannot know, of course, whether the 432 forastero men who do not report how long they had been in Oruro were temporary migrants, coming to work for a few weeks or months, or perhaps only passing through. Even if this were the case, as is likely for some of the men, forasteros, who were the vast majority of Oruro's Indian residents, were a reasonably stable population.

TABLE 5.5 Years of Residence in Oruro, Forasteros, 1683

	Forasteros Not Born in Oruro or Greater Oruro	Cumulative %	All Forasteros	Cumulative %
Less than one	7	3	7	1
1–5	104	40	119	15
6–10	63	63	74	24
11–15	21	71	38	29
16–20	27	80	177	50
21–25	18	87	84	61
26–30	11	91	120	75
31–35	13	96	49	81
36–40	4	97	60	88
41–45	5	99	14	90
46–50	0	99	30	94
51–55	3	100	7	95
56–60	0	—	29	98
61–65	0	—	0	98
66–70	0	—	7	99
71–75	0	—	1	99
76–80	0	—	5	100
81–85	0	—	0	100
86–90	0	—	1	100
More than 90	0	0	1	100
TOTAL	276	100	823	100

Source: AGN, XIII, 17-1-4.

For a more long-term view of migration patterns, it is useful to compare birthplaces with provinces of origin, which are listed in the census for all but six forastero men.[25] (See table 5.6.) First, forastero men born in Oruro gave as their origin twelve different provinces, some of them—Paucarcolla, Azangaro, Lampa, Canas y Canches— quite far distant. The greatest concentration, however, came from Paria itself and the nearby provinces of Carangas and Pacajes (43 percent). The lacustrine province of Chucuito was the place of origin for another 16 percent. Thus, most people born in Oruro had origins in provinces located on the high plateau to which the mining center was relatively accessible. Some of them, such as those originating in communities in Paria, might have been only a few kilometers away from the villages to which their ancestors had been "reduced."

The same general pattern of migration is repeated for almost all the male forasteros in Oruro. For those giving the nine most common birthplaces—Oruro, Potosí, Paria, Carangas, Pacajes, Sicasica, Chucuito, Cochabamba, and Omasuyos—most of their provinces of origin are located on the high plateau between Canas y Canches in the north and Paria in the south, with the highest number coming from the provinces closer to Oruro (see map 3, above). With only a few exceptions, people who came to Oruro were born and claimed origins in the core highland areas of Upper Peru. Even if they, or their ancestors, had migrated great distances, the basic ecology of their place of residence remained the same: they did not come in great numbers from valley or lowland zones. Coastal and valley provinces (Larecaja, Arica, Yamparaez), except for Cochabamba, are poorly represented both as places of birth and of origin. The altiplano provinces with yungas zones (Omasuyos, Sicasica) primarily sent migrants from highland communities. Cochabamba may have been exceptional because of pre-Hispanic colonization patterns and Toledan policies. Viceroy de Toledo had protected the rights of Carangas, Quillacas, and Soras—peoples from the high plateau—to lands they claimed in the Cochabamba Valley. As late as the eighteenth century, Carangas mitimaes from the town of Toledo, outside of Oruro, still worked lands in the pueblo of Capinota in Cochabamba.[26] Given these long-standing connections, some of the men recorded by colonial officials in 1683 as being from Cochabamba may still have had some ties with highland ayllus.

It is worth mentioning that the four most common provinces of origin for forasteros in Oruro (Paria, Carangas, Pacajes, and Chucuito) were areas that had been depleted by the annual obligation of the mita and by the flight of tributaries who wanted to avoid it. Indians from Paria or Chucuito who went to work in Oruro did so for reasons similar to those who migrated to temperate agricultural provinces: the high plateau was increasingly impoverished, and the mining center, like the rural haciendas, offered them the possibility of earning some money and escaping

TABLE 5.6 Birthplaces and origins of Male Forasteros in Oruro, 1683

Origins	Oruro	Potosí	Paria	Carangas	Pacajes	Sicasica	Chucuito	Cochabamba	Omasuyos	Canas y Canches
Paria	99		90				1	2		
Carangas	57	4	16	66		1		1		
Pacajes	64	3	10		28	1		1	1	
Sicasica	21	1	5			15				
Chucuito	81	4	18		2	2	19	2		
Cochabamba	30		2					8		
Omasuyos	48	3	3	1	1	1		1	16	
Canas y Canches	34	4	4							13
Chayanta	12	5	2							
Lampa	37	13	4	1	1	1				
Azaugaro	7	2		1						
Quispicanches										
Yamparaez										
Larecaja										
Condesuyos									1	
Porco		1								
Paucarcolla	21	9	2			1	1	2		
Chumbivilcas										
Arica										
Cuzco										
Not given	4					1				
TOTAL	515	49	156	69	32	23	21	18	17	13

Source: AGN, XIII-17-1-4.

TABLE 5.6 Birthplaces and origins of Male Forasteros in Oruro, 1683 (cont.)

				Birthplaces									
Chayanta	Lampa	Azangaro	Quispicanches	Yamparaez	Larecaja	Condesuyos	Porco	Paucarcolla	Chumbivilcas	Arica	Lipez	Not Given	TOTAL
1												49	242
2												56	203
		1										67	176
											1	12	55
												34	162
												10	50
												21	95
			1	1								36	93
8												9	36
	5											8	70
		5										10	25
												1	1
												1	1
					1							1	2
						2						1	4
							1						2
								1				7	44
									1				1
				1						1			2
			2									3	5
			1										6
11	6	5	4	2	1	2	1	1	1	1	1	326	1,275

the mita.²⁷ Moreover, the mining center had the additional advantage of being near their home communities.

However, the fact that forasteros stayed within the highland region, and frequently did not even go far from home, should not obscure the great amount of physical movement that had actually occurred since the creation of reducciones in the late sixteenth century. The diagonal on table 5.6 shows that only 280 men, or 22 percent of Oruro's male forasteros, were born in their province of origin. (This does not include 99 men born in Oruro with origins in Paria—that is, in their province of origin, but not place of origin.) Of these 280 men, 263 were born in their actual communities of origin. That means that by the 1680s the majority of Andean migrants in Oruro were at least one generation removed, perhaps more, from the towns their families had been assigned to in the 1570s.

Yet, in the instructions attached to his census returns, the corregidor of Oruro, Luis de Miranda, mentioned Indians who were originarios of nearby towns now working in Oruro. In his 1607 report, Felipe de Godoy also referred to workers in Oruro whose places of origin were so close that they could return in a day if they so desired and said that in their villages they owned land and houses (see chapter 4). By 1683, people may have lost land they once owned, but it is likely that some of the forasteros working in Oruro still maintained their rights in their villages of origin, even if they were not born there, and provided at least part of their subsistence through agriculture. In fact, this may have contributed to the stability of the city's work force. Instead of coming great distances, working in Oruro for short periods to pay their tribute, and then returning home (as we shall see was a common practice in the province of Pilaya y Paspaya), people may have been able to work in Oruro on a more or less regular basis while holding rights to land elsewhere. Since the altiplano was appropriate only for growing basic, native food crops and animal grazing, these lands were not much coveted by Spaniards for agricultural production. So, while Indians may have lost acreage in the valleys to aspiring hacendados, villages were more likely to hold onto property in high-altitude puna zones.²⁸ One of the nearby towns that Corregidor Miranda mentions is Toledo, approximately 40 kilometers from Oruro on the altiplano. Of 242 forasteros in Oruro who claimed origins in the province of Paria, 180 came from Toledo. Although we do not know to what extent they still shared in the community's lands and other resources, they certainly had not migrated so far as to make this impossible.

A higher proportion of Oruro's male yanaconas, compared to forasteros, were born in the city (53 percent for yanaconas, 40 percent for forasteros; see table 5.7). While the census does not indicate the yanaconas' length of residence in Oruro, given what we know about the mining industry there in the 1680s, and immigration trends among forasteros, it is safe to assume that even those who were born elsewhere were not recent arrivals to the city.

Of yanaconas not born in Oruro, about 46 percent were born in other cities: Arequipa, Trujillo, Cochabamba, Cuzco, La Paz, Potosí, La Plata, and Carangas (a mining site considered an urban area). In total, 74 percent of Oruro's yanaconas claimed to have been born in major urban areas and to have had no connections with the communities created for Indians at the end of the sixteenth century. Furthermore, examining individual returns for yanaconas not born in cities reveals that in most cases they either traced their origins to urban centers where their parents had been *yanaconas de la real corona*, or were listed as yanaconas because Oruro's census takers were uncertain as to how to categorize them. This was the situation of twenty-year-old Joseph Ignacio, who was born in Las Sepulturas, an industrial suburb of Oruro where ore was refined. Next to his name is the note: "He does not know his origin and therefore is listed with the yanaconas." Bartolomé Pérez, thirty years of age, was born in Punata in Cochabamba. The census taker wrote: "He tells me that his father was a quadroon and his mother a mestiza."[29] Obviously, the corregidor or his assistant who compiled the list was not convinced and thought Pérez was an Indian. However, since his ethnic origins were not clear, he was listed as a yanacona.

Thierry Saignes also recorded complicated combinations of personal circumstances and individual effort that resulted in identifying people as yanaconas. For instance, the illegitimate son of a family that rented land in a valley close to Potosí fled to the villa imperial, changed his name, and claimed to be a *yanacona del rey* from Oruro. Meanwhile, his legitimate half brothers had not denied their origins

TABLE 5.7 Birthplaces and Origins of Yanaconas in Oruro, in 1683

Origins	Oruro	La Paz	Potosí	La Plata	Cuzco	Cochabamba (city)	Carangas mine site*	Trujillo	Arequipa
Oruro	44	1							
La Paz	50	10							1
Potosí			4						
La Plata	3	1		3					
Cuzco	12		1	2	7				
City of Cochabamba	2					2			
Trujillo	1								
Lima	1								
Arequipa	4								
Paria	1								
Sicasica									
Cochabamba							2		
Omasuyos									
Larecaja									
Pacajes	1					1			
Chayanta									
Mizque						1			
Chichas									
Tomina			1						
Claim to be mestizos or mulattoes	2		2						
Don't know	21	2	2	4	2	1		1	
Missing data	10	3	1	3	1		2		
TOTAL	152	17	11	12	10	7	2	1	1

Source: AGN, XIII-17-1-4.

*Carangas mining site is considered an urban area.

TABLE 5.7 Birthplaces and Origins of Yanaconas in Oruro, in 1683 (cont.)

				Birthplaces							
Paria	Sicasica	Cochabamba	Omasuyos	Larecaja	Pacajes	Chayanta	Mizque	Chichas	Don't Know	Missing Data	TOTAL
13		1					1		2		62
1	3	1							1	6	73
										1	5
											7
1										3	26
											4
									1		2
											1
									1		5
2										1	4
									1		1
											2
			4								4
				1					1		2
					1						3
						1					1
									1		2
						1					1
											1
		1							1		6
6							1	1	6	1	48
1										4	25
24	3	1	6	1	1	2	2	1	15	16	285

and, although not living in their family's village of origin, had always served in the mita with the contingents from the village of Yanaoca.[30] His case and that of Bartolomé Pérez and others suggests that questions of birth had bearing on whether a person became a yanacona. Illegitimacy was frequently associated with yanacona status, because if a father was unknown it was difficult to determine where a child was a tributary;[31] so was having a parent who was not an Indian or even just having a mother and father from different communities.[32] On the one hand, it appears that individuals invented or used these circumstances to escape their communal obligations to the colonial state. On the other hand, perhaps people with unorthodox origins were offered less support by their ayllus and as a result formed a group which, although still classified as Indian, straddled the fence between Indian society and the Hispanic world.

In addition to being born in cities, 65 percent of yanacona men also traced their origins to cities, with the largest number (seventy-three) coming from La Paz. Sixty-two claimed Oruro as place of origin, a claim that has a distinctly inauthentic ring. Oruro did have a royal treasury beginning in 1607 and thus it was possible that from the early days a group of Indians there paid tribute directly to a functionary in the city instead of to official representatives from their home villages. Still, we know that Viceroy Francisco de Toledo registered yanaconas in only five cities (La Plata, Potosí, Cuzco, Arequipa, La Paz) and that although there was an encomienda named Oruro in Toledo's count, the city did not exist in 1573. Consequently, how these men came to consider themselves originarios of Oruro is unclear. A possible explanation is that some of the early Indian laborers who migrated to the city were referred to as yanaconas by Oruro's first governors and mining entrepreneurs, and were enrolled as such for tax purposes. This would be in keeping with the early colonial practice of identifying migrant Indians who worked in cities and mines as yanaconas.

Seventy-nine of the yanaconas in Oruro (28 percent) were born in their place of origin, and most were from cities. Forty-four claimed Oruro as both birthplace and place of origin. However, among yanacona males, as with forasteros, considerable geographical movement was the rule. This tends to discredit the idea that urban yanaconas and their families were tied to individual Spaniards or institutions, such as churches, more or less permanently. Instead, in general they were very mobile and probably took the initiative in seeking out economic opportunity.

Their mobility was demonstrated by the geographical extension of the yanaconas' migration. While Oruro and La Paz, the nearest city to Oruro on the altiplano, were the most common origins as well as birthplaces for yanacona men, on the whole, their birthplaces and origins were not as concentrated on the high plateau as were those of forasteros. Individuals came from valley provinces such as Tomina, Chichas, and Larecaja, from the cities of Arequipa and Lima, and twenty-six claimed the former center of the Inca empire, Cuzco, as their place of origin. If it is plausible that at least some forasteros in Oruro were still in contact with their villages of origin, the distances that many yanaconas had migrated would seem to make this unlikely for them.

If the majority of Oruro's yanaconas claimed to be descendants of early colonial urban servants and workers, there is a not insignificant group listed as yanaconas in the census who either claimed not to be Indians at all, or for whom no information on origins is given. Fully 28 percent of the yanacona males fall into these categories. Twenty-five men simply did not answer the question on origins, while forty-eight others stated that they did not know where their family came from. Here again is the issue of family and birth, but now taken beyond the nuclear family to the ayllu or community level. For instance: Domingo Chambi, thirty years of age, born in Tarapacá on what is now the coast of Chile, was "listed as a yanacona because he has never gone to the mita and did not know his origin." A very extreme case was Julio Mamani, age twenty, who "[did] not know where he was born, nor [did] he know who his parents were, nor . . . his origin."[33] It is interesting that several of the men who did not know their origins had, on various occasions, been responsible for collecting tribute from other members of the group, as if being cut off from Andean society made them more useful, or reliable, representatives of the state.

If yanaconas sought to make themselves untraceable by denying any knowledge of their origins or by saying they were from cities, it seems that they often completed their new identity by using Spanish last names. In 1663, Don Gabriel Fernández Guarache, the previously mentioned cacique from Pacajes, claimed that when men left his village of Jesús de Machaca, "they become yanaconas by adopting different clothing and last names and claiming to be free of the mita." Twenty-six years later, in 1689, the caciques of the adjacent province of Carangas maintained that Indians who left their jurisdiction "change their last names, call themselves mestizos and yanaconas, change their clothing to the Spanish style and work in craft occupations or in convents in order not to have to meet their obligations."[34]

In Upper Peru in the seventeenth century, while Spanish first names were the rule, the majority of indigenous people used Andean last names, although there was a tendency for some in urban areas to adopt Spanish last names as well. The use of Spanish surnames as an indicator of acculturation in the city of Arequipa in 1645 is discussed by Sánchez-Albornoz.[35] In Oruro the type of last names found in the 1683 census may be divided into five categories: (1) Andean names (Mamani, Yupanqui, Condori, Guanca), (2) Spanish surnames of the period (Ramos, Flores, Ramírez, Gutiérrez), (3) Spanish first names used as last names (Pablo, Nicolás, Vicente), (4) craft occupations used as last names (Herrero), and (5) indigenous place names (Sacaca, Arequipa). The last two types were quite rare in Oruro, the above examples being the only ones found in the entire census. Both forasteros and yanaconas in the city in 1683 had non-Andean last names, but their use was much more frequent among yanaconas. While 66 percent of the forasteros with legible names had indigenous surnames (837 individuals), only 33 percent of the yanaconas did (95 men). Furthermore, a much higher percentage of yanaconas used actual Spanish last names (51 percent as opposed to 23 percent among the forasteros), rather than adapting a first name for the purpose. This use of true Spanish surnames might be seen as a closer approximation of the European cultural trait.

Mita and Tribute

The reasons for the differences between forasteros and yanaconas are certainly complex, and given our present state of knowledge of Andean society of the period, cannot be established with certainty. However, we can identify two factors that contributed to the situation.

TABLE 5.8 Mita Obligations by Male Forasteros in Oruro, 1683

Age	Served in Person	Met Obligation with Money	Did Neither	Exempted from Payment[a]	No Answer	Total N
15–19	0	14	86	0	3	103
20–24	1	65	163	0	1	230
25–29	2	78	89	0	5	174
30–34	4	139	108	0	4	255
35–39	3	40	26	0	3	72
40–44	7	113	31	0	4	155
45–49	1	24	7	0	0	32
50–54	6	91	12	0	4	113
55–59	1	9	1	0	1	12
60 and older	3	96	11	10	7	127
TOTAL	28	669	534	10	32	1,273[b]
(%)	(2)	(53)	(42)	(1)	(2)	(100)

Source: AGN, XIII-17-1-4.

a. *Reservado*.

b. There were two forasteros listed in the census who were less than fifteen years old. Neither had served in the mita in person or paid for an exemption.

One, previously mentioned, is that many forasteros still participated on some level in the communal life of their villages and probably sought to establish and maintain this connection by stating their origins precisely. The other factor is the mita.

Table 5.8 indicates that only 2 percent of male forasteros in Oruro in 1683 actually served in the mita at Potosí, while 53 percent met the obligation in money. Although colonial officials frequently maintained that Indians left their villages to avoid the mita altogether, in Oruro, at any rate, approximately half of the forasteros met their service obligation in cash, paying unspecified sums to village leaders who came to the city to collect it. Further, if we look at the mita breakdown by age, we see that 249 of the males who neither paid nor went to Potosí in person were under twenty-five years of age. That means that almost 47 percent of those forasteros unaffected by the obligation were young men who might begin to pay for exemptions soon. Yanaconas, on the other hand, really were exempt from the mita: in fact, for some administrators, not serving in the mita was apparently one of the main determinants of yanacona status. The previously cited case of Domingo Chambi, who was enrolled as a yanacona because he had never gone to Potosí, is typical. Indians with traceable village origins often had to meet the forced labor obligation in one way or another. Those recognized as yanaconas did not have to do so.

The standard amount paid by mitayos in the second half of the seventeenth century who did not go to Potosí seems to have been seven pesos for each of the seventeen weeks they were supposed to work, or about 119 pesos for each year they had to serve.[36] But the census does not tell us how much men in Oruro paid not to go to Potosí, or how often they paid. It is possible, for instance, that the sum was prorated over the year, or that by paying some type of regular tax they bought a permanent exemption.[37] Whatever the amount, forasteros conceivably felt that the cost of a mita exemption was compensated by the privileges and rights they maintained by staying in their villages.

But if yanaconas did not have to serve in the mita, they did not escape paying tribute. Table 5.9 indicates that only 56 percent of the yanaconas paid tribute, while 83 percent of forasteros did. However, fifty-nine yanaconas under age twenty-five years answered that they had "not yet paid." This suggests that they expected to be made to pay at some point in the future, and that at least 77 percent of the yanacona men met their tax assessments or would soon do so. If we add the young forasteros who said that they had not yet paid taxes to those who were already paying, close to 94 percent of the forasteros in the city paid tribute or expected to do so. So, while yanaconas did not generally escape tribute, meeting the assessment was not as universal for them as it was for forasteros. Yanaconas paid their tribute to locally appointed captains or mayors (*alcaldes*), while the forasteros' taxes were collected by community leaders who came to Oruro regularly for the express purpose of collecting taxes that men living there owed in their villages.

The fact that so many forastero men paid tribute tends to contradict, at least for the city of Oruro, another commonly held belief:

TABLE 5.9 Tribute Payments by Indian Males in Oruro, 1683

Age	Paid Tribute	Did Not Pay	Had Yet to Pay	Exempted from Payment[a]	Not Given	Total N
Forasteros[b]						
15–19	33	1	65	0	4	103
20–24	151	2	76	0	1	230
25–29	160	8	0	0	6	174
30–34	240	10	2	0	3	255
35–39	66	2	0	0	4	72
40–44	149	2	0	0	4	155
45–49	30	0	0	2	0	32
50 and older	226	0	0	17	9	252
TOTAL	1,055	25	143	19	31	1,273
(%)	(83)	(2)	(11)	(2)	(25)	100
Yanaconas[c]						
15–19	6	2	21	0	4	33
20–24	20	14	38	0	1	73
25–29	22	14	2	0	0	38
30–34	41	9	0	1	0	51
35–39	18	4	0	1	0	23
40–44	17	0	0	0	1	18
45–49	5	3	0	0	0	8
50 and older	28	5	0	1	2	36
TOTAL	157	51	61	3	8	280
(%)	(56)	(18)	(22)	(1)	(3)	(100)

Source: AGN, XII-17-1-4.

a. *Reservado.*

b. Two forasteros under fifteen years of age were listed in the census, but did not pay tribute.

c. Ages of five yanacona men were not given.

that those who left their villages shifted the tax burden to the reduced number of people who stayed behind. While some forasteros may have escaped the tribute collector altogether by moving to remote areas of Upper Peru, there was little possibility of going undetected in Oruro, which was on the well-traveled road that joined Potosí to the north and to the coast. La Palata's tribute reform sought to make tax collection more uniform by having Indians pay their share where they *lived*, not in their places of origin.

A surprising finding in the 1683 enumeration with respect to tribute is that almost nobody was "reserved," or exempted from payment, even those over fifty years old. Colonial censuses from the later eighteenth century were often organized by tribute categories, with the term *reservados* denoting men over fifty who were no longer liable to taxation. Another category of *próximos* referred to youths between fourteen and eighteen years old.[38] Perhaps in the next century those over fifty really were excused from the obligation as the new generation matured to take their places, but in 1683 this does not appear to have been the case in Oruro.

How great a financial burden was the annual tribute? The amount varied from area to area, presumably reflecting the Indians' resources and ability to pay. Taxes for originarios were theoretically determined by the natural resources of their home communities and by ethnicity. Urus, for instance, often paid less tribute than Aymaras because of their generally impoverished condition.[39] The schedule established by Viceroy Francisco de Toledo in 1573 required that each community pay part of its taxes in money and part in goods (usually cloth), and sometimes a portion in animals. In Toledo's tribute assessment, the amount due in cash was broken down into the amount each individual owed. The tribute due in goods was also converted to a cash value, but applied to the community as a whole.[40] A comparison of la Palata's tribute with Toledo's shows that in many cases the amount to be paid in cash was about the same, or was even reduced somewhat by la Palata. However, now the tribute to be paid in kind was in many places simply added on to each man's assessment as a cash payment. Typical of tax levels for areas from which many forasteros in Oruro came were the tribute assessments for the town of San

Andrés de Machaca in Pacajes. In 1687 each Aymara tributary in San Andrés had to pay nine pesos and five reales (there were eight reales to the peso): seven pesos and two reales in cash, two pesos and three reales in cloth and animals. Urus in the same community paid a total of three and a half pesos in specie and in kind.[41] In the time of Toledo, the Aymara originarios of San Andrés de Machaca paid slightly more than seven pesos ensayados each, which converts to one peso *more* than originarios were obliged to pay under la Palata. The Urus in Toledo's assessment had to pay three pesos ensayados, equal to about four and a half pesos.[42]

The taxes yanaconas were required to pay were, in some cases, lower than those of Indians who lived in their reducciones. This was particularly true for yanaconas who lived on chacras, because they often lacked sufficient land or time to grow agricultural products which they could market. In his *Ordenanzas*, Viceroy Francisco de Toledo specified that yanaconas in the countryside, who lived and worked on Spaniards' chacras, should pay only one peso ensayado per year (equivalent to about one and a half ordinary pesos).[43] In his actual census and tax assessment, Toledo set the amounts to be paid by yanaconas in the cities according to his estimation of their income possibilities. For instance, in Potosí yanacona miners and ore smelters, skilled craftsmen, and those involved in trade or the sale of metals, were to pay twelve pesos ensayados per year. Yanaconas who worked in ingenios outside of Potosí, where they presumably had less opportunity for personal gain, were to pay eight pesos ensayados annually. In the city of La Plata, thirty yanaconas considered to be prosperous were taxed at a rate of eight pesos ensayados a year, while 103 others paid only five.[44]

Only in the case of La Paz can we compare the amount of taxes that yanaconas were to pay under Toledo's assessment with the sum specified in the 1680s based on la Palata's census. In the 1570s Toledo set the tax for yanaconas living in the city at five pesos ensayados per man of tributary age. In 1688 each of the city's yanaconas was ordered to pay nine and a half ordinary pesos, which represented an increase of about two pesos per person.[45] It was specifically stated by Toledo and again in the 1688 tax schedule that yanaconas in cities were to pay their entire assessment in cash. They were presumed to have both the money-making opportunities to do this, and no access to land on which to raise a portion of their tribute in food or animals.

Conclusion

The 1683 enumeration for Oruro reveals some interesting demographic and sociological features of the city's male Indian residents. For instance, although the population was quite young, with 48 percent between fifteen and fifty years of age, the overwhelming majority of adult men were married and lived with their wives. The fact that the city's immigrant population was not primarily comprised of single men or men who had left families elsewhere is an indication that, as in Potosí, the family in Oruro was the productive unit. (The complementary activities of husbands, wives, and other relatives that made survival in the colonial city more feasible are discussed in chapter 6.) Moreover, the fact that most immigrants lived in families probably contributed to another significant finding in the census: that Oruro's Indian population was quite stable.

Many of the men listed in the count were born in Oruro and in some cases their parents had been as well. Furthermore, even among those not born in the city, recent migration was not the rule. Certainly this was due in large part to the downturn in the mining industry, which reduced the need for Indian laborers. The relative permanence of the population also suggests that many of the forasteros in the city (who made up the majority of Oruro's native population) may have had lands nearby and have been able to "commute" from their villages to the mines. This means that a portion of the population was quite stable, ironically, not because the workers were totally dependent on wage labor for their survival, but because many of the forasteros and their families had worked out a complementary relationship between community agriculture and mine work in the city. In a sense, working in Oruro can be conceptualized as a substitute for ecological zones that had become inaccessible.

While one cannot maintain, as Thierry Saignes did for some rural areas, that immigrants working in Oruro were descended from mitimaes or llactarunas, it is possible to see them as fulfilling the same function.[46] Of course, as suggested in chapter 4, the economic complementarity that Oruro's migrants had developed was not always disadvantageous for the city's azogueros. In fact, Andean patterns frequently meshed well with an economic system in which relations of production were not fully capitalist, allowing entrepreneurs to pay wages below what was necessary for the workers' reproduction.

Yet, in studying relations between guarantors of work contracts and Indian contractees in seventeenth-century Cuzco, Ann Wightman found evidence that forasteros were gradually replacing kinship and reciprocity with connections based on occupation. This suggests that a sector of the indigenous population in Cuzco either found work in crafts or other fields remunerative enough to enable them to dispense with peasant agriculture and Andean economic strategies, or that for some reason they could no longer maintain ayllu connections. Distance seems to have been an important factor in this shift to occupational identification, because dependence on fellow workers as guarantors was most pronounced among forasteros in the city who came from villages outside the bishopric of Cuzco.[47]

A valid question is whether a similar change in allegiance and consciousness was occurring among the migrant population of Oruro as well. The evidence does not permit a definitive answer, but it is certainly possible that a gradual shift was taking place, especially among forasteros who were quite far from home. The workers in 1672 who stayed in city's ranchería after losing their jobs in the mills of Las Sepulturas are a case in point. However, even some forastero artisans who came from quite far away may have still relied heavily on family and ayllu ties. For instance, all the candle makers in Oruro were from the same ayllu in Cabana y Cabanilla. We also know that under the Inca state groups of mitimaes were often sent as colonists because they practiced a specific craft and that they still maintained contacts with their places of origin long after the Spanish conquest.[48] In other words, even for the group of immigrants who appeared to be the most acculturated, the craftsmen, one cannot automatically assume that occupational identification precluded essential ethnic ties.

Then there is the issue of tribute. Since forasteros paid their assigned amount to their own kuraka or his representative, instead of a tax collector appointed by the state, possibly this payment was part of a continuing reciprocal relationship. Forasteros helped shoulder the ayllu's fiscal burden, and in some instances this may have assured their continued access to land. Tristan Platt argues that the ayllus of northern Potosí through much of the nineteenth century conceived of tribute and even personal service for the state as parts of an Andean reciprocal pact that guaranteed them rights to land. If peasants in the 1800s could conceptualize their interaction with the nation-state in terms of a "moral economy" in which their taxes and labor sanctioned their ayllus' continued existence as collective entities, it is not far-fetched to imagine that forasteros two centuries earlier, who were actually paying tribute to their own leaders, did so because it maintained their connections with the kin group.[49]

Yanaconas in Oruro, however, were generally more acculturated than forasteros and at least did not admit to ties with ayllus or reducciones, so it makes sense that they indeed would have to forge new relationships based on occupation or residence. Yet, this new identity was not based on their roles as wage laborers or professional miners, as was the case with workers in eighteenth-century Mexican mining centers. The most acculturated Indians in Oruro were not industrial workers but skilled artisans who, at least according to observers, prided themselves on wearing elegant and expensive clothes and adopting Spanish mores. But culture and world view are difficult to penetrate from this historical distance, and there are indications (discussed in chapter 6) that social and family ties among yanaconas in urban areas may have been very important to their economic strategies. Nor can we rule out the possibility that some groups of yanacona artisans were descendants of specialized mitimaes and that a long tradition of craft production proved compatible with the demands of the market economy.

To shed more light on whether, or to what extent, ethnic identity was transformed by migration and how Andean customs interacted with market participation, it is necessary to analyze materials that cannot be quantified like a census but provide a more nuanced picture of urban colonial life. Although the Numeración de la Palata offers a valuable demographic and social profile of the male residents of Oruro, its one great flaw is the almost total absence of information on women. Studying native women's work and market activity within the context of household and kin-group economic strategies also provides a finer picture of the migrants' associations in the city and beyond it. The next chapter will demonstrate that by focusing on women, we also learn more about men.

· 6 ·

Gender and Social Differentiation

Women and Their Families Confront Colonialism

Even a superficial perusal of court cases or notarial records for a seventeenth-century Andean city soon reveals the extent to which indigenous people had become owners of private property. Houses and city lots always seemed to be changing hands, litigants always claiming that they had been unjustly deprived of their property rights. Less obvious at first, but present in records nonetheless, is material about other types of market activity: businesses owned, the types of work people did, the variety of economic ties among Andean people living in the city and even among urban residents and rural relatives. A particularly striking feature of the documentation in Andean urban archives, given the recent increase in scholarship about women, is evidence of how active native women apparently were in the economies of America's colonial cities. Yet historians are sharply divided about the socioeconomic power of these women. Such differences of opinion actually reflect a more essential debate about the extent to which indigenous women (or indigenous men for that matter) were the subjects of history and whether they can be portrayed as actively participating in shaping colonial society without negating the exploitation of colonialism.

Andean Women: Skillful Negotiators or Abused Victims?

A study by Frank Salomon of the processes of acculturation, miscegenation, and ethnic redefinition in Quito in the late sixteenth century depicts Andean women as using the tools at their disposal to defend their families' and kin groups' positions. Having examined the wills of a number of Indian women, Salomon suggests that Indian women may have been more important economic actors in the city than indigenous men: Indian women frequently owned property in Quito and many more women left wills than men. He demonstrates that leaving a will could be an effort by the testatrix to use the colonial legal system to influence future events and to advance a particular strategy for resisting colonialism. This could include attempts to perpetuate Andean patterns of inheritance from mother to daughter or between other female relatives, among other objectives.[1]

Elinor Burkett, who studied Indian women in sixteenth-century Arequipa, goes even further than Salomon in assessing the roles of native women in the colonial economy. She argues that they were better able to manipulate the colonial legal and social system than men primarily because of the nature of their employment as retail merchants and domestic servants. Burkett maintains that these jobs gave Indian women the opportunity to familiarize themselves with how the city functioned and put them in contact with other women like themselves with whom they formed business and personal relationships.[2] Indian men, on the other hand, because their participation in the market economy was generally limited to "gang labor in agriculture, construction and mining," had fewer possibilities for acculturation and were less adept at coping with urban life and benefiting from Hispanic institutions.[3] Burkett's views of the options open to indigenous women in colonial cities are based on an interpretation of precolonial history in which social roles were fixed by the Inca state and women in particular had virtually no access to religious or political positions.[4] From this perspective, the possibilities open to Indian women in the more individualistic culture of mercantile capitalism were considerable, even if concentrated in service jobs or petty commerce.

However, the advantages of domestic service (the most common employment for indigenous women in urban areas) may be questioned. Using a count taken in 1684 of 1,223 domestic workers in La Paz, Luis Miguel Glave describes a largely female sector of the city's Indian population that appeared to have experienced severe deterioration in personal and cultural relations. Glave's analysis reveals that large numbers of female children were separated from their parents, many unmarried mothers lived with their children in the homes of their masters, and a great number of female domestics knew nothing of their parents or communities of origin. He concludes that there was a good likelihood that many of the women accounted for in the tributary census (padrón) not only performed domestic tasks but also formed a coerced work force for various manufacturing enterprises. Taken against their will from their communities by their prospective employers, or brought to the city out of economic necessity by their parents or community leaders, the female domestics of La Paz seem to be far removed from the property-owning, will-writing women studied by Salomon and Burkett.[5]

To make sense of these disparate images, we must examine Andean women and their roles in the economy in the context of the system of private ownership and the increased social stratification that rapidly developed under colonialism. Generalizing about *all* Indian women is misleading precisely because their class positions varied widely. Furthermore, the situation of indigenous women was affected by both Hispanic and Andean ideologies of gender and the historical experience of women in each culture. Also, the economic roles of both women and men in Upper Peru were generally part of household or even kin-group strategies for coping with the exigencies of colonialism. To look at either sex separately gives an incomplete or even mistaken impression.

Frank Salomon comments, "In 1600 there were probably more different ways to be an urban Indian than there are today."[6] To study this variety with respect to indigenous women and the family economy, I broadened my scope beyond Oruro and examined civil and criminal court cases from the late seventeenth and early eighteenth centuries from the cities of La Plata and La Paz as well. La Plata (currently named Sucre) was the seat of the Audiencia of Charcas, the most important governing body in Upper Peru, with judicial as well as political and administrative functions. Not only did Andean people living in La Plata bring legal matters to the audiencia, but also cases from the entire Upper Peruvian area were heard by the court's judges. La Paz was founded in 1548 in an area previously occupied by mitimaes sent there by the Inca state to mine for gold. In the early colonial period, these colonists were joined by other Andean migrants, and in 1573 they were grouped into the reducción of San Pedro and Santiago de Chuquiabo, an Indian town facing the Spanish town across a narrow valley.[7] By the late seventeenth century, many more recent arrivals had swelled the ranks of the city's native population.

Out of the hundreds of cases reviewed in the archives of the three cities, I selected eighty-one because they contain important information about Indian women who worked, owned property, and conducted business. The cases also often incidentally reveal much about the social status, family structure, and relative power or powerlessness of the individuals involved in litigation. A small number of cases dealt with people who did not live in urban areas but who either came to the cities to conduct legal business or who were accused of crimes that were prosecuted in urban courts. Sixty-two of the records, however, dealt with Indian people who lived in one of the three cities, although it is often clear from the transcripts that they also owned property or had ties of kinship in the countryside. As a group, the judicial proceedings supply a personal dimension almost entirely missing from census documents and allow an investigator three hundred years later to appreciate something of the complexity of urban colonial existence.

Before attempting to interpret the information on women in court records, I must again underscore some of the differences between Andean and Iberian gender ideologies and discuss women's rights under Spanish law, since the most important Hispanic legal statutes also applied in the Indies. We saw in chapter 1 that, as with

Inca ideology in other spheres, rhetoric about gender did not always match the reality. While women were supposed to have political power parallel and equal to that of men, in fact the female politico-religious hierarchy was actually subordinate to that of the Inca and males. Likewise, the sexual division of labor within the family, symbolically reflecting the male-female complementarity of the universe, probably did not mean that men and women were really equal partners within the household. This supposition is an extrapolation from modern ethnographic fieldwork in Andean peasant communities, which shows that a similar division of labor continues to exist today,[8] and also indicates that complementarity in tasks required for the family's economic reproduction does not preclude considerable conflict and inequality between men and women. Household relations are only one of several determinants of social status and power, and the fact that political and religious positions in rural society are almost exclusively controlled by men has ramifications within the family group and contributes to the subordination of women.[9]

Even though women's power under the Incas was not equal to that of men, their possibilities were not as limited as Elinor Burkett suggests. Women of the nobility still had political and religious authority and were due obeisance, service, and lands according to their position within the hierarchy.[10] For ordinary people, even if the peasant household was not equalitarian, the economic contribution of women was essential and, perhaps more important, acknowledged as such. While in Spanish society peasant women or the wives of artisans may have been just as essential to their families' economic survival, Iberian ideology had no place for gender complementarity and, despite the "liberality" of Juan Luis Vives's prescriptions, was in principle patriarchal.

The legal position of women in Spanish colonial society had been established by codes written in the thirteenth century (the *Siete Partidas*) and the early sixteenth century (the *Leyes de Toro*) and was reinforced by a corporate view of society that equated the authority of the paterfamilias in the nuclear family with that of the king in the monarchical state.[11] Many of the restrictions placed on women's actions were aimed at controlling their presumed impulsiveness, poor judgment, and weak character, just as Vives's instructions were designed to correct these defects through education or training. Women were barred from virtually all political activities: they could not vote, be judges or lawyers, or hold public office.[12] In the economic sphere, married women needed the permission of their husbands to engage in many transactions, including buying or disposing of property, lending or borrowing money, or forming business partnerships. Unmarried women required their fathers' permission for these activities unless they were over twenty-five years old and had been legally "emancipated" by their fathers in the courts. Ironically, widowhood by itself freed a woman from the restrictions imposed on married or unemancipated single women.[13]

In terms of inheritance, Spanish law treated women with greater equity. Daughters and sons inherited equal shares of their parents' property, and a widow generally received half of the couple's community property on the death of her husband. Any dowry a woman brought to a marriage by law reverted to her when her husband died or if the marriage was legally dissolved. Until that time, however, the husband could administer, without his wife's permission, both the dowry and the couple's community property. Although a wife legally retained control of any belongings she brought to the marriage (other than the dowry) and any property she subsequently inherited, it seems that men commonly administered these resources as well.[14]

In the matter of guardianship of children, women's rights were extremely limited. Only the father could give consent for a child to marry, and the mother would not become her own child's legal guardian if her husband had named someone else in his will.[15] A woman also could not be named the tutor of a child who was not hers biologically; only a man appointed by the court could assume that responsibility.[16] With this truly formidable array of restrictions on their activities, Spanish American women might be supposed to be limited to the roles of wife, mother, and housekeeper. However, recent historical studies indicate that their economic activities were probably more extensive and complex than an examination of law books would lead us to believe and that, as with their male counterparts, the range of pursuits in which Spanish and creole women engaged was determined by class position. We know that elite women owned and administered property and ran businesses, particularly if a husband were absent or deceased. Less advantaged white women might seek other types of employment considered respectable: working as tutors and seamstresses and sometimes running retail businesses.[17] However, in a colonial society in which class position and race were closely related, many of the most menial female jobs were performed by Indian or other nonwhite women, just as their male counterparts did most of the heavy manual labor.

Burkett's contention that indigenous women were able to turn the situation to their advantage while men remained colonialism's superexploited labor force has not been borne out by my research. All native people were seen as a distinct, inferior caste by whites; the masses of people, both men and women, as they entered the market economy, began at the bottom rungs of the social ladder and most stayed there. The social differentiation that occurred as life in the Andes was transformed by a European class system was not a smooth process, but it certainly affected both sexes. As we have seen in the case of Oruro, by the late seventeenth century Indian men had managed to acquire sophisticated craft skills and as mine workers were sometimes able to capture a significant share of the ore for themselves. In fact, the apparently frequent sexual abuse of indigenous women, the violence toward women in general, and the discrimination they experienced simply because they were women, tend to support the argument that it was actually indigenous women who experienced the most extreme oppression under colonialism.[18]

Social Stratification, Women's Work, and Kin Networks

Perhaps more productive than studying women's or men's work and discussing the relative advantages of each is an approach that conceptualizes economic activities as aspects of household strategies. The mitayo's family, and even his ayllu, comprised the productive unit that provided inexpensive labor for the Potosí mines. Native men and women in cities who were not coerced laborers still generally structured their economic activities as couples or families. Judicial documents provide examples of the intertwining activities of urban Indian women, who often worked as retail merchants, and Indian men who were artisans or were involved in commercial activities themselves.

Gender and Social Differentiation

In the commercial structure of the colonial city, women were active in the marketplace but also frequently ran *pulperías*, or small groceries or dry goods stores. In Oruro in 1683, women ran twenty-seven out of thirty-three pulperías, while men almost entirely dominated the twenty-seven *tiendas de mercancías*, or bigger retail businesses, that generally sold imported goods. Only six of the owners of pulperías had names that identified them as Andeans, but a number of others with Hispanic surnames may have been Indians as well. The tiendas de mercancías were presumably the exclusive domain either of Spaniards or creoles, although it is possible that some of their owners were mestizos.[19] Andean men were more likely to be involved in long-distance trade either as muleteers for merchants or as independent traders.

In addition to showing the connections between husbands and wives, court cases indicate economic ties that extended beyond the nuclear family: among other relatives or ayllu members. Also documented are nonfamily business connections between some urban women and male craftsmen, particularly yanaconas. The records of these business and personal relations suggest that occupational and neighborhood ties may have in some instances replaced or supplemented kinship, as Ann Wightman concludes was the case in seventeenth-century Cuzco. However, the fact that these connections were so frequent among yanaconas makes one wonder if the people involved weren't actually part of an extended kin group. The following three cases are representative of the market activity and business networks of relatively prosperous urban Indian women.

Lucia Ursula, an Indian merchant from La Plata, left a substantial number of possessions in her 1698 will. These included two houses in the city, furniture, and a collection of religious paintings. She was the widow of Roque de la Cruz, a master chair maker, with whom she had had two children, neither of whom was alive when she made her will. She also had a natural daughter by another chair maker, a married man. To that daughter she left all of her possessions that didn't have to be sold to pay for her funeral or were not designated to pay for "masses for [her] soul and that of [her] husband."[20] In her will she listed a number of people, both men and women, who owed her small sums of money. Ursula did not specify the occupations of the women who were in her debt, but one of the men was a potter and another a carpenter. Ursula undoubtedly went to the trouble of making the will because she wanted to guarantee her natural daughter's inheritance: under Spanish law women with legitimate children were not forced to leave anything to illegitimate ones.[21]

Ana Sissa, the widow of Hernando Uscamayta, a yanacona in the service of the Convent of San Francisco in La Paz, owned several pieces of land in the city. One, inherited from her father, lay next to a parcel held by her brother. She also owned another home site, left to her by her husband, next to a site held by her husband's brother. In 1698 she and her brother-in-law together sold portions of their urban real estate to another Indian named Joseph Becerra.[22]

In 1702 Maria Fajardo, an Indian widow who ran a pulpería in Potosí, went to court to prevent a Spanish family from taking possession of the pulpería, which she said she had inherited from her deceased husband. Although it is not specified whether her husband had another occupation in addition to being a *pulpero*, the witnesses in her behalf were two yanaconas, a silversmith and a tile maker. The property next to the pulpería was reported to be owned by a yanacona chair maker.[23]

The three women just described represent a relatively privileged sector of the Indian population that participated in the market economy and used kinship and ties with other people of similar status and occupation to reinforce their position. Of perhaps approximately equivalent economic and social position were the women mentioned in nine other cases who were involved in litigation over property, usually houses in cities. Two of these nine cases show quite clearly the continued connections between women who owned private property and their ayllus. In a case from 1689, the *caciques principales* of the ayllu Chinchaisuyo in the parish of San Sebastian of La Paz claimed the land and houses of Doña Juana Sissa upon her death, saying they should belong to the ayllu as a whole because the ayllu's leaders had paid her funeral expenses. Once they had established their right to Doña Juana's property, the caciques intended to sell it to another member of the ayllu, Christobal Carita.[24] Interestingly, Indians of Chinchaisuyo had been sent to the area as mitimaes by the Incas, and although since then they had certainly been joined by more recent migrants, they still maintained a distinct identity as an ayllu.²⁵ Here we see how common it was for urban Andean people to own private property, but also that its possession and use was in some ways mediated by the kin group. The caciques claimed that the proceeds of the sale of the property should go to the community treasury not to themselves as individuals; furthermore, selling it to Christobal Carita seemed a means of guaranteeing that it stayed within the ayllu.

The second case concerned houses in Oruro owned by María Orcoma, a single woman from the town of Jesús de Machaca in the province of Pacajes. When Orcoma died without heirs, a number of people from her community, including the family of the town's kuraka, claimed her property in Oruro. In this instance, although all the various parties to the case were careful to identify their parcialidades and ayllus, their claims to the property are based on Spanish inheritance law. A striking feature of this case is that Orcoma didn't live in Oruro, which is about 100 miles away from Jesús de Machaca, but kept the houses for the rents they brought her. This then seems to be the reverse of the situation of the migrant in a city who still maintained ties with a rural community. Orcoma maintained her residence in the countryside and used her urban real estate as an investment.²⁶

In addition to the somewhat prosperous women just discussed, court proceedings also document a large number of extremely disadvantaged women who worked as servants and petty merchants, and a much smaller number of wealthy Indian women whose families held hereditary leadership positions. After the Spanish conquest, women of the native elite, like their male counterparts, took advantage of their position to acquire private property. Sometimes this meant that Andean leaders received personal titles to lands that had customarily been worked for them by peasant commoners. In other instances, noblewomen claimed as their own property that previously had been used by the entire community. Irene Silverblatt documents the legal efforts of *indios del comun* to hold on to ayllu or village lands that they claimed elite women had usurped.²⁷

Despite the restrictions placed on their rights to make contracts and engage in legally binding transactions, women of the indigenous elite appear to have had business dealings similar to those of the men in their families. For instance, Doña Lucrecia Fernández Guarache, daughter of Don Gabriel Fernández Guarache, an extremely wealthy kuraka from the province of Pacajes near La Paz, owned houses in Oruro that brought her some rental income and personally made loans totaling 3,200 pesos to the Spaniard Don Baltazar de Llano y Astorga.[28] Doña Lucrecia could sign her name and probably could read, a rare achievement for any woman in this period, but an important skill for a person with extensive business dealings.

Ana Pichu, the wife of Pedro Chipana, a somewhat less fortunate kuraka from Sicasica, was her husband's partner in two large loans he acquired in 1691 from a Spaniard in Potosí. As collateral for the total of 4,200 pesos, the couple used their various agricultural holdings, which included houses, fruit orchards, cattle ranches with 2,600 head of beef cattle, and coca fields. In the end, though, the couple was unable to repay the large debt, and Ana Pichu had to assume it alone when her husband died approximately two years later. Eventually, her creditor took legal action to embargo her property.[29]

The Guaraches, and even the less wealthy Chipana-Pichu family, were part of a tiny native elite, and unlike them the economic activity of most women was the result of dire economic necessity or even coercion. In spite of official prohibitions, women were illegally held in the homes of Spaniards and forced to weave or perform domestic work, often without pay.[30] Of the cases I reviewed, thirteen dealt with women not being paid for their services or being held against their will by their employers. Although there are some instances of both husband and wife serving in the same household, domestic service may have been, as Glave's article indicates, a major exception to the pattern of women working together with their families.

In some cases, a small debt was used as a pretext for keeping women in virtual perpetual servitude. This was the case of María Santos, who in 1706 said she had been serving Juan de Robles in order to repay seven pesos he had loaned her. Another man, Lázaro Gutiérrez, who apparently was looking for a servant, paid the debt for her and made Santos come to work for him. After she had served him for four years, Gutiérrez claimed that Santos still owed him the seven pesos plus the value of a used *ak'su* (Andean wrap skirt) which he had given her. According to Santos, when she asked to be paid for her work, Gutiérrez had her tied up, whipped, and burned with a heated metal coin. María Santos's husband, Andrés Gualpa, had also been working for Gutiérrez for ten months and in that time had received nothing for his efforts but a woolen shirt (*almilla*) and a pair of midcalf-length trousers (*calzón*). Recently, Gutiérrez had even taken back these clothes, but still refused to pay Gualpa a salary.[31]

A similar case was brought in 1689 by María Sisa, who said that she had been serving a Spanish woman named Doña Polonia Maldonado and her mother for two years. During the period of her service, she had never been paid for her labor but had been given about three meters of woolen cloth (*bayeta*) and a chicken, which together were worth approximately three pesos. When Sisa fell ill and wanted to leave, Doña Polonia claimed Sisa owed her for the goods she had given her and was holding her son prisoner to make sure Sisa didn't leave. Although in the disposition of the case a judge from the town council (*alcalde ordinario*) ruled that Sisa should be set free, he did not order Maldonado to pay her for her two years of service.[32]

Other court proceedings involved masters who claimed women as slaves, saying they were of African descent, and women who said they were Indians and therefore could not be legally enslaved.[33] Whoever was technically correct in these cases, there is ample evidence that people who had servants would go to great lengths to hold them against their will and to avoid paying them for their labor. Burkett found sixteenth-century contracts in notarial records in the city of Arequipa between employers and domestic servants that stipulated the wages to be paid. However, she estimates that probably no more than 5 to 10 percent of the Indian women working in personal service actually had contractual arrangements with their employers.[34] In seventeenth-century Cuzco, it was primarily specialized servants, wetnurses, who appeared in notarial contracts; ordinary maids and cooks probably simply had verbal agreements with the people for whom they worked.[35] Court cases show that employers often provided only room and board and an occasional small gift for their household workers and that no legal agreements whatsoever guaranteed the servants' rights.

Indeed, despite the occasional reference to a domestic servant who somehow managed to prosper,[36] it is hard to avoid the conclusion that not only were household workers among the poorest and most oppressed people in colonial cities, but also their condition resulted in a "feminization" of poverty. If the hypotheses of Glave and Silverblatt are correct, some Indian men themselves may have been complicit (willfully or through coercion) in the women's exploitation. Silverblatt quotes Guaman Poma de Ayala to prove that Indian men, desirous of the new local political and religious positions created by the colonial government, were willing to give their wives and other female relatives as servants to priests and colonial officials.[37] Glave argues less specifically that the domestic servants of La Paz who were listed in the 1684 census may have been taken from their communities by prospective employers who had "ties of dependency" with the women's ayllus.[38] This might mean that community leaders or other individuals hoped to gain personally by sending their women out to work, but it is also conceivable that tribute and labor burdens imposed by corregidores or other state officials gave them no recourse but to force their women to be servants just as they sent their men to Potosí.

Hardly any better off than household servants were the large number of Indian women who engaged in petty trading activities, some of whom may also have performed domestic work to supplement their meager earnings. In half of the cases studied (forty records), women were said to be retail merchants of one type or another. While a small group of these women had the resources to make their business activities fairly profitable, most seem to have been involved in pathetically small operations and often were in serious financial trouble. Examples are numerous: Ursula Guampa of La Paz sold other people's used articles of clothing and kept a small percentage of the sale price as a commission. Esperanza Choque was in debt for loans she had received to make the bread she sold in the plaza in La Paz. Josepha Arze was separated from her husband and said to be very poor: "maintaining herself through her intelligence in buying and selling produce." Antonia Sisa, a widow in La Plata, made *chicha* for a living and left two children and many debts when she died. Pascuala Carillo rented a pulpería in La Plata. In her husband's absence, her daughter became ill and Carillo couldn't pay the rent on the pulpería. The landlord evicted them, saying he "wasn't running a hospital." Her daughter subsequently died.[39] An interesting aspect of all of these situations is that, from what I can determine from the documents, these women

Gender and Social Differentiation 163

seem relatively isolated, lacking the family and community connections evident in the cases of women involved in litigation over houses or selling or bequeathing property.

If there was a hierarchy of occupations into which most Indian women's economic participation fell, some women were involved in activities that apparently didn't fit into the accepted structure. Two fascinating cases recount the difficulties of women working in fields that were generally reserved for men and show clearly that beyond the constraints of class and the racism of colonial society, Andean women were discriminated against just because they were women.

In 1644 an Indian woman named Bartola Sisa asked the Audiencia of Charcas to protect her rights to a silver mine in the hill of Espíritu Santo in the province of Carangas which she said a Spaniard named Cristóbal de Cotes was trying to claim as his own. Sisa said she was born in the city of Oruro but for the last three years had been in Carangas exploring for mines. She eventually discovered a vein of silver with the help of an Indian named Juan Choque, who worked for her and to whom she owed 300 pesos for his efforts. Sisa then hired an Indian named Pedro Achatta from the province of Carangas as a barretero and two other Indians to begin mining silver. According to Achatta, "Bartola Sisa, *india*, hired this witness and paid him and the others as their boss [*patrona*] who had discovered and prospected for the mine."[40]

Sisa claimed that when their first load of ore looked promising, Cristóbal de Cotes, a Spaniard, presented himself and, "seeing her alone and poor," told Sisa that she could not legally register the mine herself since she was a woman, nor could she register it in the name of her underage son. Determined to legally claim the mine somehow, Sisa went to the corregidor of the mining site and made a verbal declaration of her discovery and received a document specifying that no one should disturb her activities in the vein. Nonetheless, Cotes registered the mine in his own name and returned to the site to take over its operation. In the end, the audiencia ordered the corregidor to return the mine to Sisa and to remove Cristóbal de Cotes or anyone else who wasn't supposed to be there. The issue of whether she could actually formally register the mine as a woman was not addressed. Indians' rights (without gender specification) to register mines for themselves were protected by a special sixteenth-century royal decree, and there are indications that some fairly prosperous native miners existed in the early days at Potosí.[41] However, by the seventeenth century they were increasingly rare, so Bartola Sisa was actually quite unusual in two respects.[42]

Another case brought before the audiencia tells the story of a woman who was involved in long-distance trade, work generally considered to be for men only. (Although census and court records frequently described men as *viajeros* who brought supplies to urban areas, this is the only reference I found to a woman doing this kind of work.) María Esperanza, of the pueblo of Hayu-Hayu, set out in 1705 with her brother for Moquegua, in the south of present-day Peru, to sell her mules. In the course of the trip, her brother was struck by lightning and killed. He was buried in Pomata, in the province of Chucuito, where the village priest charged Esperanza 100 pesos for the funeral. This was all the money she had, so she changed her plans and returned as far as the pueblo of Hachacache in Omasuyo with a man named Pablo Gutiérrez. When Esperanza reached Hachacache, the town's kuraka, Don Bartolomé de Ramos (apparently trying to take advantage of a woman alone) attempted to force her into an "illicit friendship" (*ilicita amistad*), but she refused, retiring to the nearby town of Guarina. There she was taken prisoner and had her goods embargoed because of a complaint registered by the spurned Bartolomé de Ramos with the provincial corregidor. After six months she was finally released, but her property was not returned. Esperanza now appealed to the audiencia to get it back, saying, "I am single and have never been married and the goods referred to are my own acquired through my personal work."[43]

The examples of Bartola Sisa and María Esperanza suggest considerable diversity in occupations of Indian women even in the face of harassment. They also raise a number of intriguing questions for future research. First of all, with only two cases we don't know whether Sisa and Esperanza were quite unique or whether there were considerable numbers of women like them. These two accounts are also separated by more than sixty years; did native women's involvement in such activities increase or diminish over time? Were they more likely to be miners or long-distance traders in the early years of colonial rule, when social mores were in a state of flux and the Spaniards were first imposing their gender and class hierarchies? Were these activities examples of women using a market economy and cracks in the colonial system to expand their personal possibilities in ways that were not possible under the Inca state, as suggested by Burkett? Or were women like Sisa and Esperanza forced to do such work because of the decline of the Indian population and the deterioration of community life after years of colonialism? Were the limitations placed on them strictly Hispanic in origin or were their actions outside of what was considered appropriate for women in Andean society as well? For instance, it appears that both Sisa and Esperanza suffered discrimination because they were acting alone; was being economicially active as a member of a family or with the support of ayllu leaders more acceptable in both cultures?

Conclusion

At this point, perhaps the study of Andean women raises more questions than it answers. Nonetheless, I think some conclusions can be drawn about Andean women's economic situation in Upper Peru in the seventeenth and eighteenth centuries. First of all, in my research I found no evidence that Indian women were more active in the economies of colonial cities than Indian men. While it was men who were generally conscripted for gang labor, it is clear that by the mid-seventeenth century their activities—especially in cities—were by no means confined to this type of work. In contrast to the situation Burkett describes in sixteenth-century Arequipa, considerable numbers of Indian men in urban areas were now employed as artisans, miners, and traveling merchants, and these same men often owned houses or other property. They frequently spoke Spanish, wore European clothes, and may have been as adept at handling the colonial bureaucracy as Indian women.

Furthermore, even if compared to mitayos or other manual laborers, Indian women more often had occupations that permitted them some autonomy and the opportunity to familiarize themselves with the economic and legal system, this was certainly not always the case. The domestic servants studied by Luis Glave and the women who brought cases to court because they weren't being paid might have questioned just how fortunate they were. It is also questionable how often these employees had the opportunity to make contacts with other Indian women, if domestic service in the colonial period bore any resemblance to the present-day situation in which native women are given little time off and are often on call day and night.[44] Glave found that almost a quarter of the households he studied had only one domestic worker, so in many cases there might not even have been the possibility of personal contact with another servant.[45]

If a discussion of the relative advantages of Indian women compared to Indian men does not shed much light on the situation, it is because Andean women's social and economic positions and possibilities for employment were not determined merely by gender and ethnicity. The introduction of a market economy affected different groups in Andean society differently, but by the late seventeenth century large sectors of the Indian population participated in it, and with mercantilization came increased class differentiation. Although native people were generally simply relegated to the undercaste of "Indians" by Spaniards, in fact class definition now overlay and was combined with native social structure.

However, in the new colonial system, one could use both traditional relationships and the institutions of Hispanic society for survival. By the seventeenth century not only the native elite, but less privileged people as well, were accustomed to thinking of, and using, land and labor as commodities. Both men and women also sometimes found the Spanish legal system, which in so many ways disenfranchised and expropriated them, useful in achieving their goals. At the same time, though, many urban residents still relied on members of their ayllus for spiritual and material support and maintained relations of reciprocity with their kin even when their home communities were quite distant.

Andean and Hispanic conceptions of gender roles also coexisted in Upper Peru, conflicting in some instances and meshing in others, although the Catholic church and the colonial legal system guaranteed that certain precepts of Hispanic ideology became accepted practice. Here again, men and women used parts of each culture to shape their relationships. On the one hand, we know that native men some-

Gender and Social Differentiation 167

times sought to improve their position by invoking Spanish laws that gave them political authority or rights to property that according to Andean tradition were vested in women, particularly their wives.[46] We also know that women used the means at their disposal to resist this expropriation. Especially in their wills, they often found ways to circumvent Spanish inheritance laws and to adhere somewhat more closely to Andean patterns of bequeathing property along male and female lines. For instance, it may have been fear that her husband would control her property or usurp her political power that caused María Sacomecassi, in the 1590s, to refuse to marry Fernando Callacopa, kuraka of Poopo, in Paria. According to a witness, she chose not to marry Callacopa, even though she had borne him a child, because "in that time they said that when a Indian woman married she became a slave." After a brief separation, they reunited and lived together, unmarried, for the rest of their lives.[47]

So, despite Spanish legal discrimination against women, Andean conceptions of gender survived as women found mechanisms to preserve some of their political and economic prerogatives. They also survived in the belief that the universe was made up of complementary halves, male and female. The household complementarity that was the human reflection of this cosmic duality took on new meaning as families and kin groups adjusted to colonial domination and the market economy. Whether struggling through a year of forced labor in Potosí or running a pulpería in La Paz, families working together had the best chance of survival. Even though there is significant evidence of women's subjugation under colonial rule, the strong Andean women that Burkett and Salomon were struck by also continued to exist. Women's importance in the effort to adapt to the new conditions and to preserve Andean culture may have to some extent mitigated their oppression.

· 7 ·

Labor in an Agrarian Frontier Zone
Pilaya y Paspaya, 1646–1725

I N 1689 Don Bartolomé de Barrios reported in an official inquiry that he had two Indians working for him temporarily on his hacienda "La Dorada" in the province of Pilaya y Paspaya. He said they both came from Caiza in the province of Porco and that in return for their labor he paid their tribute to their kuraka because they were Indians of the *corona real*.[1]

Three years later, José Cipriano de la Cruz went before the audiencia in La Plata saying that he had unjustly been retained as a yanacona on a ranch in Pilaya y Paspaya, the *estancia* "Ingahuasi," owned by one of Potosí's wealthiest entrepreneurs, Antonio López de Quiroga. He claimed that he actually was a horse breeder on one of López de Quiroga's other properties, the estancia "Culpina," and could not legally be a yanacona because he was the legitimate son of a mestizo tailor.[2]

These accounts tell us something about two types of labor common in the agricultural province of Pilaya y Paspaya: short-term contracts arranged between kurakas and hacendados, and the hereditary servitude of yanaconaje. Both are in sharp contrast with the situation in Oruro, where individual native people themselves, not their leaders, generally arranged for their own employment, and where being a yanacona was associated with freedom through acculturation rather than perpetual service.

This chapter examines the history of labor and migration in Pilaya y Paspaya during the seventeenth and early eighteenth centuries and how Andean cultural patterns were being reworked, or even abandoned, in the commercial agricultural province. The processes of change were not consistent or unilinear, however; different groups of migrants to the province were affected by the cultural composition of the region, and influenced it themselves, in different ways. These variations were in part regional: the north of the province was more "indigenous"; it was closer to highland centers of Andean culture and had been farmed since before the Inca period by mitimaes from highland areas. The southeast, on the other hand, since pre-Columbian times had been a sparsely populated frontier zone dividing agricultural people from less sedentary populations. Alistair Hennessy mentions as one characteristic of such Latin American border regions that they were "frontiers of inclusion," meaning that in these areas cultural interchange and miscegenation were common.[3] This was certainly the case in Pilaya y Paspaya; even as early as 1646 indications of social change were already especially pronounced among migrants living in the southeastern section of the province. Chiriguanos settled down and married people from Andean ayllus, immigrants were ignorant of their provinces of origin, men adopted Spanish surnames, and many people lived permanently as renters on haciendas.

But the amount of cultural change in Pilaya y Paspaya was not only related to distance and the frontier; in addition, as in Oruro, it was also much more pronounced among yanaconas than among forasteros. However, in the agricultural province, this change took a different form: rather than emerging as a relatively prosperous group of skilled workers and artisans, the yanaconas of Pilaya y Paspaya by the early eighteenth century were an unstable group that was rapidly blending into a population of mestizo and mulatto peons. While entrepreneurs in Oruro had been unable to acquire a state-regulated system of forced labor, in Pilaya y Paspaya landowners had taken advantage of the special restrictions the colonial government had placed on rural yanaconas to reduce them to virtual serfdom.

Finally, in Pilaya y Paspaya we can look at the relationship between cultural change and a shift from ethnic to class identity from a different perspective. In Oruro, despite the mercantilization of the economy, the work force had not been proletarianized, and, at least among forasteros, ethnic ties often remained strong and helped people to negotiate the new economic system. In Pilaya y Paspaya, as we shall see, by 1725 there was significant social change among both forasteros and yanaconas, but not because they had become wage laborers or skilled artisans. More cut off from Andean culture than the immigrants in Oruro, they didn't have the advantages of workers in that city nor had they replaced their ethnic ties with class solidarity.

The Indigenous North

Pilaya y Paspaya took its unusual name from the rivers that marked its eastern boundary, the Paspaya (or Pilcomayo), and its southern border, the Pilaya. (See map 5.) The province was bounded on the northeast by Porco, in which the city of Potosí was located, and on the northwest by Tomina. On the west was the province of Chichas and to the south of the River Pilaya was the province of Tarija. Beginning in the northwest of the province, the first agricultural zone of importance in the seventeenth century was that surrounding the town of San Lucas. Although most of the territory in this corner of Pilaya y Paspaya was mountainous or high-altitude flatland primarily used for grazing, near the town of San Lucas the river of the same name flowed into a temperate valley that was good for growing grapes as well as wheat and maize. Here the College of the Company of Jesus of Potosí owned lands on which they grew grapes and grains, and nearby, at a higher altitude, grazing lands on their estancia "Cocha."

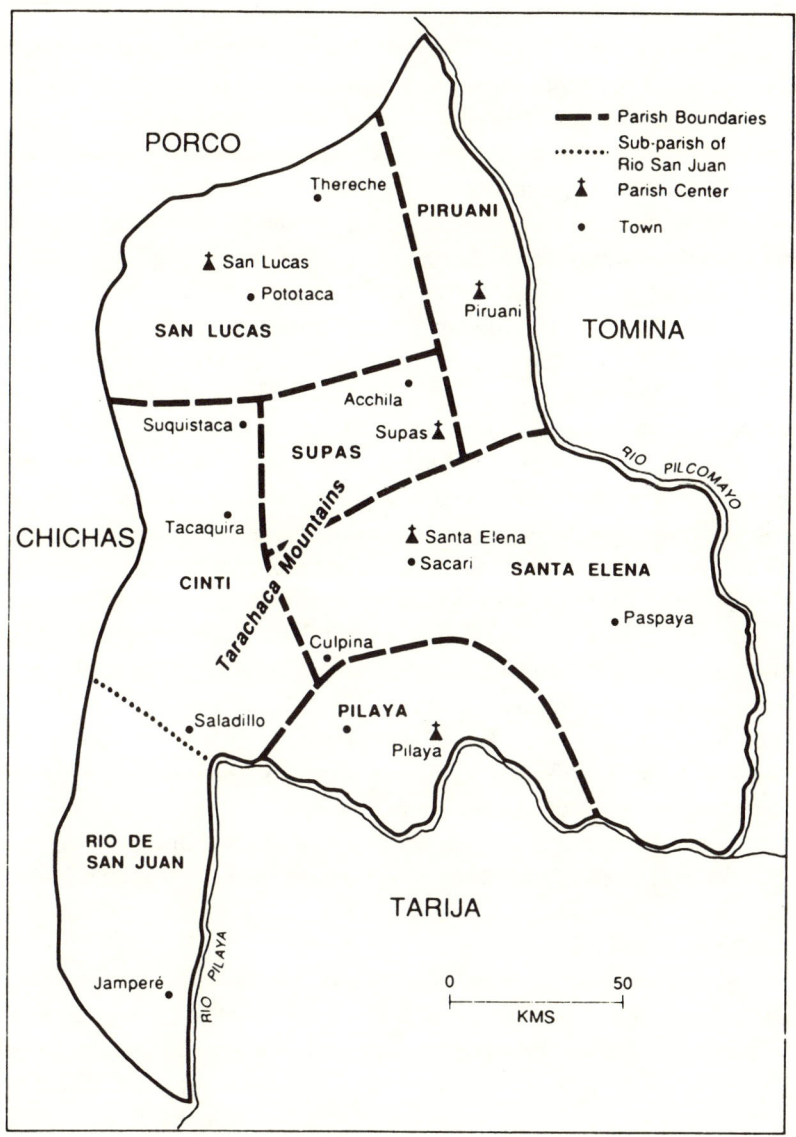

MAP 5. The Province of Pilaya y Paspaya

Source: Ann Zulawski, "Frontier Workers and Social Change: Pilaya y Paspaya (Bolivia) in the Early Eighteenth Century," in David Robinson, ed., *Migration in Colonial Spanish America* (Cambridge: Cambridge University Press, 1990), p. 113.

Father Antonio Vázquez de Espinosa, who visited the Indies between 1608 and 1620, reported that the Jesuit vineyards near San Lucas produced more than 8,000 botijas of wine a year.[4]

Other farms and ranches near San Lucas were owned by Spaniards, but in general much of the territory within the triangle formed by the towns of San Lucas, Supas, and Piruani was occupied by Indian communities, although their lands were being encroached upon by colonial settlers.[5] Most of the Indians in this area of Pilaya y Paspaya belonged to ethnic groups from the area surrounding Lake Poopo in Paria, but some were mitimaes of ayllus from the province of Porco. This was in keeping with the Andean practice whereby colonies of agricultural settlers from different highland groups shared the limited farmland in valley areas. Piecing together just when and under exactly what circumstances these people came to hold land in Pilaya y Paspaya will require considerably more detective work. What we know at this point is that since before the Spanish conquest the Quillaca-Asanaques, an Aymara kingdom that occupied the area south of Oruro, had land in the area of San Lucas. It is not clear, though, whether these mitimaes predated the Inca Empire or they were sent there by the state.[6] The Quillaca-Asanaques and a group of Yucayguaris (also from Paria) were counted as originarios of the town of San Lucas de Payacollo in the census ordered by la Palata.[7] They had been excused from serving in the mita by Viceroy Toledo because their presence was a defense against the Chiriguanos who threatened the province from the other side of the Pilcomayo River, and the government believed that if they were forced to work in Potosí they would abandon the area.[8]

In the sixteenth century, the Wisijsa people (today called Yura) of Caiza in Porco also had lands in Pototaca near San Lucas, but how long they had been there is not clear. According to Roger Rasnake, they sold these lands in the early seventeenth century to pay their tribute.[9] However, the 1725 tributary census for Pilaya y Paspaya still listed chacras near the town of San Miguel de Acchila that belonged to "the Indians of Caiza" and "the Indians of Chaqui," another group in Porco.[10]

All of the above groups were considered originarios of Pilaya y Paspaya; yet they were acknowledged by the colonial government to have been mitimaes, and we can only guess at the extent to which different groups or individuals continued to fulfill that function. Besides the so-called originarios, there were other Indians in the area who were considered forasteros. Among these was yet another group of Asanaques in the area of Supas who had been settled there some time after 1573. In addition, all ayllus of originarios contained immigrants from other areas of Upper Peru (that is, they were settled *after* Toledo's demographic policy established that those reduced to *congregaciones* were considered to be originarios of those communities).[11] These Indians were referred to as *forasteros agregados*, or forasteros incorporated into the ayllus. According to the parish priest of San Lucas, by 1689 the Indians had been joined by converted Chiriguanos. He stressed that these Chiriguanos had been persuaded to come to the communities with the promise that they would not be subject to the Potosí mita.[12] However, despite the fact that these reducciones were designed to protect the area from the depredations of the unreconstructed Chiriguanos, "uncivilized" Indians apparently still made incursions into the zone and in 1689 killed two Jesuits in the nearby town of Pototaca.[13]

In Pilaya y Paspaya, as in Oruro, by the seventeenth century there was evidence of private ownership of land by native people. In the late 1600s Don Fernando Renxifo and his wife, Doña María Fernández, *indios principales* in San Miguel de Acchila, owned five chacras near the town. Although some properties seem to have been fraudulently taken over by Spaniards, as late as the 1740s their heirs still held some of these lands.[14]

Don Fernando and Doña María, as part of the native elite, were probably more likely than ordinary people to own considerable amounts of property, some of which may have been used to help defray community expenses. Another document in fact describes how an Indian judge, the *alcalde mayor* of Pototaca, had to use his large herds of sheep and cattle to pay for the cloth and mules that the assistant corregidor had forced on the community.[15] But owning property or engaging in business transactions were not necessarily the exclusive domain of the indigenous elite. The *"indios comunes"* (common Indians) of Pototaca sold wheat and maize to Indians from Chichas and Porco who came to the province specifically to buy them.[16] And, in the records of yet another legal proceeding, we find Don Jacinto Moreno, a yanacona, bidding on a hacienda that was being auctioned, while Don Pedro Catari, an Indian, presented a notary's document establishing that he had loaned a neighboring Spanish hacendado 200 pesos.[17]

The Hispanic South

If by the seventeenth century indigenous people in the north of the province, either as communities or individuals, controlled land and were active in the regional economy, south of the parish of Supas virtually all the land in Pilaya y Paspaya was owned by individual Spanish or creole landowners. In the province, as in other parts of Upper Peru, hacendados adopted Andean vertical patterns and used lands in different altitudes to cultivate different crops. The richest, best-watered soil was found in the lower valleys, between 2,000 and 2,600 meters above sea level, and was generally used to cultivate grapes. Rising from these valleys were arid, rugged brushlands between 2,600 and 4,000 meters above sea level known as *liquinas*. Despite the limited natural vegetation, the broader liquinas that were watered by streams or lakes were suitable for growing maize, barley, and wheat. Others with less flatland were used for raising livestock.[18]

The area around Santa Elena, a town about thirty kilometers almost due south of Acchila, was an important agricultural and grazing zone. Landowners in the Santa Elena region sometimes also had vineyards in the adjacent Cinti Valley, which began just south of Tacaquira and followed the course of the Cinti River to the province's southernmost zone. The other important commercial agricultural regions of Pilaya y Paspaya lay along the River Pilaya, the province's southeastern boundary; in the east around the settlement of Paspaya; and in the San Juan River region, which protruded like a thumb to the south of the Cinti Valley. The town of Paspaya was effectively abandoned due to malaria after about 1650,[19] and the area along the Pilaya River was also malarial and therefore had a relatively sparse population. The town of Pilaya itself was the center of a church parish in 1690, but by the 1780s was said to have been abandoned due to attacks by Chiriguanos.[20]

The most important landowner in the province in the seventeenth century was Antonio López de Quiroga, who, far from fitting the

TABLE 7.1 Ownership of Estates in Pilaya y Paspaya, 1725

	No. of Landowners	No. of Properties	No. of Male Indians	Average No. of Male Indians Per Property
Owns in partnership	18	9	181	20
Owns one estate	34	34	328	10
Owns two estates	8	16	405	25
Owns three estates	2	6	170	28
TOTAL	62	65	1,084	17

Source: AGN, XIII-18-5-1.

stereotype of the colonial mining entrepreneur investing in agriculture purely for the prestige of having country estates,[21] seems to have made his holdings in Pilaya y Paspaya very profitable indeed. Although he certainly was not typical, López de Quiroga's use of his lands gives a good indication of the range of economic activities in which hacendados engaged. In the second half of the century, López de Quiroga owned the hacienda "San Pedro Mártir," the estancia "Ingahuasi," the chacra "Los Duraznos,"[22] a vineyand and hacienda called "Caraparí," and several other not insignificant properties. These were organized so that the agricultural lands produced food not only for the market but also for the residents of the vineyards, where prime land was reserved for grapes. In addition to the huge amounts of wine he sold in Potosí (see chapter 2), López de Quiroga also did a profitable business in cattle by-products and sometimes sold maize and chuño as well. Sale of these items together brought him 34,309 pesos a year between 1672 and 1689.[23]

Although no other landowner had properties as extensive as those of López de Quiroga, documents suggest that in the seventeenth century there may have been a pattern of individuals owning several different pieces of land.[24] However, only considerably later, in 1725, is documentation available that permits us to make some generalizations about property ownership in the province, and even then the size of properties is never mentioned. By that date, more than half (thirty-four) of the landowners in the province held only one property and another eighteen were joint owners of an estate (table 7.1).

Labor

The province's premier economic activity, growing grapes and making wine, required large numbers of workers to prune and fertilize the vines, maintain irrigation ditches, and harvest the grapes, and vineyard owners often bought slaves to do some of this work.[25] In fact, slaves were brought to Pilaya y Paspaya quite early in the province's development as an important producer for Potosí. We know that there were slaves on the chacras near San Lucas in the first years of the seventeenth century. Alonso Osorio Mendoza had fifty slaves on his hacienda "El Molino" in the Paspaya Valley in 1650.[26] In 1658, when Antonio López de Quiroga bought "San Pedro Mártir," twenty-six slaves were sold with the hacienda. By 1696 he had increased their number to eighty-four, giving "San Pedro Mártir" one of the biggest slave work forces in the province.[27] In 1714 the haciendas of "Rio Pilaya" and "Culpina" had forty slaves between them, thirty-four of them valued at 350 pesos each.[28] Although information on slavery in the province is fragmentary, there were enough slaves brought to Pilaya y Paspaya during the seventeenth century to account for considerable miscegenation by the early eighteenth. (This will be discussed later.)

However, slavery never became as important in Pilaya y Paspaya as it was in Peru's coastal areas of Ica and Pisco where, due to the very rapid decline of the native population during the seventeenth century, as many as 20,000 black slaves worked in vineyards.[29] From the mid-1600s to 1725, most workers in Pilaya y Paspaya were forasteros with origins in the highland areas of Upper Peru, although there were contingents of yanaconas as well.

The forasteros in the province fell into two broad categories. One group were more or less permanent residents, often referred to as *forasteros arrenderos*. These workers generally paid a labor rent for the right to use a piece of land on an estate from which they provided their subsistence. However, in some cases Indians may have paid in cash as well as in labor.[30] In his 1687 *Aranzel* regulating wages to be paid to various types of Indian workers, Viceroy de la Palata specified that Indian *arrenderos* were to be paid, like other workers who did not have land in usufruct, four reales a day.[31] However, although

I have documented that this was the going rate for one estate in Pilaya y Paspaya, there is no way of knowing if the rule applied to all resident workers or how often it was paid even to nonresident ones.[32]

In general, resident laborers were established only on properties that had liquina areas that could be parceled out for subsistence farming, since hacendados were not inclined to give renters or other permanent laborers good grape-growing land to farm. Furthermore, even owners of haciendas and chacras with renters living on them needed additional workers at certain times for tasks such as clearing irrigation ditches and picking grapes. The second group of forasteros in the province met this need for temporary labor. They were usually men, but sometimes women, who came from relatively nearby provinces, particularly Chichas and Porco, to work for short periods to raise cash to pay their villages' tribute assessments. Hacendados usually obtained these workers by making agreements with ayllu leaders rather than with the workers themselves. The workers on the estate of Bartolomé de Barrios mentioned at the beginning of this chapter were hired through such an arrangement. Another description of how these short-term contracts worked is provided by Don Pablo de Miranda, owner of the hacienda "San Francisco de la Palca." De Miranda testified that as of October 1, 1690, he employed six Indians from the town of Calcha in the province of Chichas. He said that they had been on the hacienda for two months and would be leaving within eight days because they had completed the period of the contract. Their kuraka, Don Ignacio Nuñez, had come to the hacienda a week before to collect the tribute.[33]

An interesting feature of the accounts given by Cinti Valley hacendados about their short-term workers is that in several instances workers came from the towns of Caiza and Yura in Porco and could therefore be Wisijsa, or Yura, people who originally held lands in the province. Perhaps this merely reflects a tendency for highland peoples to work in areas where they had previously had mitimaes, or it could be that when the Wisijsa kurakas gave up lands in Pilaya y Paspaya to Spaniards, they made arrangements for the employment of regular contingents of workers. Some of the estate owners interviewed specifically stated that their workers came from the same community every year.[34]

Most forasteros in Pilaya y Paspaya probably labored in vineyards, but a small number also were employed as cowboys on the province's cattle ranches. Cowboys who lived on the ranches where they worked were supposed to be paid four reales a year per head of cattle tended and be provided with food.[35] José de Cipriano, the horse breeder who claimed not to be a yanacona, said he had always been a "salaried worker" on the ranch "Culpina." However, his salary was entirely in kind, not in cash. It included the right to graze his own cattle on the ranch's lands, the use of a piece of crop land, some clothing, and food.[36]

So forasteros' arrangements with landowners seem to have been even less capitalist than those between mine workers and owners in Oruro. They paid labor rent, probably seldom received payment in cash, and community leaders often arranged and received the money for short-term work contracts. How then did forasteros' situations differ from those of yanaconas? Yanaconas also often received land in usufruct for their labor on the demesne. However, none of the government provisions dealing with yanaconas specified that they were to be paid on a regular basis, as other workers were—at least theoretically. Toledo had directed that they be allowed to work ten days a year to earn their tribute (see chapter 3). Viceroy de la Palata, in the section of his *Aranzel* dealing with the Audiencia of Charcas, simply said that the landowner should pay the tribute himself; the code did not treat yanaconas as freely contracting parties who were legally bound to be paid. Furthermore, all of Toledo's successors, including la Palata, accepted the "unfreedom" of any person who could be proven to be a descendant of a worker designated a *yanacona de chacra* at the time of Toledo.[37]

Caught between a growing philosophical commitment to free labor and the demands of entrepreneurs for forced workers in Upper Peru's most lucrative productive sector, mining, the colonial government acquiesced and organized the mita for the Potosí mines. When Indians fled this forced labor, they ran into the arms of landowners who also demanded special incentives and subsidies from the authorities. In this case, employers asked that workers be legally enserfed in return for payment of their tribute. In the end, it is difficult to say that the sanctuary of the hacienda was preferable to the mita of Potosí.

TABLE 7.2 Adult Male Indian Population of Pilaya y Paspaya, 1646, 1684, and 1725

Originarios		% Change	Forasteros	% Change	Yanaconas	% Change
1646	280	−6	667	+50	212	+18
1684	263	+16	1,001	+8	251	+39
1725	306		1,082		350	

Sources: For 1646: totals of Phelipe de Bolívar, in Zabala, *El servicio personal de los indios en el Perú* 2:109; for 1684: AGI, Charcas, leg. 270; for 1725, AGN, XIII, 18-5-1.

Patterns of Migration, 1646–1725

And yet immigrants continued to come. They arrived in large numbers from the 1640s to the 1680s, and although the migratory stream diminished somewhat after that, Pilaya y Paspaya still remained a magnet for people from the highlands well into the eighteenth century. A comparison of three tributary censuses conducted in the province in 1646, 1684, and 1725 illustrates the magnitude of immigration over a seventy-nine-year period. Closer analysis of the returns for two of these enumerations, those of 1646 and 1725, shows in what ways the immigrant population had changed during the period and how by 1725 the situation of yanaconas was strikingly different from that of other indigenous people in the province.

It is not clear whether the 1646 enumeration conducted in Pilaya y Paspaya at the request of Viceroy de Mancera was complete. A summary of the census drawn up by a deputy of the refiners' guild of Potosí, Felipe de Bolívar, and presented to the viceroy in 1646, lists 1,159 adult Indian men in the province.[38] Since the numbers are not broken down by location, there is no way of knowing if the entire province was counted; however, I assume that these figures are relatively complete and compare them in table 7.2 with the parish totals of the duque de la Palata's census of Pilaya y Paspaya[39] and the totals from the 1725 census.[40]

The comparison shows that Pilaya y Paspaya saw an overall increase (31 percent) in the number of adult male Indians between 1646 and 1684. As we saw in table 3.2 (see chapter 3), there was a large increase in Tarija between 1573 and 1683 (59 percent), and since Tarija was Pilaya y Paspaya's southern neighbor with similar economic and ecological conditions, it is possible that the amount of growth shown here is roughly accurate. Changes over the 1646–1684 period break down to a 6 percent decline in the number of originarios, a 50 percent increase in the number of forasteros, and a more modest 18 percent growth among yanaconas. There is reason to believe, however, that the number of yanaconas in the 1683 enumeration is low because the San Juan Valley section of Cinti was excluded from the count.[41]

In the forty-one years between 1684 and 1725, the male indigenous population of the province grew by 15 percent, less than half of the increase of the previous thirty-eight years between 1646 and 1684. The small increase in the number of forasteros (8 percent, compared to 50 percent between 1646 and 1683) probably indicates that migration to the area had slowed considerably, although the lesser increase may also have been the result of a fatal epidemic that struck Upper Peru about 1720. Similarly, in contrast to the 1646–1684 period, in 1725 there was a 16 percent increase in the originario population, which could mean that fewer men left the province's northern communities in a period when haciendas and other enterprises needed less labor. The apparent 39 percent growth in the yanacona population, as mentioned, may be misleading because this group seems to have been undercounted in 1684.

The Forastero Population in 1646

Returns from the 1646 census that list men individually have been located for several sections of Pilaya y Paspaya: part of the Cinti Valley, the area around Paspaya, and the agricultural zone under the jurisdiction of San Pedro Baldeolma (currently in Tarija), representing a total of 662 men.[42] I was not able to find reports for the northern area of the province, where there were ayllus of originarios, nor could I find separate returns for yanaconas, but the available data from the southern chacras and haciendas provide a fairly comprehensive sampling of forasteros, allow us to draw some conclusions about their origins, and serve as a basis for comparison with later census material.

In general, the 1646 returns, summarized in table 7.3, show that the majority of men listed came from highland provinces subject to the Potosí mita, with the largest number coming from the area that I call "Oruro-Potosí," the provinces of Porco, Paria, Carangas, and Chayanta, located between the two cities. The second greatest number of immigrants came from the La Plata area, particularly from Chichas and from Pilaya y Paspaya itself. This means that 61 percent of forasteros were from areas relatively near to the zone in which they worked. This was essentially the same pattern as among forasteros in Oruro in 1683: most people came from areas that were somewhat accessible and may even have been duplicating pre-Hispanic migration networks.

However, by disaggregating the data in table 7.3 a little, we can see that already in 1646 some sectors of the Indian population of the province were probably more cut off from their origins and more dependent on permanent or long-term work than others. Generally, three rough groups can be identified: (1) renters, among whom a considerable percentage gave no place of origin, but who also included a large number from the core Oruro-Potosí region, (2) those who were in the province for short periods and could have been functioning as mitimaes, and (3) those in the southernmost section, many of them born there, who in some cases were Chiriguanos or their descendants.

Of all the forasteros in Pilaya y Paspaya in 1646, the largest number of men who did *not* give their origins were renters in the area of Paspaya. There is a logic in this, since renters were permanent residents (compared with workers who came to the province for a few months), and perhaps some of these families had lived in Pilaya y Paspaya for a few generations. Among renters who did give their origins, there was a relatively large contingent in the Paspaya area from Aymara-speaking areas near Cuzco on the other side of Lake Titicaca. Exactly what brought these families the long distance to Pilaya y Paspaya is not clear, but it makes sense that immigrants from so far away would establish relatively permanent residence in the province. On the other hand, a considerable proportion of other renters who stated their origins came from provinces that were not so far away as to preclude returning to them.

TABLE 7.3 Origins of Male Forasteros in Pilaya y Paspaya, 1646

	No. of Renters in Paspaya	(%)	No. from Mita, Paspaya	(%)	No. in Cinti	(%)	No. in San Pedro de Baldeolma	(%)	Total	
Oruro-Potosí										
Porco	32		122		9		8		171	
Pria	6		31		1		0		38	
Carangas	15		0		3		0		18	
Chayanta	3		0		0		0		3	
SUBTOTAL	56	(34)	153	(53)	13	(19)	8	(11)	230	(39)
La Plata										
Pilaya y Paspaya	5		57		0		0		62	
Yamparez	1		0		3		0		4	
Chichas	9		16		33		8		66	
SUBTOTAL	15	(9)	73	(25)	36	(54)	8	(11)	132	(22)
La Paz										
Pacajes	22		11		0		2		35	
Sicasica	0		6		0		1		7	
Omasuyos	1		0		0		0		1	
SUBTOTAL	23	(14)	17	(6)	0	(0)	3	(4)	43	(7)

Cuzco							
Canas y Canches	14		33		1		3	51
Chucuito	6		13		0		0	19
Quispicanches	5		0		8		2	15
Azangaro	4		0		0		0	4
Chumbivilcas	0		0		1		0	1
Lampa	1		0		0		0	1
SUBTOTAL	30	(18)	46	(16)	10	(15)	5	91 (15)
La Cordillera	0		0		0		10	10
Tucumán	0		0		2		3	5
Not given	40		0		6		38	84
TOTAL	164		289		67		75	595

Source: AGN, IX, 17-1-4.

In addition to the fact that almost 25 percent of the renters in Paspaya did not know their origins, there are other indications of cultural change among these migrants. One is the presence of two men who said they were from the ayllu "Mendoza." This has a distinctly inauthentic ring. Perhaps they were actually from Mendoza in Argentina, or they may have simply adopted the surname of one of the biggest landowners in the Paspaya region in 1646, Alonso Osorio de Mendoza. One of these men from the ayllu called "Mendoza" was named Pablo Criollo, suggesting that, whatever his origin, he was probably born in Pilaya y Paspaya. The surnames of some of the other renters give further indications of change in Andean customs. The surnames of most of the men renting in Paspaya were Spanish renderings of Andean surnames: Quispe, Condori, Mamani, Cari, Ticona, etcetera. But twenty-three men (14 percent) gave distinctly Spanish last names: Ruiz, Rodríguez, Rojas, Aquilar, Ramos. Two of these have names that might identify them as artisans: Miguel Zapatero and Juan Ropa. All in all, the renters seem to have been a mixed lot—some apparently quite acculturated, but the majority still identifying their provinces and ayllus of origin.

The group of migrants who seem most likely to have acted as mitimaes in Pilaya y Paspaya, or to maintain long established vertical connections there, were in the group that Paspaya's parish priest called "Indians subject to the mita of the Cerro of Potosí."[43] The padrón does not indicate what distinguished these Indians from the *forasteros arrenderos* in Paspaya, but presumably they were not renters, and many of them may have been in the area only a short time. Andrés de Quiroga, the priest who conducted the enumeration, indicated this when he said, "[The Indians] are mobile and without stability here because most of the year they are in their villages."[44] Of the 289 men "from the mita," 88 were from Caiza, Chaqui and Tacobamba in Porco. In all three of these towns in 1592, there were settlements of the Wisijsa, or Yura, people.[45] We know the Yura also had mitimae settlements in the San Lucas area. In 1646 we find them migrating to Paspaya, another lowland zone near those they had traditionally used further north. However, now they came as hacienda laborers. Roger Rasnake speculates about the means by which the Yura paid their tribute in the late sixteenth and early seventeenth centuries. He mentions selling produce and charcoal and using the proceeds from sales of land.[46] A few decades later, they seem to have found another solution to this problem: migratory agricultural labor, which may have been as common for the Yura in the seventeenth century as it has become in the twentieth, when workers go to the Bolivian lowlands and Argentina to work.

Also among the men from the mita in Paspaya were fifty-seven from the "pueblos of Quillacas and San Lucas" in northern Pilaya y Paspaya. In this instance, we see a direct connection between the northern area of the province, which was originally settled by mitimaes, and the southern commercial area. The census does not state why these people went to Paspaya. We can assume, however, that the resources available to them in San Lucas were insufficient to pay their tribute or to meet some other needs and they had no choice but to sell their labor, like other groups from Upper Peru.

The last group of returns for Pilaya y Paspaya, those listed for San Pedro de Baldeolma, include part of the adjacent province of Tarija, apparently because the parish of San Pedro in Tarija included the southernmost section of Pilaya y Paspaya. In addition, some of the land that was within its borders in the 1640s belonged to people who lived in the city of Tarija, which was closer than the nearest settlement in Pilaya y Paspaya itself. In the enumeration of tributaries in the parish of San Pedro, about 40 percent of the men lived in Tarija (thirty-three individuals), while the remaining 60 percent were on the Pilaya side of the river.

The origins of the men in San Pedro were remarkably different from those of the mita workers in Paspaya. Only sixteen men were from Porco and Chichas (the most common provinces overall), and thirty-eight, more than 50 percent, stated no origins. Of those for whom no origin is provided, fourteen were said to be criollos of Pilaya y Paspaya, and six more criollos of Tarija—that is, they were born in the area and either did not know their origins, or saw no reason to state them. The ten men from La Cordillera are of considerable interest. La Cordillera was an adjacent area of Andean foothills in what is now the Department of Santa Cruz, which in the seventeenth century was dominated by Chiriguanos. Were these ten men, then, actually Chiriguanos who for some reason had "crossed over" both literally and figuratively? Since other forasteros were listed in the census as "sons of Chiriguanos," this is likely. One census entry gives a hint as to how long men from La Cordillera had been living and working on the estates in the Pilaya River area. Francisco Tacuri was described as being "from La Cordillera" and also a "criollo of the Tarija border." That is, his family was from the other side of the Chiriguano frontier, but was in at least in its second generation in the Pilaya-Tarija area.

Most of the Indians in the San Pedro section of the census were listed according to the property or hacienda on which they lived, although their relations with the owners were not specified. However, three men were listed in San Pedro as *indios sueltos arrenderos*, literally, loose or free Indian renters. It is not clear from whom they rented nor how they differed from the other Indians who were listed as living on chacras or other properties. Also on the Tarija side of the border, one property was listed as belonging to the descendants of the province's founder, Francisco de Tarija. After the names of the Indians living on this estate, the census listed "Indians who have lands near the aforementioned ranch." These people could conceivably have been smallholders, but there are no further clues about their activities in the census. Perhaps these few examples indicate that on the frontier, where social relations were less fixed, Indians had more freedom to live as squatters or tenants and may have been useful for protecting the boundaries of estates from Chiriguanos, rustlers, and other intruders.[47]

The general impression one receives of this southern section of Pilaya y Paspaya is that, more than the other zones discussed, it typifies the kind of social change one expects to find in frontier areas. There is less influence here of the northern indigenous cultures than in other parts of the province, and the Chiriguanos, while in many cases continuing their raids against hacendados who had taken their land, were also beginning to mix with the sedentary Indians who lived on haciendas. As Duncan Baretta and Markoff point out: "Permanent nomadism and permanent geographical stability were two extremes; . . . many wanderers had extensive ties of kinship and friendship with settled people."[48] In Pilaya y Paspaya it wasn't just that the Chiriguanos had begun to settle down, but also that the Indians from the core areas of Andean culture were losing contact with their homes.

Of the forasteros in Pilaya y Paspaya in 1646, those "from the mita" represent one extreme of short-term or seasonal migration from indigenous communities, while the group in San Pedro appear to be permanently settled and already quite acculturated. The renters in Paspaya were in some ways an intermediate group. They were not simply temporary workers, and some mentioned no connections with their ayllus, but others, particularly those from Porco, could have been maintaining traditional economic complementarity by renting land in the province. However, by 1725, as demonstrated in that year's census, the forastero population of the province had changed significantly in ways that were foreshadowed by the 1646 returns from the San Pedro region. Furthermore, the enumeration and court cases from approximately the same period reveal the servile condition and the family disintegration within the yanacona population—a particularly important sector of the work force in the south of the province early in the eighteenth century.

Yanaconas and Forasteros in 1725

A complete demographic analysis of the 1725 padrón is not possible because no ages are given for women or girls in Pilaya y Paspaya's Indian population in that year. So, while the total population of 6,778 was divided roughly equally (51 percent male, 49 percent female), we cannot know how the sexes were distributed by age.

The census reveals a number of features that were relatively unusual in colonial enumerations and may have been partly due to the epidemic, or epidemics, that ravaged the Peruvian viceroyalty between 1718 and 1722. These include a large number of widows in the population, more than a few single women with children, and marriages of both men and women to non-Indians. Other features of the 1725 count that tend to suggest that the province's Indian population was hard hit by disease were the presence of orphans who apparently were not cared for by relatives (the census specifically stated when orphans were in the custody of relatives or other adults), the relatively low proportion of married couples (64 percent), and 377 women listed as heads of households. In colonial tributary censuses, women were generally included as wives or daughters of male tributaries, with widows sometimes listed separately. The departure from this pattern in Pilaya y Paspaya in 1725 suggests an extreme disruption of family groups. About half of the women listed separately were widows (194), and the others were single mothers, women who had married outside their ethnic group or tribute status, and orphans.

On the other hand, signs of social disruption were not equally pronounced in all sectors of the Indian population in Pilaya y Paspaya in 1725, suggesting that it was not disease alone that caused the dislocation. Examining the returns for the originarios, forasteros, and yanaconas separately will highlight these variations and permit some speculation on the causes.

Looking at the age distribution of male originarios in Pilaya y Paspaya in 1725, given in table 7.4, we see that it differed from that of forasteros primarily in the ratio of active adult males (those fifteen to forty-nine years old) to the elderly (age fifty and above). The originario population had a higher proportion of old men (15 percent compared to 12 percent for the forasteros), while among forasteros the active adult group was larger (41 percent as opposed to 37 percent in the originario group).[49] Male originarios in their economically productive years probably tended to migrate. Elderly originarios may also have returned to their communities after years of living and working elsewhere, as López-Beltrán suggests for Livitaca in 1689 (see chapter 5). Both the originario and the forastero populations had high proportions of male children under five years of age, indicating that if these groups were affected by the epidemic, they were making a rapid demographic recovery.

If the number of male originarios between fifteen and fifty years of age was reduced because of migration or flight, one can assume that the ranks of the forasteros of the same age range were swelled for the same reason. The census does not state how long forasteros had lived in the province, but of those who gave their origin (an indication that they may have migrated fairly recently), more than 50 percent were between twenty and twenty-nine years of age (table 7.5 shows the origins of forasteros in the province in 1725). On the other hand, the fact that more than 69 percent of forasteros gave no place of origin in 1725 suggests that most of them had been born in the province. This is strikingly different from the situation seventy-nine years before, in 1646, when only about 13 percent failed to state their home province. We

TABLE 7.4 Age of Indian Males in Pilaya y Paspaya, 1725

	No. of Originarios	(%)	No. of Forasteros	(%)	No. of Yanaconas	(%)	Total N	(49)
Children		(48)		(47)		(54)		(49)
0–4	110		415		146		671	
5–9	129		400		128		657	
10–14	48		168		123		339	
Economically active adults		(37)		(41)		(45)		(41)
15–19	53		175		88		316	
20–24	32		157		54		243	
25–29	26		175		60		261	
30–34	34		122		32		188	
35–39	40		111		40		191	
40–44	22		71		32		125	
45–49	16		50		19		85	
Elders		(15)		(12)		(1)		(10)
50–54	41		110		9		160	
55–59	8		34		0		42	
60–64	14		46		0		60	
65 and older	25		50		0		75	
TOTAL	598		2,084		731		3,413	

Source: AGN, XIII-18-5-1.

do not have records of the origins of forasteros in the province at the time of the la Palata census, but comparing the figures from 1646 with those from 1725 bears out the findings of table 7.3: migration had slowed down considerably.[50]

Table 7.5, which gives the origins for the 363 men who *did* state their family homes, indicates that there had been some changes since 1646. First of all, while the the most common province of origin in 1725 (as in 1646) was still Porco, the number stating that they were from that province fell both absolutely and as a percentage of all forasteros in the province. Unfortunately, in most instances the 1725

TABLE 7.5 Origins of Male Forasteros in Pilaya y Paspaya, 1725

Province	Number
Porco (including Potosí)	152
Pilaya y Paspaya	132
Tarija	15
Tomina	11
Pacajes	10
Paria	9
Yamparaez	8
Chichas	8
Omasuyos	6
Sicasica	4
Carangas	3
Cochabamba	3
Chucuito	2
Not given	819
TOTAL	1,182

Source: AGN, XIII, 18-5-1.

count simply gives province of origin without specifying town or ayllu, so we cannot know if the forasteros in Pilaya y Paspaya who were originally from Porco belonged to groups that had traditionally sent colonists to the province. It is clear, though, that if these groups still had lands in the area or arrangements with individual hacendados to provide workers in exchange for tribute, they were not as common as they had been earlier. In 1725, only eight men were recorded as coming from Chichas, the other province that sent many temporary migrants to Pilaya y Paspaya in the seventeenth century.

The reduced number of men from provinces that generally sent short-term migrants and the fact that so many forasteros gave no place of origin indicates that more of the work force lived permanently in the valley than in 1646. Perhaps landowners didn't need so many extra hands for the harvests, given the economic malaise of the early eighteenth century. Yet, since we know that wine from the province continued to be very saleable in Potosí in the eighteenth century, it is possible that in 1725 there were enough people in the province to meet the demand for temporary workers and that contracts with indigenous communities were no longer necessary.

In 1725 the second most common origin given for forasteros was Pilaya y Paspaya itself. The returns are somewhat ambiguous on this point, but since the men from Pilaya y Paspaya did not report what villages and ayllus they came from, they were probably not really originarios of the province at all, but simply born there. They were what the 1646 count referred to as "criollos" of the Pilaya y Paspaya. This means that by 1725 in Pilaya y Paspaya, the concept of having an *origin* distinct from a *birthplace* was beginning to lose its meaning.

Returning to table 7.4: note that the age distribution of male yanaconas differed markedly in several respects from that of both forasteros and originarios. First of all, elderly men made up only about 1 percent of the male yanacona population, and, in fact, none was older than fifty-four. The lack of elderly men is primarily compensated by the very large percentage of boys younger than fifteen, which means that the adult, economically active sector of the population was not significantly larger among yanaconas than among the other groups.

Part of the reason for the apparent lack of men in their most productive working years is the very large number of yanaconas listed in the census as "belonging" to various landowners but said to be absent. Altogether, 273 yanaconas were said to be missing, including forty-four female yanaconas who were listed separately in the census. In some instances, the missing yanaconas were apparently working on other properties belonging to the same hacendado. This appears to have been the case for the hacienda and ranch "Ingahuasi," where fifty-four "missing" yanaconas were probably working on the hacienda of "San Pedro Mártir" at the time of the census (see Appendix 2). This was an arrangement that Antonio López de Quiroga specifically outlined in his will.[51] But most of the missing were said to have been gone for a long time, and hacendados generally claimed to know nothing of their whereabouts. Since only yanaconas were listed as absent in the census, one might assume that landowners may simply have wanted to go on record as having once had these servants to facilitate reclaiming them should they eventually be found.

TABLE 7.6 Marital Status of Indian Women Listed Separately in Pilaya y Paspaya, 1725

	No. of Originarios	No. of Forasteros	No. of Yanaconas	Total N	% of Total
Married	1	3	36	40	(11)
Single	4	18	51	73	(19)
Widowed	23	79	92	194	(51)
Not given	0	0	70	70	(9)
TOTAL	28	100	249	377	(100)
(%)	(7)	(27)	(66)	(100)	

Source: AGN, XIII, 18-5-1.

The absence of so many adult yanacona men also helps to explain another finding peculiar to the group: the extremely high number of women counted as individuals. While only 9 percent of the originarios and forasteros listed were women or girls, among yanaconas, 42 percent of those listed as household heads were females. Of the female heads of household, thirty-six were married to non-yanaconas (table 7.6). Of these, twenty-five were married to "free" Indians—that is, men who were not legally bound to the estates on which they worked. The other women were married to men of different ethnic groups: one to a mestizo, three to black slaves, one to a free black, two to mulatto slaves, two to free mulattos, and two to Spaniards. The fact that husbands of women not married to Indians were mostly slaves or freemen of color suggests that yanaconas were closely associated with the most disadvantaged socioeconomic groups in the province. Of the other yanacona women listed separately in the census, ninety-two were widows and the remaining one hundred twenty-one were either single or gave no marital status at all. Forty-six of these were single mothers, while the other seventy-five female yanaconas were probably orphans or children abandoned when their parents left the estates for one reason or another. (I deduced this because these females were frequently listed with brothers who were minors.)

A little more light is shed on the reasons for the presence of so many unmarried women, and for exogamy among yanacona women,

TABLE 7.7 Age and Marital Status of Missing Male Yanaconas, Pilaya y Paspaya, 1725

	Married	Single	Widowed	Not Given	Total Number
5–9	0	3	0	0	3
10–14	0	4	0	0	4
15–19	0	13	0	14	27
20–24	8	10	0	29	47
25–29	8	3	3	12	26
30–34	2	5	1	10	18
35–39	11	4	3	3	21
40–44	15	6	1	6	28
45–49	11	1	1	2	15
50–54	4	2	1	2	9
55–59	0	0	0	1	1
Not given	13	2	5	11	31
TOTAL	72	53	15	90	230
(%)	(31)	(23)	(7)	(39)	(100)

Source: AGN, XIII, 18-5-1.

by studying the marital status and ages of the men from the group who were recorded as absent. In table 7.7 we see that ninety-one men, or about 40 percent, of those missing were between twenty and thirty-four years of age, and that of these only eighteen were said to be married. Another eighteen men in this age range were listed as single, but no marital status was given for the greatest number—fifty-one men. Even if these fifty-one yanaconas were married, the evidence suggests that they did not leave the haciendas with their wives and families; such information is specifically given in the census. This means that some of the women listed individually could be the wives of men who abandoned the estates on which they worked. And the absence of so many young men, many of whom must have been single, certainly decreased the number of eligible males for young women to marry.

Table 7.7 also indicates that 57 percent of absent men forty years old and older were married and left the estates accompanied by their wives. Herbert Klein notes that in the Yungas coca-growing region of Chulumani in the late colonial period yanaconas not only came willingly to haciendas, but also when times were hard landowners apparently allowed, even forced, them to leave. In this way, they did not hold on to an unnecessary resident labor force, and also did not have to pay the tribute for so many men.[52] The number of absent yanaconas in Pilaya y Paspaya in 1725 suggests that hacendados there may have taken a similar approach: dispensing with men over forty could have eliminated an aging and therefore less productive sector of the work force and freed the lands they occupied for younger workers or for direct cultivation by the hacendado.

Despite the absence of eligible male yanaconas, the number of unmarried mothers and women married to men of different ethnic groups helped to maintain the group's birthrate at a level approximately equal to that of forasteros and originarios. For all three groups, it is difficult to calculate the number of children per couple, because there were considerable numbers of widows and widowers, and among yanaconas (as noted), so many single mothers. Dividing the number of children by the number of married couples, and adding widowed and single parents, we get an average of 2.25 children for the originarios, 1.93 among forasteros and 2.03 for yanaconas. Thus, despite their apparently greater social disorganization, yanaconas maintained their population size, albeit with the reproductive help of other racial and cultural groups. However, miscegenation was a harbinger of the time when the yanaconas would cease to exist as a distinctly Indian sector of the population.

The hacendados' desire to reinforce the supposed servile condition of the yanaconas cannot be forgotten and is evident even in the census returns. Originarios and forasteros were listed in a relatively straightforward manner according to place of residence. If a man had grown sons, sometimes these were listed in sequence after the father's name, with a note stating the family relationship. In general, the *padrones* (returns) of originarios and forasteros maintain the adult male as the primary unit of inquiry, except for the previously mentioned cases of orphans, widows, and relatively few single women. Yanaconas, on the other hand, when possible, were counted by families. Presumably this portion of the census was organized in this manner to lend legitimacy to the landlords' claims to yanaconas, since rights of "ownership" were usually established in courts by tracing the lineage of the person in question.[53] The practice of naming all the members of a family went to such extremes that in some cases several generations of dead people were listed. For instance: "Juan Mamani, dead, son of Francisco Caio, dead, was married to María Sissa, dead, their children Joseph Santos, twenty-three years old and María."[54] In this case, obviously, the important facts were that Joseph Santos was a twenty-three-year-old male and that he had a sister named María. Nonetheless, the family was traced back to the grandfather, perhaps because high mortality in the epidemic had obscured the hereditary chain that the hacendado saw as entitling him to yanacona labor.

From the hacendado's point of view, the yanacona might have been preferable to a black slave in several respects. He cost the landowner nothing in initial investment and, in fact, had often even asked for the asylum of yanacona status. Furthermore, since the yanacona did not come from a distinct racial group like the slave, should it seem expedient he could be "let go" to join Indian society in some other context: to return to his community, live on the periphery of a Spanish city, or seek work on another hacienda. But, being ethnically Indian and resembling the majority of rural workers cut both ways; it was also an advantage for the yanacona. Land was relatively accessible, and other hacendados were always threatening to woo away their workers; perhaps these factors explain why landowners emphasized their hereditary rights to yanacona workers and were ready to fight legal battles to hold on to them. The records of the Audiencia of Charcas contain many court cases between Indians who claimed their freedom from yanaconaje and estate owners who either wanted to keep them or to get them back. Always the onus was on the laborer to prove that he was *not* a yanacona.

In 1717 Claudio and Gonzalo Sánchez Paniagua, owners of the "Agua de Castilla" hacienda in the Cinti Valley, complained that "their" yanacona, Juan Flores, frequently ran away; on one such occasion, he changed his last name and went to the audiencia with a "sinister account" that was "contrary to all truth" of why he should be free of *yanaconasco*. The basis of Flores's case was that his father had been an orphan raised in Sánchez Paniagua's house, but that the family had no hereditary connections to other yanaconas on the property.[55] In this case, the difference between being a yanacona on a rural estate and in a city is strikingly clear. Don Gabriel Fernández Guarache, the previously mentioned kuraka from Jesús de Machaca, when trying to track down recalcitrant tributaries in the cities, referred to them as having become "free yanaconas." Claudio Sánchez Paniagua said that Juan Flores wanted "to be free of *yanaconasco*."

Another case from Pilaya y Paspaya involved Pascual Wallpa, who brought his petition before the court in 1703. Wallpa claimed that when he could not pay a debt to the corregidor in Cinti, the magistrate sold him as a yanacona to Doña Francisca Ibañez, who owned a ranch in the area. He said that Doña Francisca was supposed to deduct from his debt four reales a year for each head of cattle he tended. Wallpa maintained that instead of doing this, she claimed the right to hold him in perpetual servitude. Doña Francisca, for her part, denied purchasing Wallpa from the corregidor. The final resolution of the case is unknown. The audiencia eventually freed Wallpa, but the corregidor then imprisoned his wife and children for the debts he had incurred.[56]

Wallpa's situation points to the apparently frequent role of the corregidor in helping landowners acquire yanaconas. Toledo probably was only acknowledging a precedent when he specified in his regulations on yanaconas that corregidores should help hacendados find "vagrant" Indians who could legally be forced to work for them (see chapter 3). Since the time of Toledo, many had protested that these magistrates worked hand-in-glove with hacendados to hold workers as yanaconas who should have been serving in the mita of Potosí.[57] José Cipriano, who claimed he was being unjustly held as a yanacona on the estate of Antonio López de Quiroga, may have had a particularly hard time in this regard: not only was López de Quiroga the most powerful hacendado in the province, but at least two of his relatives had served as corregidor of Pilaya y Paspaya.[58]

A final interesting case illustrates not only that hacendados would go to considerable lengths to retain yanaconas whom they claimed were rightfully theirs, but also that the number of yanaconas a landowner possessed might somehow miraculously increase despite the proprietor's contention that he had only *yanaconas originarios*, that is, yanaconas designated as such in the time of Toledo. In 1697 Felix Belásquez, owner of the hacienda "Ympora y Ympora" in the San Juan River region of Pilaya y Paspaya, asked the Audiencia of Charcas to uphold his "possession or quasi-possession" of the yanacona Juan Paco. To strengthen his case, Velásquez stressed his poverty, saying that he had to care for his mother and his unmarried sister as well as his own family. He said Paco was his only yanacona and that if he didn't get him back, he would lose his crop.[59]

How one yanacona could make the difference between getting the crop in or not is unexplained. Nor is the fact that in 1697 Velásquez claimed to have only one yanacona, but in 1725 the hacienda had thirty-eight. In the 1697 complaint, Velásquez lists the yanaconas he had at the time of the 1683 census. In 1725 not one name of the yanaconas on the hacienda, then owned by his son, was even remotely similar to the earlier ones, nor were any of them said to be descendants of those present in 1683. On the contrary, most of the yanaconas in 1725 seemed to be members of two families, the Tolavas and the Chipanis, neither of whom was mentioned at the time of la Palata. The case of Felix Belásquez suggests, then, that despite landowners' attempts to make it appear that families of yanaconas lived on their estates in perpetuity, the yanacona work force may actually have fluctuated considerably. Workers could be allowed to absent themselves when no longer needed, freeing the hacendado from the burden of their tribute or an aging work force. But the very fact that they so often had to be claimed as serfs suggests that the yanaconas' economic need was not great enough to hold them; they had to be made to stay against their will.

Conclusion

By 1725 the trend toward separation from Andean culture in Pilaya y Paspaya was quite pronounced. What Thierry Saignes suggested for other areas of Upper Peru seems to have been even more the case in Pilaya y Paspaya: there was a qualitative difference between the seventeenth century, when most forasteros could identify the kin groups to which they belonged, and the eighteenth, when the migratory flow was diminished and the connections between immigrants and their villages of origins had become attenuated.[60] By the third decade of the eighteenth century, most forasteros seem to have been born in the province and to know nothing of connections with highland ethnic groups. Yanaconas had become a dependent work force of hacienda peons gradually blending with other non-Indian agricultural workers in the province. While they sometimes experienced considerable mobility, there are few indications that it was upward. In fact, the servile condition and the disrupted families in the group made them more similar to the female domestic servants studied by Luis Glave than to any other group of workers examined in this book, although even the maids' period of service was not supposed to last forever.

On the whole, the philosophical trend toward free paid labor seems to have scarcely penetrated the countryside. Although there are occasional references in documents to wages, they seem to have been paid infrequently, and even then, they were generally in kind rather than in cash. As late as the 1730s, wages were usually in food and goods on the province's huge Jesuit-owned estate, "Trigo Pampa."[61] People mostly received small plots of land for their labor and perhaps had their tribute paid by their hacendados.[62] Migration to Pilaya y Paspaya's agricultural estates may have caused greater cultural change than did working in Oruro's mines, but it wasn't because relations of production had evolved in a capitalist direction. To a certain extent, those who advance theories of dependency find evidence to support their views in Pilaya y Paspaya: mercantile capitalism had created plenty of change in the area, but it had not created capitalist relations of production and it didn't give residents of the area the commonly accepted advantages of the system: a living wage, personal mobility, and the possibility of solidarity with others based on a consciousness of common class interests as a replacement for dwindling ethnic identification.

However, if the general tendency of the (apparently incomplete) census from 1778 is any indication,[63] many workers in Pilaya y Paspaya eventually found a way to escape the oppression of yanacona status or the burdens of being Indian. The count of the province taken in that year reported 257 Spanish men, 328 Indians, and 742 mestizos (55 percent), results that plausibly reflect more than a century of cultural and demographic evolution. People had used a familiar and reliable strategy: they changed their ethnic and legal status to minimize discrimination. Whether through miscegenation or guile, many now were mestizos, just as in the seventeenth century their forebears had become yanaconas to avoid the mita of Potosí.

Conclusion

BY STUDYING the formation of an indigenous labor force in Upper Peru, this book addresses two intrinsically related themes in colonial Latin American history: (1) the degree of capitalist transformation of native economies that resulted from Spanish mercantilism in the New World and (2) the range of cultural change caused by the imposition of a new economic system. With regard to the first point, this study has found considerable transformation but not necessarily in a capitalist direction, if by capitalist one means the entire separation of the workers from the means of production and their dependence on wage labor. Yet it is also clear that the systems of labor that emerged in the Andes in the seventeenth and eighteenth centuries were not "traditional" in the sense of being pure survivals of Andean economic organization. Instead, new, but noncapitalist, relations of production developed, and some have continued to be useful to the accumulation of capital on a world scale well into the twentieth century.

The process of creating a work force was full of conflict; Andeans did not allow their labor to be turned into a commodity without a struggle. And in the effort to mitigate exploitation, they used various tools of the new social order when they met their needs—the colonial legal system, European technology, the market economy—as well as their own kin networks, patterns of inheritance, and concepts of gender. This dynamic process of constantly responding to and attempting to gain some advantage in a situation largely beyond their control meant that the very efforts to stave off immiseration and social disintegration also led to cultural transformation.

Nor was there contention simply between Spaniards and Indians. Philosophical differences and variations in socioeconomic change within each society made the interaction more complex. Spanish policy, while incrementally encouraging the commodification of labor and the right of native Americans to sell it, still exhibited the inconsistencies inherent to a colonial power that had not yet completed the transition to capitalism. Vying with liberal conceptions were corporatist beliefs that condoned the use of force and exonerated servitude. These ideas were reinforced by Spanish prejudice and racism, which encouraged administrators and entrepreneurs to perceive Andeans as even more idle and vicious than Spain's own peasant masses. Yet, this viewpoint was also in part an accurate reaction on the part of the ruling group to a society in which class differentiation and separation from the means of production were not nearly as advanced as they were in Spain. Nonetheless, there were always a few Spaniards who for religious and moral reasons opposed coercion. Many more were concerned about the long-term effects of superexploitation of the native population, and some began to realize that Andeans might not be impervious to material incentives after all. Felipe de Godoy could say in 1607, "Indians always go where there is the most to be gained."

Thus, the decision on the part of Spanish administrators to gradually introduce a policy based more consistently on market incentives was not merely idealistic nor was it founded only on the Iberian socioeconomic situation. The realization that such an approach might

Conclusion

succeed in Upper Peru reflected an understanding by colonial rulers of the growing class stratification in Andean society. This had begun before the Europeans' arrival, and it was no coincidence that it was often those native people who had been most privileged before the conquest who took fullest advantage of the opportunities offered by the colonial market. Sometimes they did this to enhance their groups' welfare, selling the produce of chacras or starting businesses to help defray tribute costs, for instance. But mercantile strategies did not always benefit the community. Sometimes the process was reversed, and ayllu ties and principles of reciprocity were marshaled by kurakas to advance their own personal fortunes in the new world order. We know this was so because eventually many "common Indians" themselves used a colonial institution, the legal system, to denounce their own leaders.

In 1629 the *indios comuneros* of Santiago Cotagaita in Chichas filed a complaint against their cacique, Don Juan Calla, for appropriating a community flour mill. They said that all the men and women of the community had provided free labor to build the mill, with the understanding that it would belong to the group as a whole and be used to grind their own grains and those of Spaniards, with the proceeds from the venture going to pay their tribute. However, Don Juan Calla had located the mill on his own property and for twenty-four years had used it solely for his own benefit. He charged everyone, Indian and Spaniard alike, six reales per fanega for grinding maize, a price witnesses said was exorbitant, and was said to have an income of 2,000 pesos a year from the mill alone. In addition to never giving the people of the community any help with their tribute, Calla was accused of forcing eighty Indians of the community to work without pay in the mill.[1]

This particular complaint is illuminating not only because of Don Juan's exploitation of his own people, but also because the indios comuneros demonstrated a considerable familiarity with market mechanisms themselves. They had not been paid for their initial labor, but had accepted that condition because they believed they, as community members, were going to own the mill. They were overcharged for grinding their maize, and their work in the mill was not remunerated. Don Juan had not kept his side of the bargain; he had not used the mill as part of a group survival strategy, and since he had not, the collectivity was calling him to account. If the kuraka would not operate according to principles of Andean communal reciprocity, the members of the community were determined that he should at least treat them as freely contracting workers.

The mobilization of labor power also both reinforced and undermined Andean ideas about the proper economic and social roles of men and women. In some situations, the gender complementarity that reflected a parallel division of the cosmos clearly enhanced possibilities for survival or prosperity in colonial circumstances. In other instances, Andean men seemed ready to forgo even the principle, let alone the practice, of gender equality if it appeared to be in their interest. But, just as the ideological and practical conflict about labor did not break down along neat Andean-European lines, gender was also mediated by class and ethnic ties.

Indigenous women working as domestic servants were among the poorest people in Upper Peruvian cities, and indigenous men may have been in part responsible for their condition. It is not hard to imagine Don Juan Calla of Santiago Cotagaita sending the daughters of his poorer "kin" to serve in the homes of Spaniards with whom he had business dealings. On the other hand, women who prospered in urban areas seem to have used either kin networks or ties with people of similar occupations, particularly yanacona artisans, to enhance their position. Whether these business and personal relationships with craftsmen actually represented a new alignment along class, or at least occupational, lines is difficult to say. In some cases they may have, but possibly there were also kin or communal ties among some or many of the people described as yanaconas in offical documents.

In many ways, the yanaconas are the real enigma of seventeenth-century Upper Peru. And the differences between the social and economic condition of yanaconas in Oruro and those in Pilaya y Paspaya are emblematic of the range of relations of production and cultural change in the region. In Oruro they were highly acculturated and often described as "free": free from the mita, free from communal responsibilities. Interestingly, they were primarily concentrated in crafts, working as assistants to Spaniards, or in some cases on their own, not in the mining industry. So, the most hispanicized native peo-

Conclusion

ple in the city were not those most likely to develop into an industrial proletariat; if anything, yanacona men who worked in crafts, and the women retail merchants with whom they were often associated, seem more like an incipient petty bourgeoisie than a working class. On the other hand, those who worked in the mines in most cases didn't really seem to be developing into a proletariat either. Primarily forasteros, well into the seventeenth century they could identify their ayllus and parcialidades, and many were close enough to their homes to go there frequently. This connection with their communities and with land seems to have put them in a position, especially in times of labor shortage, to resist the mine and mill owners' efforts to eliminate the practice of ore sharing.

If becoming acculturated in Oruro was a way of protecting oneself and minimizing the exploitation of the colonial state, it is debatable whether the same was true for yanaconas in Pilaya y Paspaya. While they did escape the hardship of the mita by fleeing to the agricultural province and while they certainly did become acculturated, it is difficult to maintain that by this means they avoided exploitation. Although yanaconas may have had some leverage with employers because of the scarcity of workers in the province, they also seem to have traded the burdens of being Indian for the (arguably) equally onerous ones of legal serfdom. As time went on, through miscegenation and subterfuge, many descendants of yanaconas undoubtedly became mestizos and, along with the children of black slaves, Chiriguanos, and other Andean migrants, made up a regional work force of renters and peons.

According to Erick Langer, although there were wide variations among different types of haciendas, in the nineteenth century the most typical relation of production in the region was still labor rent. Arrenderos were provided with plots of land and in return had to work a certain number of days each year on the demense, to provide other specified services for the landowner, and to pay a cash rent as well.[2] While it is conceivable that some smallholders, who were relatively common in the southwest of the province in the nineteenth century, were descendants of colonial yanaconas or forasteros, in general it does not appear that immigrants in Pilaya y Paspaya had had even the limited material success of their counterparts in Oruro.

There were probably a number of reasons for this. Certainly land in Pilaya y Paspaya was more valuable commercially than land on the high plateau, so migrants to the zone, unless they had extraordinary resources, were less likely to become proprietors. Also, while sometimes those who held land in usufruct may have been able to market some of the subsistence crops they raised, this practice was not nearly as remunerative as selling shares of ore in Oruro. But it also seems that being cut off from their kin groups eliminated one of the main material, as well as spiritual, props for many of the immigrants in Pilaya y Paspaya. It is probably not coincidental that in colonial legal documents references to native people owning land are all from the north of the province. While land was less valuable in that section, it was nonetheless still coveted by Spaniards, so the kin-group connections of proprietors and the fact that communal lands were protected by the colonial state must have been instrumental in allowing native people to acquire private property as well.

Clearly, despite the skill with which Andeans devised means of coping with the new system, their options in many circumstances were extremely limited. The woman and her daughter evicted from their pulperia in La Plata, the domestic servants of La Paz, the workers held against their wills as yanaconas, the thousands of people who fled their homes to avoid the mita are dramatic testimony to this fact. There are also limits to the amount of control a historian can "give" native Americans in shaping the colonial world without denying their exploitation and espousing a kind of relativism that scarcely distinquishes between colonized peoples and colonists. While Andean people certainly were subjects, not merely objects, of history, the surplus extracted from the New World through the use of indigenous labor, coerced or otherwise, after all, *did* facilitate the development of capitalism in Europe, and it is absurd to suggest that this process was effected without enormous suffering and emotional and cultural loss on the part of indigenous Americans.

Today native peoples throughout the Western Hemisphere are conscious both of past exploitation and past achievements and are overcoming long-term ethnic rivalries to form a pan-American movement for indigenous rights. In Bolivia, lowland groups such as the Chiriguanos and Guaranis are joining highland Quechua and Aymara

Conclusion

speakers in recovering their history, reclaiming their lands and demanding bilingual education.[3] Obviously, as suggested in the introduction, these ethnic movements are not independent of the dominant culture and do not seek to create an entirely distinct and separate social construct. The very fact of uniting as "Indians" is an example of accepting an ethnic category invented long ago by Europeans.

Nor does the hard-won unity of various Native American groups preclude other types of conflicts. If, as this book demonstrates, in the seventeenth century ethnic identity was mediated by class and gender, the same is even more true today. Indigenous rights organizations include professionals, business people, and employees of nongovernmental aid organizations, whose perspectives may be very different from those of unionized peasants and workers who belong to the same organizations. Furthermore, activists make decisions not only according to ethnic and class position but also as women or as men.

In a sense, the story that began in the 1530s is still being told. Despite the social diversity evident in the Andes in 1600, perhaps there are even *more* ways of being Andean on the eve of the twenty-first century. Capitalism has not made ethnicity less compelling; it has manipulated it, reformulated it, made it more complicated. And, in continuing efforts to create not only economic development but also social justice in Latin America, the points at which ethnicity, class, and gender intersect will be the vortices of debate about the society of the future.

Appendixes
Notes
Glossary
Bibliography
Index

Appendix 1

Quinto Real in Pesos Ensayados: Oruro, 1611–1730

1611	230,721	1635	164,952	1659	—
1612	222,092	1636	160,486	1660	19,700
1613	220,682	1637	166,452	1661	19,700
1614	204,359	1638	149,432	1662	18,768
1615	277,476	1639	137,933	1663	10,608
1616	298,987	1640	163,333	1664	10,608
1617	318,964	1641	168,179	1665	10,608
1618	322,776	1642	187,831	1666	52,822
1619	—	1643	—	1667	52,312
1620	136,337	1644	—	1668	51,700
1621	118,244	1645	—	1669	—
1622	—	1646	174,019	1670	—
1623	—	1647	161,142	1671	—
1624	232,844	1648	158,634	1672	—
1625	164,808	1649	180,676	1673	28,908
1626	311,146	1650	110,309	1674	25,960
1627	263,774	1651	73,693	1675	26,184
1628	247,692	1652	66,360	1676	30,650
1629	238,453	1653	56,168	1677	—
1630	219,121	1654	48,510	1678	—
1631	204,407	1655	—	1679	—
1632	191,326	1656	52,776	1980	—
1633	172,714	1657	52,776	1681	—
1634	164,952	1658	—	1682	—

(continued)

Quinto Real in Pesos Ensayados. Oruro: 1611–1730 (cont.)

1683	46,025	1699	79,272	1715	52,992
1684	39,428	1700	—	1716	80,376
1685	36,216	1701	—	1717	104,664
1686	45,492	1702	—	1718	148,392
1687	46,320	1703	—	1719	141,868
1688	39,284	1704	—	1720	80,968
1689	42,972	1705	—	1721	60,744
1690	44,768	1706	95,764	1722	93,304
1691	47,948	1707	85,780	1723	81,048
1692	50,408	1708	98,600	1724	74,380
1693	65,380	1709	118,356	1725	83,064
1694	85,608	1710	118,628	1726	84,986
1695	99,380	1711	99,484	1727	92,928
1696	103,091	1712	83,584	1728	91,576
1697	—	1713	72,952	1729	82,032
1698	79,272	1714	59,548	1730	76,744

Sources: AGN XIII-8-2-4; 8-2-5; 8-2-6; 8-2-7; BMO, Libro Real de la Real Hacienda, March 9, 1611 to March 29, 1612; 1649; 1678; 1684; 1695; Libro Comun de 1639; Libro Real de Contador 1646; 1647; 1648–49; 1656–57; 1664–65; 1667–68; 1673; 1699; Libro de Tesorero 1637–38; 1638–39; 1640–41; AGI, Charcas, 37, 18; TePaske and Klein, *The Royal Treasuries*, vol. 2, pp. 188–213; Bakewell, "Registered Silver Production," pp. 101–03.

Note: Annual figures for years with months missing were arrived at by calculating monthly averages.

Appendix 2

Population Distribution by Place of Residence,
Pilaya y Paspaya, 1725

Parish	Place	Type	Total Trib.	Origi- narios	Fora- steros	Yana- conas
San Lucas	San Lucas	T	130	107	23	0
	Thoroche	NG	27	12	15	0
	Ancomaio	NG	12	4	8	0
	Guanaia	CL	56	48	8	0
	Cocha	R	11	4	7	0
	Zabala	P	87	23	64	0
	Munipaia	NG	15	0	15	0
	Uruchiri	P	11	0	10	1
	Aitacara	P	4	0	4	0
	Pototaca	T	41	30	11	0
	Total		394	228 (58%)	165 (42%)	1
Supas	Curini	Ch	4	0	4	0
	Ancomarca	NG	20	7	13	0
	Acchila	T	30	8	22	0
	Cailli	CL	41	27	14	0
	Saiarani	CL	43	10	33	0
	Chiguamarca	Ch	23	15	8	0
	Soctolo	CL	18	5	13	0

(continued)

Population Distribution by Place of Residence, Pilaya y Paspaya, 1725 (cont.)

Parish	Place	Type	Total Trib.	Origi- narios	Fora- steros	Yana- conas
	Motila	Ch	18	10	8	0
	Pugllala	NG	22	0	22	0
	Sacasaca	Ch	39	0	39	0
	Supas	Ch	16	0	16	0
	Total		274	82 (30%)	192 (70%)	—
Piurani	Piruani	T	18	18	0	0
	Piruani	CL	12	0	12	0
	Tomola	R	9	0	9	0
	Savilque	Ch	58	0	58	0
	Sierra Chica	Ch	23	0	23	0
	Sierra Grande	Ch	8	0	8	0
	Sunchu	Ch	23	0	23	0
	Urcupiña	Ch	19	0	8	11 (10)
	Cholcosi	Ch	2	0	2	0
	Colpa	Ch	19	0	6	13 (14)
	Yatina	Ch	1	0	1	0
	Avioma	Ch	23	0	18	5 (15)
	Pulquiña	Ch	26	0	26	0
	Total		241	18 (7%)	194 (81%)	29 (12%)
Santa Elena	Sta. Elena	T	42	0	42	0
	Los Duraznos	Ch	16	0	16	0
	Ingahuazi	H;R	98	0	26	72 (54)
	Sacarí	Ch	31	0	31	0
	Pucara	Ch	3	0	3	0
	Yatina	Ch	33	0	33	0
	Condoriri	Ch	7	0	7	0
	Machaca	Ch	15	0	15	0
	Tipani	Ch	20	0	20	0
	Lambrani	Ch	15	0	15	0

Appendixes

Population Distribution by Place of Residence, Pilaya y Paspaya, 1725 (cont.)

Parish	Place	Type	Total Trib.	Originarios	Porosteros	Yanaconas
	Obexa Cancha	Ch	3	0	3	0
	Sacani	Ch	14	0	14	0
	Zumaya	Ch	14	0	14	0
	Cotani	Ch	13	0	13	0
	Cañaguaico	Ch	12	0	12	0
	Chicha Pampa	Ch	19	0	19	0
	Guaicoma	Ch	15	0	15	0
	Papachacra	Ch	20	0	20	0
	Tangoia	Ch	12	0	12	0
	San Marcelo	Ch	5	0	5	0
	Agua de Castilla	Ch	4	0	4	0
	Culpina	Ch, R	42	0	20	22 (13)
	Pacariri	Ch	6	0	6	0
	Guizana	R	10	0	10	0
	Total		469	0	375 (80%)	94 (20%)
Pilaya	La Loma	NG	14	0	14	0
	Copavilque	Ch	4	0	4	0
	Laramendi	Ch	10	0	10	0
	Pedro de Aguirre	Ch	6	0	6	0
	S. Francisco Cocha	Ch	10	0	10	0
	La Lechera	Ch	7	0	7	0
	Valle de Pilaya	Ch	4	0	4	0
	Cerro Redondo	Ch	8	0	8	0
	Total		63	0	63 (100%)	0
Cinti	Valle de Cinti	NG	6	0	6	0
	Stgo. de Vera	T	5	0	5	0
	Tacaquira	NG	15	0	15	0
	Guacacancha	NG	14	0	14	0
	Moroquiri	Ch	7	0	7	0

Population Distribution by Place of Residence, Pilaya y Paspaya, 1725 (cont.)

Parish	Place	Type	Total Trib.	Origi- narios	Fora- steros	Yana- conas
	Parintaca	R	2	0	2	0
	Alzuri	Ch	8	0	8	0
	Suquistaca	T	25	8	17	0
	Sillata	R	5	0	5	0
	La Dorada	H	1	0	1	0
	La Torre	H	5	0	5	0
	Nalcastaca	NG	2	0	2	0
	Tota	R	7	0	7	0
	Aranjuez	NG	3	0	3	0
	Sta. Rosa	H	2	0	2	0
	F. Rivera	H	4	0	4	0
	Romo de Aguero	H	3	0	3	0
	A. Varrio	H	4	0	4	0
	P de Aguirre	H	3	0	3	0
	J. Rodrigues	H	1	0	1	0
	S. Pedro Martír	H	8	0	2	6 (1)
	L. Salinas	H	2	0	2	0
	M. A. Valanza	H	1	0	1	0
	Lintaca	H	10	0	10	0
	Cairani	NG	1	0	1	0
	Pampa Quemada	H	3	0	3	0
	Guaranguai	H	4	0	4	0
	S. A. de Palca	H	21	0	1	20 (1)
	A de Rivera	H	2	0	2	0
	Ruiz G	H	9	0	9	0
	Viuicha	H	1	0	1	0
	Mollepampa	H	1	0	1	0
	Populo	H	3	0	3	0
	Nausa	H	5	0	5	0
	Saladillo	H	2	0	2	0
	La Cueba	H	20	0	4	16 (3)
	Camataqui	H	15	0	5	10 (5)
	Taracana	H	6	0	6	0
	TOTAL		236	8 (3%)	176 (74%)	52 (22%)

Population Distribution by Place of Residence, Pilaya y Paspaya, 1725 (cont.)

Parish	Place	Type	Total Trib.	Origi-narios	Fora-steros	Yana-conas
Valley of San Juan	R. de S. Juan	T	5	0	5	0
	Impora	H	41	0	3	38 (7)
	Taraia	H	54	0	7	47 (17)
	Yzuma	H	9	0	0	9 (4)
	S. J. de la Dorada	H	6	0	0	6
	Sactapa	H	15	0	0	15 (5)
	Rio Limi	H	9	0	0	9 (1)
	Taraya	H	61	0	0	61 (27)
	Altamirano	H	49	0	0	49 (5)
	Farfán	H	23	0	0	23 (10)
	Libi Libi	H	2	0	0	2
	S. J. Tirahoyo	H	151	0	0	151 (78)
	Sivinga-mayo	H	5	0	0	5
	San Geronimo	H	8	0	0	8 (3)
	TOTAL		438	0	15 (3%)	423 (96%)

Key to Types: T = Town, NG = Not given, R = Ranch, CL = Community lands, P = Paraje, Ch = Chacra, H = Hacienda
Source: AGN, Sala XIII, 18-5-1.
Note: Numbers in parentheses at the far right are missing yanaconas.

Notes

Abbreviations Used in Notes

AGI   Archivo General de Indias (Sevilla)
AGN   Archivo General de la Nación (Buenos Aires)
ALP   Archivo Histórico de La Paz (La Paz)
ANB   Archivo Nacional de Bolivia (Sucre)
BMO   Biblioteca Municipal de Oruro (Oruro)
BN   Biblioteca Nacional de España (Madrid)
BNP   Biblioteca Nacional del Perú (Lima)
TI   Tierras e Indios Collection, ANB

Introduction

1. Raymond Williams, *Marxism and Literature* (Oxford: Oxford University Press, 1977), 113–14, 109–27, *passim*.

2. Jorge Basadre, "El regimen de la mita," *Letras* (Lima, 1937), 325–64; Alberto Crespo Rodas, "La 'mita' de Potosí," *Revista Histórica* 22 (1955–56), 169–82; and "El reclutamiento y los viajes de la 'mita' del cerro de Potosí," *Minería hispana e hispano-americana* (Leon, Spain: Catedra de San Isidoro, 1970), 1:467–81; Jeffrey A. Cole, *The Potosí Mita, 1573–1700: Compulsory Indian Labor in the Andes* (Stanford: Stanford University Press, 1985); "An Abolitionism Born of Frustration: The Conde de Lemos and the Potosí Mita, 1667–73," *HAHR* 63:2 (1983), 307–33; "Viceregal Persistence Versus Indian Mobility: The Impact of the Duque de la Palata's Reform Program on Alto Perú, 1681–1692," *Latin American Research Review* 19:1 (1984), 37–56; Ramon Ezquerra Abadia, "Problemas de la mita de Potosí en el siglo XVIII," *Minería hispana e hispano-americana*, 1:483–511.

3. Particulary important works in the dependency debate are: Andre Gunder Frank, *Capitalism and Underdevelopment in Latin America* (New York: Monthly Review Press, 1967); Immanuel Wallerstein, *The Modern World-System: Capitalist Agriculture and the Origins of the European World-Economy in the Sixteenth Century* (New York: Academic Press, 1974); *The Modern World-System II: Mercantilism and the Consolidation of the European World-Economy, 1600–1750* (New York: Academic Press, 1980); Fernando Henrique Cardoso and Enzo Faletto, *Dependency and Development in Latin America* (Berkeley: University of California Press, 1979); Ernesto Laclau, "Feudalism and Capitalism in Latin America," *New Left Review* 67 (May–June 1971), 1938. For a review, see Steve J. Stern, "Feudalism, Capitalism, and the World-System in the Perspective of Latin America and the Caribbean," *American Historical Review* 93 (1988), 829–72.

4. Modes of production were generally understood as referring to the core or esssential nature of an economic system: the material forces of production (technology, division of labor) and relations of production (how labor is organized, how profit is extracted). Examples of modes of production are feudalism and capitalism, but some Latin American scholars proposed new modes, which did not exist in Europe, that they believed better defined the situation in the New World. Others argued that instead of having one mode that defined a society, it was possible to locate two or more modes, joined in relations of dominance and subordination, in the colonial setting. See Aidan Foster-Carter, "The Modes of Production Controversy," *New Left Review* 107 (1978), 47–78; Ciro F. S. Cardoso, "Sobre los modos de producción coloniales de América," in Carlos Sempat Assadourian, *Modos de producción en América Latina* (Mexico City: Cuadernos de Pasado y Presente 1979); Enrique Semo, *Historia del capitalismo en México: los origenes, 1521–1763* (Mexico City: Ediciones Era, 1973).

5. This is the position of Florencia Mallon in *The Defense of Community in Peru's Central Highlands: Peasant Struggle and Capitalist Transition, 1860–1940* (Princeton: Princeton University Press, 1983). Brooke Larson also argues that, while there was significant social differentiation, capitalism did not emerge in the region during the eighteenth or early nineteenth centuries (*Colonialism and Agrarian Transformation in Bolivia: Cochabamba, 1550–1900* [Princeton: Princeton University Press, 1988]).

6. On the seventeenth-century migrations, see Nicolás Sánchez-Albornoz, *Indios y tributos en el Alto Perú* (Lima: Instituto de Estudios Peruanos, 1978); "Migraciones internas en el Alto Perú. El saldo acumulado en 1645," *Historia boliviana* 2:2 (1982), 11–19; "Migración urbana y trabajo: los indios de Arequipa, 1571–1645," *De historia e historiadores. Homenaje*

a José Luis Romero (Mexico City: Siglo XXI, 1982), 259–81; "Migración rural en los andes: Sipesipe (Cochabamba), 1645," *Revista de Historia Económica* 1:1 (1983), 13–36; "Mita, migraciones y pueblos: variaciones en el espacio y en el tiempo. Alto Perú, 1573–1692, *Historia boliviana* 3:1 (1983), 31–59; Ann M. Wightman, *Indigenous Migration and Social Change: The Forasteros of Cuzco, 1570–1720* (Durham: Duke University Press, 1990); Karen M. Powers, "Indian Migration and Sociopolitico Change in the Audiencia of Quito, 1534–1700," Ph.D. diss., New York University, 1990.

7. Peter Bakewell, *Miners of the Red Mountain: Indian Labor in Potosí, 1545–1650* (Albuquerque: University of New Mexico Press, 1984), 181. See also Carlos Sempat Assadourian, *El sistema de la economía colonial: mercado interno, regiones y espacio económico* (Lima: Instituto de Estudios Peruanos, 1982), 314, 318.

8. June Nash, *We Eat the Mines and the Mines Eat Us: Dependency and Exploitation in Bolivian Tin Mines* (New York: Columbia University Press, 1979), esp. chaps. 5 and 9.

9. Thierry Saignes, "Políticas étnicas en Bolivia colonial, siglos XVI–XIX," *Historia boliviana* 3:1 (1983), 130; "Valles y punas en el debate colonial: la pugna sobre los pobladores de Larecaja," *Histórica* 3, no. 2 (Dec. 1979), 141–64; "De la filiation à la residence: les ethnies dans les vallées de Larcaja," *Annales* 33:56 (1978), 1160–81. Also see Sánchez-Albornoz, "Migración rural."

10. Felipe de Godoy, "Relación de asiento, minas y población de San Felipe de Austria, llamados de Oruro" [1607], *Boletín de la Oficina Nacional de Estadísticas* (La Paz, 1912), 7:438, 455.

11. Noble David Cook, *Demographic Collapse: Indian Peru, 1520–1620* (Cambridge: Cambridge University Press, 1981), 151.

12. Nicolás Sánchez-Albornoz, *La población de América latina desde los tiempos precolombinos al año 2000*, 2d ed. (Madrid: Alianza Editorial, 1977), 119.

13. Godoy, "Relación," 451, 453. In that year Oruro also had 127 Spanish vagabonds in its population.

14. Thierry Saignes, "Valles y punas en el debate colonial," 141; Waldemar Espinosa Soriano, "El reino Aymara de Quillaca-Asanaque, siglos XV–XVI," *Revista del Museo Nacional* 45 (Lima), 202.

Chapter 1. Societies in Transition

1. Reinterpreting cooperative or communal values to include even apparently opposite meanings is what Raymond Williams calls the incorpora-

tion of *residual* culture traits into the dominant culture: "effectively formed by the past but still active in the cultural process." Since the dominant culture may find it risky to allow these residual traits to exist as alternatives outside of official ideology, they are frequently reinterpreted, diluted, and incorporated into the cultural tradition in new ways (Williams, *Marxism and Literature*, 122–23). On reciprocity, see Steve J. Stern, "The Rise and Fall of Indian-White Alliances: A Regional View of Conquest History," *Hispanic American Historical Review* 61:3 (August 1981), 461–91; Tristan Platt, *Estado boliviano y ayllu andino: tierra y tributo en el norte de Potosí* (Lima: Instituto de Estudios Peruanos, 1982); and Erick Langer, "Labor Strikes and Reciprocity on Chuquisaca Haciendas," *Hispanic American Historical Review* 65 (1985), 255–78.

2. John V. Murra, *Formaciones económicas y políticas del mundo andino* (Lima: Instituto de Estudios Peruanos, 1975), 194; Therese Bouysse-Cassagne, "L'espace Aymara: Urco et Uma," *Annales* 33 (1978), 1058–59.

3. Murra, *Formaciones*, 59–115; Norio Yamamoto, "The Ecological Complementarity of Agro-Pastoralism: Some Comments." In *Andean Ecology and Civilization: An Interdisciplinary Perspective on Andean Ecological Complementarity*, ed. Shozo Masuda, Izumi Shimada, and Craig Morris (Tokyo: University of Tokyo Press, 1985), 95; Elias Mujica, "*Altiplano*-Coast Relationships in the South-Central Andes: From Indirect to Direct Complementarity." In *Andean Ecology*, ed. Shimada et al., 125–30. Mujica postulates the development of coastal agricultural colonies by people from the Lake Titicaca region between 500 and 1200 A.D. during the Tiwanaku period.

4. On the term *ayllu*, see Roger Rasnake, *Domination and Cultural Resistance: Authority and Power among an Andean People* (Durham, N.C.: Duke University Press, 1988), 49–51.

5. See Amalia Castelli, Marcia Koth de Paredes and Mariana Mould de Pease, *Etnohistoria y antropología andina* (Lima: Museo Nacional de Historia, 1981), particularly Gabriel Martínez, "Espacio Lupaqa: algunas hipotesis de trabajo," 264–80; Franklin Pease G. Y., "Ayllu y parcialidad: reflexiones sobre el caso de Collaguas," 19–33; María Rostworowski de Diez Canseco, "La voz parcialidad en su contexto en los siglos XVI y XVII," 35–45; Waldemar Espinosa S., "El fundamento territorial del ayllu serrano. Siglos XV y XVI," 93–130. See also Karen Spalding, *Huarochirí: An Andean Society Under Inca and Spanish Rule* (Stanford: Stanford University Press, 1984), 28–34.

6. Waldemar Espinoza Soriano, "El reino Aymara de Quillaca-Asanaque, siglos XV–XVI," *Revista del Museo Nacional* 45:193–94, 202.

7. Luis Capoche, *Relación general de la villa imperial de Potosí* [1585], *Biblioteca de Autores Españoles* (Madrid: Ediciones Atlas, 1959), 122:140.

8. Garci Diez de San Miguel, *Visita hecha a la provincia de Chucuito . . . en el año 1567* (Lima: Ediciones de la Casa de la Cultura del Perú, 1964), 37.

9. Bouysse-Cassagne, "L'espace aymara," 1061–65, 1067–68.

10. María Rostworowski suggests that for groups based on the coast survival was easier than for highland people since they could produce most of the staples of their diet within one ecosystem and thus more readily produce an economic surplus which could be used to support full-time artisans and other specialists. This specialization was more conducive to commercial exchange than organizing the economy around vertical ecological niches. María Rostworowski de Diez Canseco, *Étnia y sociedad: Costa peruana prehispánica* (Lima: Instituto de Estudios Peruanos, 1977), 211–71. See also Frank L. Salomon, "*Pochteca* and *mindala*: A Comparison of Long-Distance Traders in Ecuador and Mesoamerica," *Journal of the Steward Anthropological Society* 9 (1978), 231–46; Terence N. D'Altroy and Timothy K. Earle, "Staple Finance, Wealth Finance, and Storage in the Inka Political Economy," *Current Anthropology* 26:2 (1985), 194–97.

11. John V. Murra has done the most extensive research on the use of ecological niches and the absence of markets among the Aymara; see articles on this subject in *Formaciones*, including: "El control vertical de un máximo de pisos ecológicos en la economía de las sociedades andinas," 59–115, and "Un reino aymara en 1567," 193–223.

12. Murra, "Un reino aymara en 1567," in *Formaciones*, 220–21.

13. Much has been written on the ideal and the reality of reciprocal relations in the Andes. See Murra, "Un reino aymara en 1567," in *Formaciones*, esp. 211–21; Spalding, *Huarochirí*, esp. 25–32; Steve J. Stern, *Peru's Indian Peoples and the Challenge of Spanish Conquest* (Madison: University of Wisconsin Press, 1982), 8–11; Nathan Wachtel, *The Vision of the Vanquished* (Hassocks, Sussex: Harvester, 1977), 67–70.

14. Murra, "El control vertical," in *Formaciones*, 64, 68.

15. Murra, "Un reino aymara in 1567," in *Formaciones*, 213.

16. Spalding, *Huarochirí*, 38–39.

17. On reciprocity and conflict and on language expressing conflicting meanings, see ibid., 56–61.

18. John V. Murra, "The Limits and Limitations of the 'Vertical Archipelago' in the Andes," in *Andean Ecology*, ed. Masuda et al., 15.

19. Murra, "Un reino aymara en 1567," in *Formaciones*, 217.

20. Ibid., 212–13, and table II, between these pages.

21. John V. Murra, "Nueva información sobre las poblaciones *yana*," in *Formaciones*, 225–42, 227, 231–33, 236, 239–40.

22. John H. Rowe, "Absolute Chronology in the Andean Area," *American Antiquity* 10:3 (1945), 269, 277–79; Alfred Metraux, *The History of the Incas* (New York: Schocken Books, 1970), 47–48.

23. Craig Morris, "From Principles of Ecological Complementarity to the Organization and Administration of Tawantinsuyu," in *Andean Ecology*, ed. Masuda et al., 478–81.

24. Irene Silverblatt, *Moon, Sun and Witches: Gender Ideologies and Class in Inca and Colonial Peru* (Princeton: Princeton University Press, 1987), 41–44. Silverblatt reproduces a diagram drawn by an Andean chronicler, Pachacuti Yamqui, to demonstrate the Incas' structuring of the universe.

25. Irene Silverblatt, "Imperial Dilemmas, the Politics of Kinship, and Inca Reconstruction of History, *Comparative Studies in Society and History*, 1988, 86.

26. Nathan Wachtel, *The Vision of the Vanquished*, 65–66.

27. Espinoza Soriano, "El reino Aymara," 204.

28. Ibid., 197, 200.

29. Ibid., 204.

30. Nathan Wachtel, "The *Mitimas* of the Cochabamba Valley: The Colonization Policy of Huayna Capac," in *The Inca and Aztec States, 1400-1800*, ed. George A. Collier, Renato I. Rosaldo and John D. Wirth (New York: Academic Press, 1982), 202–03 and *passim*.

31. Silverblatt, *Sun, Moon, and Witches*, 5, 21.

32. Ibid., 9–14.

33. For a review of Marxist and non-Marxist explanations of the position of women in state societies, see Irene Silverblatt, "Women in States," *Annual Review of Anthropology* 17 (1988), 427–60.

34. Silverblatt, *Sun, Moon and Witches*, 45.

35. Ibid., chap. 3, esp. 60–66.

36. John V. Murra, "The Economic Organization of the Inca State," Ph.D. diss., University of Chicago, 1956, 228.

37. Silverblatt, *Moon, Sun and Witches*, 89–90.

38. Ibid., 91.

39. Thierry Saignes, *Los andes orientales: Historia de un olvido* (Cochabamba: CERES, 1985), 109, 113, 142.

40. Henry Kamen, *Inquisition and Society in Spain in the Sixteenth and Seventeenth Centuries* (Bloomington: Indiana University Press, 1985). Jaime Vicens Vives, *An Economic History of Spain* (Princeton: Princeton University Press, 1969), 292.

41. Ibid., 210–11.

42. Integration was not limited to any particular social class. Nobles in southern Spain married into merchant families of *converso*, or New Christian, origin. Jews were not only important to the economic and cultural life of Castile and Aragon but even valued confidants of the Catholic monarchs. Both conversos and converted Moslems, or *moriscos*, worked as artisans in contact and competition with old Christians. See Ruth Pike, *Aristocrats and Traders: Sevillian Society in the Sixteenth Century* (Ithaca: Cornell University Press, 1972), 21–22, 141–43, 150; Kamen, *Inquisition and Society*, 1-5; Joseph F. O'Callaghan, *A History of Medieval Spain* (Ithaca and London: Cornell University Press, 1975), 282–330; J. H. Elliott, *Imperial Spain, 1469–1716* (New York: New American Library, 1977), 103–04, 120; Vicens Vives, *An Economic History*, 298–99, 334–35.

43. According to Vicens Vives's estimates, there were perhaps 250,000 conversos in Spain in 1480. Of these perhaps 2,000 were burned at the stake, another 20,000 returned to Catholicism with renewed zeal and the rest emigrated, severly affecting the mercantile cities of Catalonia, Valencia and Sevilla (*An Economic History*, 292).

44. Ibid., 335.

45. Richard Konetzke, "Entrepreneurial Activities of Spanish and Portuguese Noblemen in Medieval Times," *Explorations in Entrepreneurial History* 6 (1953), 115–20; William D. Phillips, Jr., and Carla Rahn Phillips, "Spain in the Fifteenth Century," in *Transatlantic Encounters: Europeans and Andeans in the Sixteenth Century*, ed. Kenneth J. Andrien and Rolena Adorno (Berkeley: University of California Press, 1991), 18; David E. Vassberg, *Land and Society in Golden Age Castile* (Cambridge: Cambridge University Press, 1984), 91–93; Elliott, *Imperial Spain*, 112; Pike, *Aristocrats and Traders*, 21–26, 31–34.

46. Vassberg, *Land and Society*, 90–91, 100–03; Elliott, *Imperial Spain*, 115, 111, 109.

47. Vassberg, *Land and Society*, 79–83; Vicens Vives, *An Economic History*, 302–03.

48. Elliott, *Imperial Spain*, 116.

49. O'Callaghan, *A History of Medieval Spain*, 618; Henry Kamen, *Spain 1469–1714: A Society of Conflict* (London: Longman, 1991), 48–51; Vicens Vives, *An Economic History*, 306, 350–52.

50. Vicens Vives, *An Economic History*, 113.

51. One of the earliest formulations of liberalism is John Locke, *Treatise on Government* (1689). Also see John Stuart Mill, *On Representative Government* (1862).

52. José Antonio Maravall, *Estado moderno y mentalidad social* (Madrid: Ediciones de la *Revista de Oriente*, 1972), 2:369, 354.

53. Ibid., 2:371.
54. Ibid., 2:354, 356.
55. Nicolás Sánchez-Albornoz, "El trabajo indígena en los andes: teorías del siglo XVI," in *Historia económica y pensamiento social. Estudios en homenaje a Diego Mateo del Peral* (Madrid: Alianza Editorial, 1983), 24.
56. Vicens Vives, *An Economic History of Spain*, 306.
57. Sancho de Moncada, *Restauración política de España*, discurso I, folios 3–4 (1618), cited in Maravall, *Estado moderno*, 2: 377. On Sancho de Moncada, see Marjorie Grice-Hutchinson, *Early Economic Thought in Spain, 1177–1740* (London: George Allen and Unwin, 1978), 122, 139, 140–42.
58. Sánchez-Albornoz, "El trabajo indígena," 22–23.
59. Ibid., 22.
60. Maravall, *Estado moderno*, 363.
61. Ibid., 361. Elsewhere in Europe in approximately the same period merchants were circumventing the guilds, which often deliberately limited supply to keep prices up, by commissioning craft production by farm families. Without the protection of the guilds, these families were more likely to accept merchants' offers to supplement what they produced on the land. See Peter Kriedte, *Peasants, Landlords and Merchant Capitalists: Europe and the World Economy, 1500–1800* (Cambridge: Cambridge University Press, 1983), 10–12.
62. Maravall, *Estado moderno*, 358.
63. Vicens Vives, *An Economic History of Spain*, 334.
64. Ibid.
65. Vassberg, *Land and Society*, 103–04, 147–50; Maravall, *Estado moderno*, 364–66.
66. Inflation caused by the influx of silver from the Indies priced Spanish textiles out of both foreign and domestic markets. As more foreign cloth was imported, the lower quality of Castilian textiles was also starkly revealed. See Vicens Vives, *An Economic History of Spain*, 339, 354. Spanish industries also suffered from the development of manufacturing in the American colonies, an eventuality the mercantile system was supposed to prevent but actually ended up encouraging. See chap. 2.
67. Mary Elizabeth Perry, *Gender and Disorder in Early Modern Seville* (Princeton: Princeton University Press, 1990).
68. Valerie Wayne, "Some Sad Sentence: Vives' *Instruction of a Christian Woman*," in *Silent But for the Word: Tudor Women as Patrons, Translators, and Writers of Religious Works*, ed. Margaret Patterson Hannay (Kent, Ohio: Kent State University Press, 1985), 20.

69. Foster Watson, ed. *Vives and the Renascence Education of Women* (New York: Longmans, Green; London: Edward Arnold, 1912), 12–13.
70. Watson, *Vives*, 8.
71. Wayne, "Some Sad Sentence," 258, n1.
72. Ibid., 19; Perry, *Gender and Disorder*, 53.
73. Wayne, "Some Sad Sentence," 17.
74. Gloria Kaufman, "Juan Luis Vives on the Education of Women," *Signs* 3:4 (Summer 1978), 895.
75. Ibid.
76. Kaufman, "Juan Luis Vives," 893.
77. Wayne, "Some Sad Sentence," 21.
78. Perry, *Gender and Disorder*, 49.
79. For instance, Valentina Pinelo, an Augustinian nun, published a critical interpretation of the life of Saint Anne, and María de Zayas y Sotomayor wrote two books, one of which included a spirited defense of women's right to independence and education. Perry, *Gender and Disorder*, 73–74, 91–92.
80. Silvia Marina Arrom, *The Women of Mexico City, 1790–1857* (Stanford: Stanford University Press, 1985), 56–58.
81. Arrom, *The Women of Mexico City*, 58–59.
82. Roland H. Bainton, *Women of the Reformation: From Spain to Scandinavia* (Minneapolis: Augsburg Publishing House, 1977), 18–19; Perry, *Gender and Disorder*, 112.
83. Bainton, *Women of the Reformation*," 35–37.
84. Perry, *Gender and Disorder*, 98, 110–16.
85. Maravall, *Estado moderno*, 385; Grice-Hutchinson, *Early Economic Thought in Spain*, 102, 144.
86. See Perry, *Gender and Disorder*, chap. 1.
87. Ibid., 123–26.
88. Ibid., 14–17; Pike, *Aristocrats and Traders*, 33.

Chapter 2. Colonial Economy and the Organization of Labor

1. Elliott, *Imperial Spain*, 66–69.
2. Silvio Zavala, *La encomienda indiana*, 2d rev. ed. (Mexico City: Editorial Porrua, 1973), 15.
3. Lesley Byrd Simpson, *The Encomienda in New Spain: The Beginning of Spanish Mexico* (Berkeley and Los Angeles: University of California Press, 1950), chap. 2.
4. Elliott, *Imperial Spain*, 68.

5. Zavala, *La encomienda indiana*, 20–23; Simpson, *The Encomienda in New Spain*, chap. 3.

6. According to Nicolás Sánchez-Albornoz: "Even accepting conservative estimates, the pre-Columbian population of Hispaniola must have fallen from about one hundred thousand to only a few hundred in 1570." *The Population of Latin America: A History* (Berkeley and Los Angeles: University of California Press, 1974), 41–42.

7. Spalding, *Huarochirí*, 127–28; Steve J. Stern, *Peru's Indian Peoples*, 31–35; and "The Rise and Fall of Indian-White Alliances."

8. Encomiendas in the viceroyalty of Peru were at first totally unregulated as to how much and what types of tribute encomenderos could extract from their Indians. On July 19, 1536, a royal decree stipulated that the Peruvian governor, Francisco Pizarro, and Vicente de Valverde, bishop of Cuzco, should determine and enforce just tribute rates because the Indians were being overtaxed by encomenderos. Silvio Zavala, *El servicio personal de los indios en el Peru* 1 (Mexico City: El Colegio de Mexico, 1978–1980), 4.

9. Espinoza Soriano, "El reino Aymara de Quillaca-Asanaque," 107; Alberto Crespo Rodas, "La fundación de la Villa de San Felipe de Austria y asiento de minas de Oruro," *Documentos orureños* (Oruro: Editorial de la Universidad Boliviana Técnica de Oruro, 1976–1977), 2:22.

10. Espinoza Soriano, "El reino Aymara de Quillaca-Asanaque," 207.

11. Crespo Rodas, "La fundación," 22.

12. Espinoza Soriano, "El reino Aymara de Quillaca-Asanaque," 213; Crespo-Rodas, "La fundación," 2:23.

13. Thierry Saignes, "Valles y punas en el debate colonial," 141. On the Indians from Porco: AGN, XII, 18-5-1.

14. AGN, IX, 10-3-7, "Representaciones y quejas de las provincias, 1689–91," f. 123.

15. Thierry Saignes, "Une frontière fossile: la cordillère chiriguano au XVIII siècle," 2 vols. Thèse du troisième cycle, Université de Paris, 1974.

16. "Ordena el presidente La Gasca la repatriación de los indios llevados por fuerza a trabajar a Potosí," 29 de julio de 1549, in Silvio Zavala, *El servicio personal* 1:13.

17. Tristan Platt, "Acerca del sistema tributario pre-Toledano en el Alto Perú," *Avances* 1 (1978), 35.

18. Wachtel, *The Vision of the Vanquished*, 175–76; Stern, *Peru's Indian Peoples*, 69–70.

19. Stern, *Peru's Indian Peoples*, 51–71; Wachtel, *The Vision of the Vanquished*, 179–83.

20. Studies of campaigns against idolatry show that they were sometimes a counterattack after charges of abuse were brought against the clergy by the

Indians of their parishes. See Rafael Varón Gabai, "El Taki Onqoy: las raizes andinas de un fenómeno colonial," in *El retorno de las huacas: Estudios y documentos del siglo XVI*, ed. Luis Millones (Lima: Instituto de Estudios Peruanos and Sociedad Peruana de Psicoanálisis, 1990), 388–403; Henrique Urbano, "Cristóbal de Molina, el Cusqueño: Negocios eclesiásticos, mesianismo y Taqui Onqoy," *Revista Andina* 8:1 (1990), 265–83; Antonio Acosta, "La extirpación de las idolatrías en el Perú: Origen y desarrollo de las campañas a propósito de *Cultura andina y represión*, de Pierre Duviols," *Revista Andina* 5:1 (1987), 171–95; Antonio Acosta, "Religiosos, doctrinas y excedente económico indígena en el Perú a comienzos de siglo XVII," *Historica* 4:1 (1982), 1–34.

21. As early as 1535 a report was issued by Tomás de Berlanga, bishop of Tierra Firme, accusing Francisco Pizarro of putting his own interests above those of the crown and of assigning the best repartimientos to individual encomenderos instead of to the crown (Zavala, *El servicio personal* 1:3).

22. Juan de Matienzo, *Gobierno del Perú*, ed. Guillermo Lohmann Villena (Paris-Lima: Institut Français d'Études Andines, 1967), 98–100, 74–77.

23. *Bartolomé de Las Casas: A Selection of His Writings*, trans. and ed. George Sanderlin (New York: Knopf, 1971), 164–65, 193.

24. For instance, "Instrucciones al licenciado Cristóbal Vaca de Castro," Madrid, June 15, 1540, in Zavala, *El servcio personal* 1:5–6.

25. Spalding, *Huarochirí*, 151–52.

26. Zavala, *La encomienda*, 79–84.

27. Josep M. Barnadas, *Charcas, 1535–1565: Orígenes históricos de una sociedad colonial* (La Paz: Centro de Investigación y promoción del Campesinado, 1973), 248.

28. Richard Konetzke, *Colección de documentos para la historia de la formación social de Hispanoamérica, 1493–1810*, vol. 1: *1493–1590* (Madrid: Consejo Superior de Investigaciones Científicas, 1953), 252–55.

29. Cole, *The Potosí Mita*, 5–8.

30. Peter J. Bakewell, "Technological Change in Potosí: The Silver Boom of the 1570s," *Jarhbuch fur Geschichte von Staat, Wirtschaft und Gesellschaft Lateinamerikas* 14 (Cologne and Vienna, 1977), 57–58, 75–76.

31. On the reducciones, see Nicolás Sánchez-Albornoz, *La población de América latina*, 2d ed. (Madrid: Alianza Editorial, 1977), 66–67; and Daniel W. Gade and Mario Escobar, "Village Settlement and the Colonial Legacy in Southern Peru," *Geographical Review* 2:4 (1982), 430–49.

32. On the new systems of religious and civil positions established in Indian communities and how they interacted with older ayllu structures, see Karen Spalding, "Los escaladores sociales: patrones cambiantes de movilidad en la sociedad andina bajo el régimen colonial," in *De indio a campesino:*

Cambios en la estructure social del Perú colonial (Lima: Instituto de Estudios Peruanos, 1974), 61–87.

33. Zavala, *El servicio personal* 1:115–223, 2:3–55; Juan A. Villamarin and Judith E. Villamarin, *Indian Labor in Mainland Colonial Spanish America* (Newark: University of Delaware, Latin American Studies Program, 1975), 16–19, 32–37, and case studies.

34. Cole, *The Potosí Mita*; Bakewell, *Miners of the Red Mountain*; Alberto Crespo Rodas, "La 'mita' de Potosí;" Jorge Basadre, "El regimen de la mita."

35. Peter J. Bakewell, "Registered Silver Production in the Potosí District, 1550–1735," *Jahrbuch für Geschichte von Staat, Wirtschaft und Gesellschaft Lateinamerikas* 12 (Cologne and Vienna, 1975), 67–103.

36. "Descripción de la villa y minas de Potosí. Año de 1603," in *Relaciones geográficas de Indias*, ed. Marcos Jiménez de la Espada, 1:382.

37. Carlos Sempat Assadourian, *El sistema de la economía colonial: mercado interno, regiones y espacio económico* (Lima: Instituto de Estudios Peruanos, 1982); Peter J. Bakewell, *Silver and Entrepreneurship in Seventeenth-Century Potosí: The Life and Times of Antonio López de Quiroga* (Albuquerque: University of New Mexico Press, 1988).

38. For instance, Charles V encouraged the development of the silk industry in New Spain while ordering the destruction of olive groves in Peru (Elliott, *Imperial Spain*, 196). A similar inconsistency was evident in the orders issued for textile factories in the viceroyalty of Peru. Maximiliano Moscoso, "Apuntes para la historia de la industria textil en el Cuzco colonial," *Revista Universitaria* (Cuzco, 1962–63), 68.

39. L. A. Clayton, "Trade and Navigation in the Seventeenth-Century Viceroyalty of Peru," *Journal of Latin American Studies* 7:1 (May 1975), 3.

40. Ibid., 5–10.

41. On the commercialization of agriculture in Cochabamba in the late sixteenth and early seventeenth centuries, see Brooke Larson, *Colonialism and Agrarian Transformation*, esp. chap. 2.

42. "Descripción de la villa y minas de Potosí," 380; Antonio Vazquez de Espinosa, *Compendio y descripción de las Indias Occidentales* [1629], *Biblioteca de Autores Españoles* (Madrid: Ediciones Atlas, 1969), 231:410.

43. "Descripción de la villa y minas de Potosí," 382.

44. Assadourian, *El sistema*, 165–66.

45. Pedro Cieza de Leon, *La crónica del Perú*, ed. Manuel Ballesteros (Madrid: Historia 16, 1984), 346–47; John Murra, "Notes on Pre-Columbian Cultivation of Coca Leaf," *Coca and Cocaine: Effects on People*

and Policy in Latin America (Cambridge, Mass.: Cultural Survival, Inc.; Latin American Studies Program, Cornell University, 1986), 49–52.

46. Cieza de Leon, *La crónica del Perú*, 347; "Descripción y relación de la ciudad de La Paz," Marcos Jiménez de la Espada, *Relaciones geográficas de Indias: Peru* 1:343.

47. Assadourian, *El sistema*, 156.

48. Bakewell, *Silver and Entrepreneurship*, 142.

49. Peter J. Bakewell, *Antonio López de Quiroga (industrial minero de Potosí colonial)* (Potosí: Universidad boliviana "Tomás Frias," Division de Extensión Universitaria, 1973), 14.

50. Jorge A. Flores Ochoa, "Pastores de alpacas de los Andes," in *Pastores de puna*, ed. Flores Ochoa (Lima: Instituto de Estudios Peruanos, 1977), 23–26.

51. Ibid., 184; Assadourian, *El sistema*, 44.

52. In the Andean version, the kurakas or other leaders provided the fibers for women to spin and weave. Now the encomendero or representative of the state had the community supply its own primary materials to make the tribute items (Assadourian, *El sistema*, 192).

53. Mary Money, *Los obrajes, el traje y el comercio de ropa en la Audiencia de Charcas* (La Paz: Instituto de Estudios Bolivianos, 1983), 18:3, 5.

54. Fernando Silva Santisteban, *Los obrajes en el virreinato del Perú* (Lima: Publicaciones de Museo Nacional de Historia, 1964), 15.

55. Ibid., 20.

56. Many obrajes in the southern Andean region were destroyed during the rebellions of the 1780s. Also in the eighteenth century, with more trade legally permitted with Europe, particularly with England, inexpensive imported textiles began to have a negative effect on South American production. Silva Santisteban, *Los obrajes*; Teresa Gisbert, Silvia Arze, and Martha Cajias, *Arte textil y mundo andino* (La Paz: Gisbert y Cia., 1987), 282.

57. The results of the census conducted under Toledo's orders and the tributes assessed are available in Noble David Cook, ed., *Tasa de la visita general de Francisco de Toledo* (Lima: Universidad Nacional de San Marcos, 1975).

58. AGI, Charcas, 54, "D. Raphael Ortiz de Sotomayor sobre la mita de Cerro de Potosí," Potosí, 1620. In "Acerca del sistema tributario pretoledano," Tristan Platt shows that even before tribute was actually collected in money, the amount of food or goods communities had to supply was pegged to their market value.

59. In 1606 the *oidores* of the Audiencia of Charcas wrote to the king explaining that because workers who finished their shifts had sold their ani-

mals and clothes, they did not have the resources to go home and either went elsewhere to work or stayed on in Potosí (AGI, Charcas, 18, Audiencia of Charcas to King, March 1, 1606).

60. Antonio de Ayans, "Breve relación de los agravios que reciben los indios que hay desde cerca del Cuzco hasta Potosí," [1596]. In *Pareceres jurídicos en asuntos de indios*, ed. Rubén Vargas Ugarte (Lima, 1951), 39–40.

61. "Some go with their wives and children to very remote places, two hundred and three hundred leagues away from [Potosí] where they work for the owners of chacras and ranches . . . because for a small payment they are free . . . and exempt from the mita" (AGI, EC, 868A, "Don Gabriel Fernández Guarache . . . sobre puntos tocantes a la mita y remedios contra los agravios que padecían los dhos caciques").

62. AGI, Charcas, 54, "Don Raphael Ortiz de Sotomayor sobre la mita de Potosí."

63. AGI, Charcas, 270, "El virrey del Perú, conde de la Monclova, remite testimonio . . . sobre entero de la mita," f. 8v. Monclova refers specifically to the impact of the Viceroy Marques of Mancera's (1639–1648) policy of selling crown lands.

64. Ann Wightman, "'. . . residente en esa ciudad . . .': Urban Migrants in Colonial Cuzco," in *Migration in Colonial Spanish America*, ed. David J. Robinson (Cambridge: Cambridge University Press, 1990), 91–101; Elinor C. Burkett, "Indian Women and White Society: The Case of Sixteenth-Century Peru," in *Latin American Women: Historical Perspectives*, ed. Asunción Lavrin (Westport: Greenwood Press, 1978), 111.

65. Sánchez-Albornoz, "El trabajo indígena," 39.

66. The decree of 1601 is published in Miguel de Agia, *Servidumbres personales de indios* [1603], (Seville: Escuela de Estudios Hispanoamericanos, 1946), xxi–lii.

67. Miguel de Agia, *Servidumbres*, 57 and *passim*; Mario Góngora, *Studies in the Colonial History of Spanish America* (Cambridge: Cambridge University Press, 1975), 147–48.

68. Juan Matienzo, about 1570, quoted by Alberto Crespo Rodas in "La mita de Potosí," 70–71.

69. Sánchez-Albornoz, "El trabajo indígena," 42.

70. Personal servitude was again prohibited in a royal decree of 1633, but this had to be followed by others to the same effect (ibid.). In 1670 Viceroy de Lemos proposed, to no avail, that the mita be discontinued (Cole, "An Abolitionism Born of Frustration").

71. Scholars who maintain that there was a drop in production and a general economic decline include Woodrow Borah, *New Spain's Century of*

Depression (Berkeley: University of Califronia Press, 1951); Francois Chevalier, *Land and Society in Colonial Mexico* (Berkeley and Los Angeles: University of California Press, 1963); J. I. Israel, "Mexico y la 'crisis general' del siglo XVII,' in *Ensayos sobre el desarollo económico de México y América latina, 1500–1975*, ed. Enrique Florescano (Mexico City: Fondo de Cultura Económica, 1979), 128–53. Those who hold that instead of a depression New Spain experienced an economic reordering and increased internal self-sufficiency in the 1600s, include Bakewell, *Silver Mining and Society in Colonial Mexico: Zacatecas, 1546–1700*; John Lynch, *Spain Under the Hapsburgs*, vol. 2 (New York: Oxford University Press, 1969); Richard Boyer, "Mexico in the Seventeenth Century: Transition of a Colonial Society," *HAHR* 57:3 (1977), 455–78. Basically in agreement but taking a more cautious approach based on royal treasury records are: John TePaske and Herbert Klein, "The Seventeenth Century Crisis in New Spain: Myth or Reality?" *Past and Present* 90 (1981), 116–35.

72. TePaske and Klein, "The Seventeenth Century Crisis," 120–23; D. A. Brading and Harry E. Cross, "Colonial Silver Mining: Mexico and Peru," *HAHR* 52:4 (1972), 573–76. Several scholars have argued that, as in the Mexican case, it was not that less silver was produced in the viceroyalty of Peru but that less arrived in Spain. See: Clayton, "Trade and Navigation;" Lynch, *Spain Under the Hapsburgs*, vol 2.

73. Brading and Cross, "Colonial Silver Mining," 573–76; Assadourian, *El Sistema*, 121–22; Bakewell, "Registered Silver Production," 89.

74. ANB, Minas, t. 86, no. 18, 1656, "Visita que el contador Juan de Garagalza, alcalde mayor de minas de Oruro, tomó del socavón nombrado Escobar"; ANB, Minas, t. 87, no. 1, 1672–1673, "El bachiller Francisco Gaitán de Encinas, cura de la doctrina de las Sepulturas, sobre que se modere la cuarta decimal asignada a dicha doctrina en consideración al descaecimiento que experimenta toda esa ribera por el paro de los ingenios que alli habia; AGI, Charcas, 32, Cabildo of Oruro to Viceroy, Oct. 26, 1656; AGI, Charcas, 37, Royal Treasurer of Oruro to King, March 2, 1639.

75. Henry Kamen, "The Decline of Spain: A Historical Myth?" *Past and Present* 81 (Nov. 1978), 24–50. J. I. Israel's response is in *Past and Present* 91 (May 1981), 170–80, followed by a rejoinder by Kamen on pp. 181–85. Also see: J. H. Elliott, "The Decline of Spain," in *Crisis in Europe, 1560–1660*, ed. Trevor Aston (New York: Basic Books, 1965), 167–93.

76. Martínez de Mata, *Octavo discurso*, cited in Kamen, "The Decline of Spain," 30.

77. Elliott, *Imperial Spain*, 329–37.

78. Israel, "Debate: The Decline of Spain: A Historical Myth?" 171–72.

79. Elliott, *Imperial Spain*, 190–91; Vicens Vives, *An Economic History of Spain*, 427–31.

80. There has been much debate about the causes of Spanish inflation. See Earl J. Hamilton, *American Treasure and the Price Revolution in Spain, 1501–1650* (Cambridge: Harvard University Press, 1934); see also Elliott, "Crisis in Spain"; and Vicens Vives, *An Economic History of Spain*, 432–55.

81. Andrien, *Crisis and Decline*, 11–12, 17–19, and *passim*.

82. See esp. Larson, *Colonialism and Agrarian Transformation*; Assadourian, *El sistema*. Their arguments are discussed below.

83. Bakewell, *Silver and Entreprenuership*.

84. The figure for Oruro is an estimate based on the results of a census taken in that year (see chap. 5). For Potosí in 1779, see Sánchez-Albornoz, *La población*, 142.

85. Larson, *Colonialism and Agrarian Transformation*.

86. Assadourian, *El sistema*, 126–27; Chevalier, *Land and Society in Colonial Mexico*.

87. Enrique Tandeter and Nathan Wachtel, *Precios y producción agraria: Potosí y Charcas en el siglo XVIII* (Buenos Aires: Centro de Estudios de Estado y Sociedad, n.d.), 32–37, 39, 42. Also see Cieza de Leon, *La crónica del Perú*, 347.

Chapter 3. Indian Population and Migration

1. Padre Pablo José de Arriaga al General de la Compañía de Jesús, May 21, 1590, cited in José Toribio Polo, "Apuntes sobre las epidemias en el Perú," *Revista Histórica* 5 (1913), 102–03.

2. Ayans, "Breve relación," 56.

3. Noble David Cook, *Demographic Collapse: Indian Perú, 1520–1620* (Cambridge: Cambridge University Press, 1981), 247.

4. Henry F. Dobyns, "An Outline of Andean Epidemic History to 1720," *Bulletin of the History of Medicine* 37:6 (1963), 496.

5. Ibid., 499.

6. Polo, "Apuntes sobre las epidemias," 51–54, 56; Dobyns, "An Outline," 497–500.

7. Dobyns, "An Outline," 500.

8. Polo, "Apuntes sobre las epidemias," 58.

9. From a report by Viceroy del Villar, in Dobyns, "An Outline," 505.

10. Polo, "Apuntes," 68; Dobyns, "An Outline," 509.

11. Dobyns, "An Outline," 509–10.

12. Polo, "Apuntes," 73–74.
13. Dobyns, "An Outline," 511–12.
14. Sánchez-Albornoz, *Indios y tributos en el Alto Perú*, 22–23, 34.
15. Gade and Escobar, "Village Settlement," 430.
16. Catherine J. Julien, *Hatunqolla: A View of Inca Rule from the Lake Titicaca Region* (Berkeley and Los Angeles: University of California Press, 1983), 10–11.
17. Saignes, *Los andes orientales*, 111.
18. Gade and Escobar, "Village Settlement," 430.
19. "Relación de la provincia de los Pacajes," in *Relaciones geográficas de Indias: Perú*, ed. Marcos Jiménez de la Espada, 334–35. No date is given for this document, but internal evidence suggests a date from the 1580s.
20. Sánchez-Albornoz, *La población*, 66–68.
21. Gade and Escobar, "Village Settlement," 434.
22. Saignes, *Los andes orientales*, 113.
23. AGI, Charcas, 54, Viceroy Principe de Esquilache to King, April 24, 1620.
24. Thierry Saignes, "De la filiation à la residence," 1174–77; "Políticas étnicas," 13–14.
25. Saignes, *Los andes orientales*, 137–39.
26. Bakewell, *Miners of the Red Mountain*, 65–66, 123, 134, 180–85; Cole, *The Potosí Mita*, 29–30.
27. The same phenomenon in the late colonial period has been discussed by Enrique Tandeter, "La rente comme rapport de production et comme rapport de distribution: le cas de l'industrie minière de Potosí, 1750–1826," Thèse de 3e cycle, Ecole des Hautes Etudes en Sciences Sociales, 1980, 96–167.
28. It is not clear if these were family expenses or only those of the mitayo (Ayans, "Breve relación," 38).
29. BNP, B575, Autos sobre el despacho de la mita de Potosí ... Villa de la Concepción, Oct. 24, 1669; BNP, B585, Despacho de la mita de Potosí ... Puno, Nov. 2, 1673.
30. AGI, EC, 686A, Don Gabriel Fernández Guarache ... sobre puntos tocantes a la mita ..., Potosí, 1663.
31. AGI, Charcas 54, Viceroy Principe de Esquilache to King, April 14, 1620.
32. Ayans, "Breve relación," 56.
33. These phenomena are illustrated in the discussion of Oruro and Pilaya y Paspaya in chaps. 4–7. See also Nicolás Sánchez-Albornoz, "Migraciones internas en el Alto Perú;" Ann Wightman, *Indigenous Migration and*

Social Change; Noble David Cook, "Migration in Colonial Peru: An Overview," in *Migration in Colonial Spanish America*, ed. David Robinson (Cambridge: Cambridge University Press, 1990), 41–61.

34. Sánchez-Albornoz, "Migraciones internas," 13.

35. This is true even if only six provinces are counted in Wachtel's study, i.e., if Paria and Carangas are not counted twice.

36. See Wachtel's review of Sánchez-Albornoz's *Indios y tributos* in *Annales* 5–6 (1978), 1208.

37. Larson, *Colonialism and Agrarian Transformation*, 80.

38. Ibid., 30–32; Wachtel, "Mitimas," 220.

39. Larson, *Colonialism and Agrarian Transformation*, 78–81.

40. AGN, 18-7-4, Representaciones y quejas de Paria. Also see "Información testimonial tomado por el corregidor de Potosí en 1690," in *Indios y tributos*, ed. Sánchez-Albornoz, Apendice 2, 113–49.

41. Saignes, *Los andes orientales*, 178.

42. AGI, Charcas 31, Audiencia of Charcas to King, 1599 (day and month not given), ff. 3–5.

43. Wachtel, *The Vision*, 132.

44. BN 20.065-30, "Noticia del origen de los indios llamados yanaconas del Perú y a continuación el extracto de lo dispuesto en las ordenanzas del Virrey D. Francisco de Toledo y de las leyes de la recopilación de Indias que tratan de los indios yanaconas." Toledo's "Ordenanzas de los yanaconas de Charcas" were issued in La Plata on February 6, 1674; they are published in Roberto Levillier, *Governantes de Perú* (Madrid, 1921–1926) 8:241–56.

45. Saignes, *Los andes orientales*, 177.

46. BN 20.065-30, "Noticia del origen de los indios llamados yanaconas."

47. AGI, Charcas 31, Cabildo of La Plata to King, La Plata, April 1, 1604.

48. Figures for Alfaro visita and quote: AGI, Charcas 54, Viceroy Principe de Esquilache to King, April 24, 1620.

49. Capoche, *Relación general*, 135.

50. N. D. Cook, ed., *Tasa de la visita*, 38–39.

51. AGI, Charcas 54, Don Raphael Ortiz de Sotomayor sobre la mita . . . 1620, f.18v. Also see chap. 5.

52. Sánchez-Albornoz, "Migración rural en los andes," 30; Saignes, *Los andes orientales*, esp. chap. 4. Polo de Ondegardo describes mitimaes as "people from the site," that is, those permanently settled in lowland areas. Llacturunas he said were "outsiders" who often went to the same places as mitimaes but later returned to their highland communities (Juan Polo de Ondegardo, "Relación de los fundamentos acerca del notable daño que

resulta de no guardar los indios sus fueros," cited in Saignes, *Los andes orientales*, 117).

53. Sánchez-Albornoz, "Migración rural en los andes," 33–34. As late as 1683 the summary for the census taken at the orders of Viceroy de la Palata describes some of the forasteros in the valley province of Larecaja as llacturunas (AGI, Charcas 270).

54. This was the case of forasteros living in indigenous communities in Pilaya y Paspaya in 1645 and as late as 1725: AGN, IX, 17-1-4 and XII, 18-5-1. Ann Wightman writes about the existence of an *ayllu forastero* in Yucay in Cuzco. During the seventeenth century, forasteros in Yucay who rented land from regional ayllus were grouped into "an artificially created but self-perpetuating social group" (Wightman, *Indigenous Migration*, 89).

55. See testimony from yanaconas in the 1683 census for Oruro, discussed in chap. 5.

56. Sánchez-Albornoz, "Migraciones internas," 16.

57. For census summary, see Phelipe de Bolívar, "Padrones de los indios naturales, forasteros y anaconas con distinción de provincias tocantes al repartimiento general de mita de Potosí," Lima, Nov. 29, 1646, published in Silvio Zavala, *El servicio personal de los indios en el Perú* 2:109. Table 3.3 is reproduced from Sánchez-Albornoz, "Migraciones internas" and is based on Bolívar's summary.

58. Sánchez-Albornoz, "Migraciones internas," 17.

59. On forasteros in Cochabamba see Larson, *Colonialism and Agrarian Transformation*, chap. 3, esp. 93–96, 100–01, 108–13.

60. AGI, Charcas 270, "Libro y relación sumaria que de orden del exmo. Sr. Duque de la Palata . . . a formado D. Pedro Antonio de Castillo . . . de todo lo obrado . . . en la numeración general de yndios del dho reino, que en virtud de zédulas suyas se hisso en el año de 1682." The census summary undoubtedly underrepresents yanaconas because it omits major cities and yanaconas were not included in some provincial totals.

61. AGI, Charcas 54, "Don Raphael Ortiz de Sotomayor sobre la mita," f. 6v.

Chapter 4. A Colonial Andean Mining Center: Oruro, 1607–1720

1. Felipe de Godoy, "Relación del asiento, minas y población de San Felipe de Austria, llamados de Oruro," *Boletín de la Oficina Nacional de Estadística* (La Paz: 1912), 7:439.

2. Ibid., 450.

3. In economic systems where slaves and free workers perform the same jobs, free workers tend to be poorly paid and their work demeaned.

4. José de Mesa and Teresa Gisbert, "Oruro: origen de una villa minera," *Documentos orureños* (Oruro: Editorial de la Universidad Técnica de Oruro, 1976), 1:70–71.

5. Ibid., 74–78; the cathedral has been replaced by the prefectura.

6. Godoy writes, "Han acudido tantos indios de tan diversas partes que hay más número de seis mil con los que allí en los ingenios donde tienen hechas sus casas y rancherías" (438); and again, "Lo que es la población de indios hay en la dicha villa y en los ingenios de la ribera de ella más número de 6,000 indios que como acostumbra generalmente son casados y con muchos hijos" (455).

7. Mesa and Gisbert, "Oruro: origen," 82–82.

8. Godoy, "Relación." 451.

9. On Oruro's place in the conflict between Lima and Charcas, see Alberto Crespo Rodas, "La fundación de la Villa de San Felipe de Austria y asiento de minas de Oruro," in *Documentos orureños* 1:46–50; and Cole, *The Potosí Mita*, 70.

10. Albert Crespo maintains that Maldonado de Torres actually accused one of the Audiencia's oidores, Manuel Castro y Padilla, who had founded Oruro in 1606, of having alloted the best lands for ingenios to his relatives and of having also guaranteed members of his family seats on the city's cabildo (Crespo, "La fundación," 46).

11. Godoy, "Relación," 440, 442. His recommendations included the provision of mercury and forced labor to miners in the site.

12. "Real cédula que los indios pueden tener y labrar minas de oro y plata como los españoles," Madrid, Dec. 17, 1551, in Konetzke, *Colección de documentos* 1:294.

13. Godoy, "Relación," 451.

14. Ibid., 437.

15. This figure, which compares favorably with Potosí, was also given by other people who visited the mines in 1607 (Godoy, "Relación," 422–423); AGI, Charcas 18, "Testimonio del estado en que estan las minas de la villa de S. Phelipe de Austria," Oruro, April 8, 1607. García de Paredes Ulloa, the corregidor, and Bartolomé Ruvio de Rivera visited the mines in the Cerro de San Cristobal.

16. Godoy, "Relación," 435–36, 450.

17. The first ores mined in Oruro were *pacos*, which were relatively soft and in some cases required only smelting to separate the silver from the lead and copper compounds. When pacos did need to be refined through amal-

gamation with mercury, a relatively small amount of quick silver was sufficient. The ores mined and refined in Potosí were also primarily pacos. However, after the first years most of the minerals in Oruro were those known as *negrillos* because of their dark color. Although high in silver content, negrillos were difficult to refine, requiring substantial amounts of mercury (Carlos F. Stubbe, *Vocabulario minero antiquo. Compilación de terminos antiguos usados por los mineros y metalurgistas de América Ibérica*. Buenos Aires: El Ateneo, 1944).

18. Godoy "Relación," 444–46.
19. Luis Capoche, *Relación general*, 122–24.
20. Godoy, "Relación," 447–48.
21. AGI, Charcas 18, "Testimonio del estado;" Godoy, "Relación," 440.
22. ANB, Minas 86, no. 10, Audiencia de Charcas to Consejo de Indias, La Plata, March 17, 1608; ANB, Minas 86, no. 2, Viceroy Marques de Montesclaros to Audiencia de Charcas, Lima, January 13, 1608; Godoy, "Relación," 457.
23. Godoy, "Relación," 437.
24. Ibid., 438,
25. In some cases, mitayos in Potosí like the free workers in Oruro managed to help themselves to ore to supplement their meager earnings. See Carlos Sempat Assadourian, "La producción de la mercancía dinero en la formación del mercado interno colonial," *Economía* [Lima] 1:2 (1978): 40–41. For the kajchas, or weekend miners, of the late colonial Potosí see Enrique Tandeter, "La producción como actividad popular: 'Ladrones de mina' en Potosí," *Nova Americana* 4 (1981), 43–65.
26. Godoy, "Relación," 435–36.
27. Ibid., 438–39.
28. AGI, Charcas 18, Maldonado de Torres to King, April 8, 1606.
29. Ibid., 450. Enrique Tandeter also remarks that in Potosí in the eighteenth century free workers required much more supervision than mitayos for whom the task system functioned as a foreman ("Trabajo forzado y trabajo libre en el Potosí colonial tardío," *Estudios CEDES* 3:6 (1980): 37).
30. Godoy, "Relación," 452–58.
31. Ibid., 452. Marcello Carmagnai discusses a similar system that developed in the Norte Chico of Chile in the beginning of the eighteenth century, where the practice was also referred to as "la dobla" or "the double" (*El salariado minero* [Santiago: Editorial Universitaria, 1963], 52–54).
32. Godoy, "Relación," 453, 455.
33. AGI, Charcas 18, Alonso Maldonado de Torres to King, April 8, 1606.

34. AGI. Charcas 18, "Testimonio del estado."

35. Brading and Cross, "Colonial Silver Mining," 570.

36. If, as contemporaries estimated, two-thirds of the silver from Potosí may have left Peru illegally and untaxed via Buenos Aires, a similar situation must have existed in Oruro. Tax evasion may have been more common when silver production was in decline, as a means of offsetting dropping incomes (Blakewell, "Registered Silver Production," 80–81). This could explain why tax evasion in Oruro is so often mentioned in the late seventeenth and eighteenth centuries. See ANB, Minas 88, no. 5, "Autos obrados con motivo de haber soltado los mineros y azogueros de Oruro el agua a sus labores y cesado el trabajo en ellas," Oruro, 1720.

37. John J. TePaske and Herbert Klein, *The Royal Treasuries of the Spanish Empire in America*, vol. 2: *Upper Peru (Bolivia)* (Durham, N.C.: Duke University Press, 1982); Peter J. Bakewell, "Registered Silver Production," 67–103.

38. AGI, Charcas 18, Maldonado de Torres to King.

39. ANB, Minas, 87, no. 1, "El bachiller Francisco Gaitán de Encinas, cura de la doctrina de las Sepulturas, jurisdicción de la Villa de Oruro, sobre que se modere la quarta decimal asignada a dicha doctrina en consideración al descaecimiento que experimienta toda esa rivera por el paro de los ingenios que allí habia," Oruro, 1672–1673, f. 84. This document compares the dismal state of the ingenios in the early 1670s with their productivity in 1612.

40. AGI, Charcas 54, Audiencia to King, 1626.

41. AGI, Charcas 54, Antonio de Salinas Ruberto to King, Oct. 26, 1628. No description of the process was included in the document.

42. Ibid.

43. Bakewell, *Silver and Entrepreneurship*, 72–94, 135–39, 165–67.

44. ANB, Minas 86, no. 17, "Información de los servicios prestados por el capitán Jusepe Cuterillo en las labores de minas de la Villa de Oruro, 1630–1638;" AGI, Charcas 37, Gaspar Elosu Echevarria (Judge of the Treasury in Oruro) to crown, March 6, 1631.

45. A. V. Chayanov, "Peasant Farm Organization," in Chayanov, *The Theory of Peasant Economy*, ed. D. Thorner, B. Kerblay, and R.E.F. Smith (Homewood, Ill.: Irwin, 1966), 80, 87, and 70–89, *passim*; Hans Medick, "The proto-industrial family economy: the structural function of household and family during the transition from peasant society to industrial capitalism," *Social History* 3 (1976): 299.

46. ANB, Minas 87, no. 1.

47. Ibid.

48. Court cases from the period indicate that during the depression numerous entrepreneurs went bankrupt and lost their mines and mills. Usually

these debts were to their *aviadores*, or outfitters, for mercury and for cash advances for operating expenses. For instance, Geronimo Rodrígues lost his mines and ingenio to his aviador, Antonio de Alos, for 6,000 pesos he owed for "personal services" and for 4,000 libras of mercury (ANB, Minas 88, no. 9, "Antonio de Alos sobre que d. Geronimo Rodrígues, azoguero y dueño de minas de Oruro le quedó debiendo en razón de servicios personales," 1720). A similar fate befell the heirs of Cristobal Gómez de Montemaior, who lost the ingenios of Polo and Sacasaca for the 18,000 pesos Gómez owed to Fray Luis de la Presentación (ANB, Minas 92, no. 10, "Fray Luis de la Presentación . . . sobre lo que le estan debiendo los ingenios de Polo y Sacasaca, provincia de Paria, 1720").

49. AGN, XIII, 17-1-4.

50. AGI, Charcas 37, Gaspar de Elosu Echevarria, Tesorero Juez Oficial Real de la Villa de S. Felipe de Austria, to King, March 2, 1639.

51. ANB, Minas 88, no. 17, "Don Marcelo Gómez de Castro sobre lo que quedó debiendole d. Miguel de Buruega, difunto, 1731–1738." The accounts included with the testimony are from the year de Buruega died, 1714.

52. In 1663, a Potosí mitayo had to haul twenty to twenty-four sacks out of the mines per day. If he could not do this every day for a week, he was paid for only a half week, or 10 reales, even if he had delivered more than half of the task set. He had to pay 24 reales to the mine owner for not completing his quota, leaving a deficit of 14 reales (AGI, Escribanía de Cámara, 686a, Don Gabriel Fernández Guarache . . . sobre . . . la mita, Potosí, 1663).

53. ANB, Minas 88, no. 17.

54. On the repartimiento de mercancías, see Alfredo Moreno Cebrián, *El corregidor de indios y la economía peruana en el siglo XVIII* (Madrid: Consejo Superior de Investigaciones Científicas, 1977); Jurgen Golte, *Repartos y Rebeliones* (Lima: Instituto de Estudios Peruanos, 1980); Brooke Larson and Robert Wasserstrom, "Coerced Consumption in Colonial Bolivia and Guatemala," *Radical History Review* 27:49–78.

55. Guillermo Cespedes del Castillo, "Lima y Buenos Aires: Repercusiones económicas y políticas de la creación del virreinato de La Plata," *Anuario de estudios americanos* 3 (1946): 667–874; Golte, *Repartos y rebeliones*, esp. 22–24; Larson and Wasserstrom, "Coerced Consumption," esp. 52–54.

56. AGI, Charcas 32, Cabildo of Oruro to Viceroy, October 26, 1656.

57. AGI, Escribanía de Cámara, 857A, Residencia de Alonso de Ortega, corregidor de la provincia de la villa de S. Felipe de Austria por d. Faustino de Solarzano, su succesor, 1658; Escribanía de Cámara, 857B, Residencia de Faustino de Solorzano para d. Juan Nicolás Proloan, su succesor, 1664; Escribanía de Cámara, 858A, Residencia d. Juan Nicolás Proloan, corregidor

de la provincia de S. Felipe de Austria, 1675; Escribanía de Cámara 859A, Residencia d. Alonso del Corral, corregidor del asiento y minas de Oruro, 1680; Escribanía de Cámara 859C, Se tomó residencia d. Luis de Miranda, corregidor del asiento y minas de Oruro, 1685.

58. ANB, Minas 148, E CAN no. 59, "Don Antonio de Elizondo y d. Andres de Ocana, mineros asistentes en el asiento de la Joya, jurisdicción de la villa de Oruro, sobre los excesos cometidos en su perjuicio por d. Francisco de Miranda, teniente de corregidor en dicho asiento," 1722.

59. ANB, Minas 88, no. 5, "Autos obrados con motivo de haber soltado los mineros y azogueros de Oruro el agua a sus labores y cesado el trabajo en ellas," 1720.

60. Ibid.

61. Tandeter, "La rente," 189.

62. Ibid., 194.

63. ANB, Minas 88, no. 5, f. 4.

64. Henry F. Dobyns, "An Outline," 511; Toribio Polo, "Apuntes," 77–78; ANB, Minas 126, no. 13, "D. Juan Bautista Uri-siri, alcalde mayor y capitán enterador de la mita de pueblo de Corquemarca, provincia de Carangas, sobre que se suspenda dicho servicio hasta que cese la peste en Potosí;" AGN, XIII, 18-4-3, "Informes de retasas de Paria, 1725–1725."

65. AGN, XIII, 17-1-4. Retasa de Aciento y Minas de Oruro, 1722. This enumeration found only 482 tributary Indians in Oruro and all of its surrounding ranches and industrial suburbs.

66. ANB, Minas 88, no. 5, f. 4.

67. Ibid., f. 12v.

68. David Brading, *Miners and Merchants in Bourbon Mexico: 1763–1810* (Cambridge: Cambridge University Press, 1971), 148–49; Doris Ladd, *The Making of a Strike: Mexican Silver Workers' Struggles in Real del Monte, 1766–1775* (Lincoln: University of Nebraska Press, 1988), esp. chap. 5.

69. ANB, Minas 88, no. 5, f. 12v.

70. Ibid., fs. 35, 38, 41v.

71. Ibid., 12v.

72. ANB, Minas 86, no. 16, "Información de los servicios del licenciado Diego Ordoñez de Villaquiran en las labores de minas de las villas de Potosí y Oruro, 1623–1630;" ANB, Minas 87, no. 4, "Diego Gómez de Samadal y Salvatierra con Juan Duran sobre la mina nombrada N.S. de la Soledad, Villa de Oruro, 1702–1704."

73. Tandeter, "La rente," 212.

74. ANB, Minas 88, no. 9, "Antonio de Alós sobre que d. Gerónimo Rodríques . . . le quedó debiendo."

Chapter 5. The Indian Labor Force of Oruro in 1683

1. AGN, XIII, 18-4-2, Duque de la Palata to King, letter attached to census instructions, Lima, July 24, 1683.
2. AGN, XIII, 17-1-4, "Padrón de Oruro," 1683.
3. Cole, *The Potosí Mita*, 106, 108–09.
4. Brian Evans, "Census Enumeration in Late Seventeenth-Century Alto Perú: The Numeración General of 1683–1684," in David J. Robinson, ed., *Studies in Spanish American Population History*, Dellplain Latin American Studies, no. 8 (Boulder: Westview Press, 1981), 35; Nicolás Sánchez-Albornoz, "Mita, migraciones y pueblos," 36.
5. Evans, "Census Enumeration," 41.
6. Clara López-Beltrán, "Envejecimiento y migración en una comunidad andina: Livitaca en 1689," *Revista de Historia Económica* 5:2 (1987), 250.
7. Evans, "Census Enumeration," 40.
8. Sánchez-Albornoz, "Mitas, migraciones y pueblos," 36.
9. AGN, XIII, 17-1-4, Padrón de Oruro, 1683.
10. In the 1683 count the majority of forastero and yanacona men over the age of fifty still paid tribute. Using the Numeración de la Palata and parish registers, Brian Evans estimates that the life expectancy for Indians in Upper Peru in this period was twenty-five years. See "Census Enumeration," 42.
11. Magnus Mörner, *Perfil de la sociedad rural del Cuzco a fines de la colonia* (Lima: Universidad del Pacifico, 1978), pp. 7–29.
12. López-Beltrán, "Envejecimiento," 253.
13. Evans, "Census Enumeration," 42.
14. Brian Evans commented on this tendency in his study of the 1683 returns from fifteen villages ("Census Enumeration," p. 40). Sánchez-Albornoz also remarks upon it in the 1646 count for the community of Sipesipe ("Migración rural," p. 20).
15. López-Beltrán, "Envejecimiento," 255–56.
16. AGI, Charcas, 37, Royal Treasurer to King, Oruro, 1637.
17. *Residencías* of corregidores list master craftsmen who do not appear to be Indians. See AGI, Escribanía de Cámara, 857A, Residencía de Alonso de Ortega, corregidor de la provincia de la villa de S. Felipe de Austria, 1658; Escribanía de Cámara, 859C, Se tomó residencía de d. Luis de Miranda, corregidor del Asiento y Minas de Oruro, 1685.
18. Wightman, *Indigenous Migration*, 118–22, and " '... residente en esa ciudad ...': urban migrants in colonial Cuzco," 101–07; Spalding, *Huarochirí*, 275, 280.

19. Thierry Saignes, "Ayllus, mercados y coacción colonial: el reto de las migraciones internas en Charcas (siglo XVII)," in *La Participación indígena en los mercados surandinos: estrategias y reproducción social, siglos XVI a XX*, ed. Olivia Harris, Brooke Larson, and Enrique Tandeter (La Paz: Centro de Estudios de la Realidad Economica y Social, 1987), 135.

20. Rolando Mellafe, "Evolución del salario en el virreinato peruano (esquema y sugerencias)," *Ibero-Americana Pragensia* 1 (1967), 104.

21. AGN, XIII, 17-1-4. Auto de Luis de Miranda, Oruro, September 16, 1683, f. 1v.

22. I wish to thank Daniel Santamaría for providing me with a statistical analysis of this census. The padrón itself is in AGN, XIII, 23-10-2, "Padrón de los indios yanaconas de la Villa de Potosí," 1672.

23. AGI, Escribanía de Cámara, 868A, "Dn. Gabriel Fernández Guarache, cacique principal del pueblo de Jesús de Machaca ... con los diputados del gremio de azogueros de la villa de Potosí, sobre puntos tocantes a la mita," Potosí, 1663.

24. Saignes, "Ayllus, mercados," 134–38.

25. It is often difficult to decide what province a town belonged to during the colonial period: boundaries have changed and early maps are unreliable. I refer to the total census figures for the 1683 numeración de la Palata (AGI, Charcas, 270), which groups towns according to the province to which they were subject. Confusion often arises because people customarily identified themselves by ethnic group, saying, for instance, that they were "Pacajes" or "Carangas," while the towns they came from had been arbitrarily placed in a province with another name by colonial officials.

26. Larson, *Colonialism and Agrarian Transformation*, 77–78, 147.

27. Sánchez-Albornoz, "Mitas, migraciones y pueblos," 41.

28. AGI, Charcas 54, Don Raphael de Sotomayor sobre la mita del cerro de Potosí, 1620.

29. AGN, XIII, 17-1-4.

30. Saignes, "Ayllus, mercados," 138.

31. Escribanía de Cámara, 868a. Gabriel Fernández Guarache claimed that it was particularly widows and single mothers who took their male children to cities and gave them to religious institutions or arranged for them to learn a craft.

32. Saignes, "Ayllus, mercados," 138.

33. AGN, XIII, 17-1-4.

34. Escribanía de Cámara, 868a; AGN, XIII, 18-7-4, Representaciones y quejas de provincias, f. 581v.

35. Nicolás Sánchez-Albornoz, "Migración urbana y trabajo," 279–80.

36. AGN, XIII, 23-10-2, Repartimiento de la mita de Potosí, 1665, Lima, July 25, 1665.

37. Enrique Tandeter reports that in the late colonial period in Potosí some men had what might be called "second-class" exemptions for the mita, for which they paid considerably less than the 119 pesos referred to here. He suggests that something similar may have been the rule in Oruro: that the workers there did not pay the large sums supplied by mitayos who still lived in their home villages (personal communication).

38. Census data from 1786 for Pacajes and Chulumani used by Herbert Klein were organized this way. "*Hacienda* and Free Community in Eighteenth Century Alto Perú: A Demographic Study of the Aymara Population of the Districts of Chulumani and Pacajes in 1786," *Journal of Latin American Studies* 7:2 (1975), 193–220.

39. Wachtel, "Hommes d'eau," 1127–59.

40. Cook, *Tasa de la visita*.

41. AGN, XIII, 18-7-4, "Libro de retasas hechas en virtud de la Numeración General que tiene las provincias y caxas que comprehenden, en la manera siguiente: Pacajes, Ciudad de la Paz, Omasuyos, Caravaya, Larecaja, Paucarcolla, Azangaro." The tax schedule based on la Palata's enumeration, while it lists each community's originarios and forasteros separately, makes no distinction in the amount of tribute they were to pay. La Palata's instructions ordered that land be provided for Indians who had been living outside their reducciones and wanted to return home, but who might find that their lands had been rented by the village's leaders. He did not specify that forasteros who did not go back to their reducciones should be given land.

42. Cook, *Tasa de la visita*, 45.

43. BN, 20.065-30, "Noticia del origen," Item 14, La Plata, February 6, 1574.

44. Cook, *Tasa de la visita*, 38.

45. Ibid., 78; AGN, XIII, 18-7-4, f. 211v.

46. Saignes, "Políticas étnicas," pp. 1–30; "Valles y punas," 141–64; "De la filiation," 1160–81.

47. Wightman, *Indigenous Migration*, 120–23, and " '. . . residente en esa ciudad . . . ,' " esp. 109–11.

48. For instance, in 1562 a man living in the village of Tancor, in the province of Huanuco, said that his ancestors, from Caure, had been settled there by the Incas as potters (John V. Murra, ed. *Visita de la Provincia de Leon de Huanuco* [Huanuco: Universidad Nacional Hermilio Valdizan, 1967], 2:81).

49. Tristan Platt, *Estado boliviano y ayllu andino: tierra y tributo en el norte de Potosí* (Lima: Instituto de Estudios Peruanos, 1982), esp. 94–111. On the concept of moral economy, see James Scott, *The Moral Economy of the Peasant: Rebellion and Subsistence in Southeast Asia* (New Haven: Yale University Press, 1976); E. P. Thompson, "The Moral Economy of the English Crowd in the Eighteenth Century," *Past and Present* 50 (1971), 76–136. For a review of the literature, see Brooke Larson, "Exploitation and Moral Economy in the Southern Andes: A Critical Reconsideration," paper presented at the NYU/Columbia University Conference on Patterns of Social Change in the Andes, December, 1988.

Chapter 6. Gender and Social Differentiation

1. Frank Salomon, "Indian Women of Early Colonial Quito as Seen Through Their Testaments," *The Americas* 44:3 (1988), 326–30.
2. Elinor C. Burkett, "Indian Women and White Society: The Case of Sixteenth-Century Peru," in *Latin American Women: Historical Perspectives*, ed. Asunción Lavrin (Westport, Conn.: Greenwood, 1978), 117, 119.
3. Ibid., 121.
4. Ibid., 103–05.
5. Luis Miguel Glave, "Mujer indígena, trabajo doméstico y cambio social en el virreinato peruano del siglo XVII: La ciudad de La Paz y el sur andino en 1684," *Bulletin de l'Institut Français d'Etudes Andines* 16:3–4 (1987), 47, 50–52, 55.
6. Salomon, "Indian Women," 326.
7. Saignes, *Los andes orientales*, 198–99.
8. For instance, Bernd Lambert, "Bilaterality in the Andes," in *Andean Kinship and Marriage*, ed. Ralph Bolton and Enrique Mayer (Washington, D.C.: American Anthropological Association, 1977), 1–27; Billie Jean Isbell, " 'Those Who Love Me': An Analysis of Andean Kinship and Reciprocity Within a Ritual Context," in ibid., 81–105; Jim Belote and Linda Belote, "The Limitation of Obligation in Saraguro Kinship," in ibid., 106–16.
9. Olivia Harris, "Complementarity and Conflict: An Andean View of Women and Men," in *Sex and Age as Principles of Social Differentiation*, ed. J. LaFontaine (London: Academic Press, 1978), esp. 32–34.
10. Silverblatt, *Moon, Sun and Witches*, 62.
11. Silvia Marina Arrom, *The Women of Mexico City, 1790–1857* (Stanford: Stanford University Press, 1985), 77.
12. Ibid., 58. Arrom does mention a few instances of women inheriting their husbands' public offices in the early colonial period.

13. The rule on emancipation also applied to single men (ibid., 61).
14. Ibid., 67–68.
15. Ibid., 70.
16. ALP, C15–EC9, 1641, "Maria Yapoma reclama sobre la herencia de Francisco Renjifo."
17. Asunción Lavrin, "Women in Spanish American Colonial Society," in *The Cambridge History of Latin America*, ed. Leslie Bethell (Cambridge: Cambridge University Press, 1984), 2:327, 330. Also see Asunción Lavrin, "In Search of the Colonial Woman in Mexico: The Seventeenth and Eighteenth Centuries," in *Latin American Women*, ed. Asunción Lavrin, 23–59. No comparable work has been published on Spanish women in the Viceroyalty of Peru although Elinor Burkett makes some comparisons between Spanish elite women and other women in Peru during the sixteenth and seventeenth centuries in "In Dubious Sisterhood: Class and Sex in Spanish Colonial South America," *Latin American Perspectives* 4:4 (1977), 18–26.
18. Listed are just a few examples of court cases dealing with the abuse of women: ALP, C43–EC1, 1704, "Ana Orcoma, india natural de La Paz, parroquia de San Sebastian, querella civil y criminalmente con un indio llamado Sebastian, oficial sastre por estrupro de su hija Magdalena"; ALP, C43–EC2, 1704, "Maria Rosa contra Juan Cruz y Lucia Martinez, india, por maltratos de obra"; ALP, C44–EC10, 1705, "Declaraciones de testigos, sobre malos tratos a Josepha Arce por parte de su marido Dionicio Millares"; ANB, TI, 1672.8, "Juicio criminal contra Juan Francisco Quispe, cacique de los indios de San Lazaro, por maltratmientos a su mujer"; ANB, TI, 1672.32, "Juicio criminal contra Juan Francisco Quispe, indio Gobernador de la Parroquia de San Lazaro, por haber envenenado a su mujer."
19. AGI, Escribanía de Cámara, 859C.
20. ANB, TI, 1698.16, "Expedientes sobre la averiguación de la memoria hecha por la india Lucia Ursula Sisa y de los bienes que quedaron a su muerte."
21. Arrom, *Women of Mexico City*, 69.
22. ALP, C36-EC4, 1692, "Venta de sitio y aposentos de Ana Sissa a Don Joseph Becerra."
23. ANB, TI,1702.48.1, "Autos sequidos por María Fajardo, india, con los nietos de Juan Gaitán, sobre una tienda de pulpería en Potosí."
24. ALP, C34-EC2, 1689, "Lorenzo Camita Limanche y Lorenzo Camita, caciques, indios principales de ayllu chinchaisuio, solicitan el solar de Juana Sisa, difunta, por ser del común de ayllu."
25. Saignes, *Los andes orientales*, 191–92.

26. ANB, TI 1702.24, "Autos seguidos por Petrona Gonzalez, india, con Pedro Nina, sobre unas casa ubicadas en Oruro."

27. Silverblatt, *Moon, Sun and Witches*, 116–19.

28. ALP, C30-EC1, 1685, "Lucrecia Fernández Guarache manifiesta que el capitán Baltazar de Llano y Astorga le es deudor de dos escrituras en su favor con la suma de 3200 pesos."

29. Roberto Choque Canqui, "Los caciques aymaras y el comercio en el Alto Perú," in *La participación indígena*, ed. Olivia Harris, Brooke Larson, and Enrique Tandeter, 371–72 (La Paz: Ceres, 1987).

30. Felipe Guaman Poma de Ayala, "De corregidores, escribanos, tenientes, jueces" and "De padres, fiscales, cantores," in *El primer nueva corónica y buen gobierno* (Mexico City: Siglo Veintiuno, 1980), 2:454–664.

31. ANB, TI, 1706.14, "Juicio criminal contra Lázaro Gutiérrez por azotes y otros maltratamientos inferidos a la india María Santos."

32. ALP, C34-EC6, 1689, "María Sisa, india, pide al corregidor y justicia mayor para que Doña Polonia Maldonado le pague por sus servicios."

33. ANB, TI, 1698.13, "Doña María Sánchez de Doria, con el protector de naturales, sobre el derecho a una esclava llamada María"; ANB, TI, 1705.35, "La india Juana Feliciana con Doña Petronilla Medellín solicitando su libertad por haber sido libre."

34. Burkett, "Indian Women and White Society," 111.

35. Wightman, "Residente," 100–01.

36. Frank Salomon discusses the case of Francisca Vilcacabra of Quito, who although describing herself as a servant, also ran a *chichería* and left large sums of money in her 1596 will. "Indian Women," 337–38.

37. Silverblatt, *Moon, Sun and Witches*, 154.

38. Glave, "Mujer indígena," 55.

39. ALP, C54-EC17, 1722, "Ursula Guampa denuncia... el robo de una lliclla y un par de medias que le había dado para vender y que no puede pagar por ser muy pobre"; ALP, C36-EC3, 1694, "El protector de naturales solicita... que la india Esperanza Choque, vendedora de pan en la plaza pública, pague cada seis meses a 50 pesos"; ALP, C44-EC10, 1705, "Declaraciones de testigos sobre malos tratos a Josepha Arce por parte de su marido Dionicio Mellares," (including quote); ANB, TI, 1713.12, "Pedro Coaquira, contra la india Bárbara de la Cruz sobre maltratamientos con palo y piedra en compañía de muchos"; ANB, TI, 61697.21, "Pascuala de Carrillo contra Juan de Leiseca atribuyendole la muerte de su hija Petrona Carrillo" (including quote).

40. ANB, Minas, T 96, 2, "Bartola Sisa, india, pidiéndose le ampare en la posesión de la mina que tiene registrada en el cerro del Espíritu Santo,

provincia de Carangas, la cual pretende usurparle Cristóbal de Cotes, 1644.VI.23–28."

41. "Real cédula que los indios pueden tener y labrar minas de oro y plata como los españoles," Madrid, Dec. 17, 1551, in *Colección de documentos para la historia de la formación social de Hispanoamérica, 1493–1810*, ed. Richard Konetzke (Madrid, 1950), 1:294. Bartolomé Arzans de Orsua y Vela mentions a few Indian miners in Potosí who became rich. See *Historia de la Villa Imperial de Potosí* (Providence, R.I.: Brown University Press, 1965), 2:118.

42. While doing the research on Oruro in the seventeenth and eighteenth centuries, I never encountered references to Indian mine owners although some mestizos owned mines. Neither Peter Bakewell (*The Potosí Mita*) nor Jeffrey Cole (*Miners of the Red Mountain*) refers to Indians owning mines in Potosí.

43. ANB, TI, 1708.33, "María Esperanza, india de Hayu-Hayu, Caracollo, sobre un cacique de Urinsaya por despojo y otros atentados."

44. Lesley Gill, "Painted Faces: Conflict and Ambiguity in Domestic Servant-Employer Relations in La Paz, 1930–1988," *Latin American Research Review* 25 (1990).

45. Glave, "Mujer indígena," 46.

46. Silverblatt, *Moon, Sun and Witches*, 150–52.

47. ANB, TI, 1616.1, "Jerónimo Guarache, chacique principal de Poopo, contra Diego Copatele, sobre derecho a las tierras de Totocala en Molle Molle."

Chapter 7. Pilaya y Paspaya, 1646–1725

1. AGN, IX, 10-3-7, Representaciones y quejas de provincias.

2. ANB, Minas 19, 6, "José Cipriano de la Cruz, indio residente en Culpina, provincia de Pilaya y Paspaya, contradiciendo el yanaconazgo," 1692.

3. Alistair Hennessy, *The Frontier in Latin American History* (Albuquerque: University of New Mexico Press, 1978), 19.

4. Antonio Vázquez de Espinosa, *Compendio y descripción general de las Indias occidentales* (Madrid: Biblioteca de Autores Españoles, 1969), 411. On the Jesuit holdings in the area, see Ana María Presta, "Hacienda y comunidad: un estudio en la provincia de Pilaya y Paspaya, siglos XVI–XVIII," *Andes: antropologia e historia* 1 (1990), 31–45. On Cocha's acquisition by the Jesuits: Ana Maria Presta, "Ingresos y gastos de una hacienda jesuitica altoperuana: Jesús de Trigo Pampa (Pilaya y Paspaya),

1734–1767," *Anuario del Instituto de Estudios Histórico–Sociales* (Universidad del Centro de la Provincia de Buenos Aires) 4 (1989), 89–90.

5. ANB, TI, 1648, 18, "Amparo de posesión en favor del indígena Pablo Mamani de las tierras en Guanaya en el pueblo de San Lucas," La Plata, July 25, 1648; ANB, TI, 1715, 29, "Los indios de San Lucas de Paacollo (Pilaya) contra los jesuitas de Potosí por despojo de las tierras de Pilalo, Chinpara, Guanaya," La Plata, 1715.

6. Espinoza Soriano, "El reino Aymara," 202.

7. AGI, Charcas 270, "Libro y relación sumaria que de orden del exmo. Sr. Duque de la Palata . . . a formado don Pedro Antonio del Castillo."

8. AGN, IX, 10-3-7, "Representaciones y quejas de las provincias."

9. Rasnake, *Domination and Cultural Resistance*, 103, 114.

10. AGN, XII, 18-5-1.

11. AGI, Charcas, 270.

12. AGN, IX, 10-3-7, "Representaciones y quejas," f. 124.

13. Ibid.

14. ANB, TI, 1740, 40, "Reclamo de los indígenas Andrés Marco y Ursula Collquema, sobre parte de las tierras de Pullaya Pampachacra y la Loma . . . en Aschilla, Provincia de Pilaya.

15. ANB, TI, 1723, 18, "Querella de los indios Sebastian Lucana y Pascual Ortiz contra d. Antonio Carabeo, teniente general de Pilaya, por excesos cometidos por haber repartido mulas y efectos."

16. Ibid. These sales are also mentioned in AGN, IX, 10-3-7.

17. ANB, TI, 1695, 48, "Antonio de Acosta con José de Saldana sobre nulidad de remate de las tierras de Mollemolle situadas en la jurisdicción de Pilaya."

18. Erick D. Langer, *Economic Change and Rural Resistance in Southern Bolivia, 1880–1930* (Stanford: Stanford University Press, 1989), 90.

19. Antonio de Alcedo, *Diccionario geográfico*, 3:194–95.

20. AGN, IX, 10-3-7; Alcedo, *Diccionario geográfico*, 3:194.

21. D. A. Brading, "Government and Elite in Late Colonial Mexico," *HAHR* 53:3 (August 1973).

22. From the will of Antonio López de Quiroga, in ANB, TI, 1714, 26, "Autos sobre 8.000 p. que piden a censo principal el capitán don Pablo Vaca Flores y su mujer sobre las haciendas de Rio Pilaya, Caraparí, etc.

23. Bakewell, *Silver and Entrepreneurship*, 142.

24. A tributary census of the province in 1646 (AGN, IX, 17-1-4, Alto Perú, padrones, 1645–1686) and ANB, TI, 1650,6 "Expediente de juicio seguido a nombre del Convento de la Merced," both indicate that in the mid-

1640s Alonso Osorio de Mendoza owned at least four vineyards, a sugar cane plantation and a cattle ranch. ANB, TI, 1660, 16, "Don Nicolás de Salazar contra el tesorero público de Espinosa, sobre pesos 1200 de composición de las tierras de Caraparí en Pilaya y Paspaya," contains a list of *composiciones de tierras* which shows that in the 1640s out of fourteen proprietors, four owned more than one estate. One owned two chacras, three ranches, and one hacienda.

25. Assadourian, *El sistema*, 156; ANB, TI, 1709,45, "Ejecución seguido por d. Joseph de Azurduy, administrador de monasterio de Remedios de la Plata, contra las Haciendas de Populo;" ANB, TI, 1707, 49, "Autos seguidos por don Diego Felipe Bernal de Ortega con d. Domingo de Escalante sobre división y partición de los bienes de Doña Maragarita Gonzales, entre estos la hacienda de Caraparí.

26. ANB, TI, 1650, 6.

27. Bakewell, *Silver and Entrepreneurship*, 141.

28. ANB, TI, 1714, 26.

29. Assadourian, *El sistema*, 156; Nichoas P. Cushner, *Lords of the Land: Sugar, Wine, and Jesuit Estates of Coastal Peru, 1600–1767* (Albany: State University of New York Press, 1980), 81–112.

30. AGN, IX, 17-1-4. Antonio López de Quiroga's will says that on his "Cerro Redondo" chacra he had arrenderos who paid him 125 pesos annually (ANB, TI, 1714, 26).

31. "Aranzel de los jornales ... mandado ordenar por el ... Duque de la Palata ... Lima, 1687," in Zavala, *El servicio personal*, Appendix B, 2:211.

32. ANB, TI, 1703, 15, "Capitulos interpuestos por el indio Pascual Wallpa, contra el General D. Luis de Castro, corregidor y justicia mayor de la provincia de Pilaya y Paspaya," July 28, 1703.

33. AGN, IX, 10-3-7, "Representaciones y quejas de las provincias, 1689-90," fs. 134, 134v.

34. Ibid., fs. 132v–39.

35. ANB, TI, 1703, 15.

36. ANB, M, 19, 6.

37. "Aranzel," in Zavala, *El servicio personal*, 2:211.

38. Zavala, *El servicio personal*, 2:109.

39. The 1683 totals are in AGI, Charcas 270, "Memorial ajustado de los autos de la Numeración Genl que se executo de orden de el Virrey Duque de la Palata." The actual returns for the province have not yet been found, although contemporary documents make frequent references to the count in

the province. Complaints from Pilaya y Paspaya about the enumeration are in AGN IX, 10-3-7, and many court cases of the period cite the count as a precedent in argument, a few even give limited local results (the number of Indians found on a particular chacra, for instance). For example: ANB, TI, 1697, 45, "Diligencias de D. Felix Belasquez sobre el reclamo."

40. The apparently complete count of the province from which these totals is taken is in AGN, XIII, 18-5-1.

41. Haciendas in the region were important as early as 1646, and there are records of yanaconas working on them in the first half of the century, yet only twelve yanaconas are said to live in Cinti in 1683. See AGN, IX, 17-1-4, and ANB, Caja de Comunidades de Indios de la Caja Real de Potosí, "Nomina general de todos los deudores a la caja genl. de censos que corre desde este año de 1842 para en adelante."

42. Returns in AGN, IX-1-4. Viceroy Mancera ordered the enumeration to be conducted in May 1645. Most of the provinces affected probably complied during 1645. However, in Pilaya y Paspaya the count was not taken until 1646. The returns discussed here were completed between February and June 1646. Bolívar directed his summary to the viceroy on November 29, 1646.

43. However, this was not strictly the case, since we know that the colonial government exempted Indians from San Lucas, included as having origins in Pilaya y Paspaya, from the mita to encourage them to settle there and to form a buffer against the Chiriguanos.

44. AGN, IX, 17-1-4, Alto Perú, Padrones 1645-1686.

45. Rasnake, *Domination and Cultural Resistance*, 102-03.

46. Ibid., 113-15.

47. This type of function is discussed by Mario Góngora in *Origen de los "inquilinos" de Chile central* (Santiago de Chile: Editorial Universitaria, 1960), 44, 113-17. Although Góngora mentions that there were *declassé* Indians among the *arrendatarios* in Chile in the eighteenth century, he found no evidence of their existence in the seventeenth. Also see Góngora's *Studies in the Colonial History of Spanish America*, 154.

48. Silvio R. Duncan Baretta and John Markoff, "Civilization and Barbarism: Cattle Frontiers in Latin America," *Comparative Studies in Society and History* 20:4 (1978), 603.

49. This was the same percentage of men that López-Beltrán found in the adult age group among originarios in Livitaca in Cuzco. See chap. 5.

50. If we had figures for the 1600-1646 period, we might find that the intensity of migration to the province was greatest in these years. See Sánchez-Albornoz, "Migraciones internas," 11-19.

51. ANB, TI, 1714, 26, "Autos sobre 8.000 p."

52. Herbert S. Klein, "The State and the Labor Market in Rural Bolivia in the Colonial and Early Republican Periods," in *Essays in the Political, Economic and Social History of Colonial Latin America*, ed. Karen Spalding (Newark: Latin American Studies Program, University of Delaware, 1982), 102.

53. For instance, in 1697 Felix Belasquez, owner of the hacienda "Ympora y Ympora" in the San Juan River zone claimed Juan Paco as his yanacona on the ground that his mother and father, Pablo Paco, were his yanaconas; Juan Paco denied that these were his parents (ANB, TI, 1697, 45, "Diligencias de d. Felix Belásquez sobre el reclamo del indígena Juan Paco, como a yanacona de sus haciendas de Ympora y Ympora").

54. AGN, XIII, 18-5-1, La Plata, 1725–1754, Padrones.

55. ANB, TI, 1717, 20, "Juicio seguido por don Claudio Sánchez Paniagua y su hermano Gonzalo, contra un indio Juan Flores, alegando ser yanacona de su hacienda de Agua de Castilla, en Cinti, provincia de Pilaya."

56. ANB, TI, 1703, 15, "Capitulos interpuestos por el indio Pascual Wallpa."

57. AGI, EC, 868a; AGI, Charcas 54, "D. Rafael Ortiz de Sotomayor sobre la mita."

58. Bakewell, *Silver and Entrepreneurship*, 132–33.

59. ANB, TI, 1703, 15, "Diligencias de D. Felix Belasquez."

60. Saignes, *Políticas étnicas*, 26–28.

61. Presta, "Ingresos y gastos," 99–100.

62. Tribute payments were also an expenditure listed for Trigo Pampa (ibid., 99).

63. The total number of men in the province seems far too low, and the census records no blacks or mulattos (Erick Langer, "Mano de obra campesina y agricultura comercial en Cinti, 1880–1930," *Historia boliviana* 3:1 [1983], 72).

Conclusion

1. ANB, TI, 1629.9, "Los indios comuneros de Santiago de Cotagaita contra el Gobernador sobre un molino de ese pueblo."

2. Langer, *Economic Change*, 96–97.

3. *Aquí* (La Paz), Friday August 9, 1991; Susanna Rance, "The Hand That Feeds Us," NACLA, *Report on the Americas* 25:1 (1991), 35–36.

Glossary

Aclla: Girl selected to remain a virgin by the Inca state.
Agregado: Indian living in an Indian community that is not his own. Sometimes also used to refer to *forasteros* on haciendas or other estates.
Aguardiente: Sugarcane alcohol.
Alcabala: Value-added sales tax.
Alcalde ordinario: Member of colonial town council who also functioned as a judge for minor crimes.
Alferez real: Member of *cabildo*, or town council, who carried the royal standard in civic ceremonies.
Altiplano: Arid, flat, high plateau area extending from the northern side of Lake Titicaca through the province of Paria in the south with an average altitude of 3,800–4,000 meters (or about 13,000 feet) above sea level.
Apiri: Worker who hauled ore out of silver mines.
Arrendero: One who rents land and pays with labor; see also *Forastero arrendero*.
Arriero: Mule driver.
Audiencia: Colonial governing body with judicial and policy-making functions in a relatively large geographical zone.
Aviador: Merchant who bought silver from producers and loaned money to miners to cover operating expenses.
Ayllu: Andean kin group that generally traced its descent to a common real or mythical ancestor and had collective rights to land.
Ayni: reciprocal labor exchange.
Azogue: Mercury.
Azoguero: Owner of a silver refinery that used mercury (*azogue*) in the refining process.
Barretero: Mine worker who excavated mine face with pick and hammer.

Botija: A liquid measure equivalent to one hundred pounds.
Cabeza: Head, or grinding wheel, of a refining mill.
Cabildo: Colonial town council.
Caja Real: Royal treasury office.
Cédula real: Royal decree.
Cerro Rico: Literally, "rich hill," used to refer to the mountain of silver at Potosí.
Chacarero: Owner of a *chacra*.
Chacra: Agricultural property or farm.
Chicha: Fermented beverage made from maize.
Chicheria: Establishment in which *chicha* is served.
Chuño: A type of freeze-dried potato, ch 2, also table 3.1
Composición de tierra: Legalization of landholding through payment of an assessed fee to a designated official. CH 2?
Concierto: Labor contract between individuals or between community leaders and employers.
Congregaciones: Villages to which Indians were forced to move by the colonial government in the 1570s.
Corpa: Share of ore carried out of the mines by workers to sell or to smelt themselves.
Corregidor: Local magistrate responsible for maintaining order, administering justice, and in Indian areas, collecting tribute.
Criollo: Spaniard born in America.
Encomendero: Holder of an *encomienda* grant.
Encomienda: The grant of the right to collect tribute from Indians from certain communities, usually as a reward for service to the royal government.
Estancia: Ranch.
Forastero: Indian who had left a native community to take up residence in another community, in a Spanish city, or on an estate.
Forasteros arrenderos: More or less permanent settlers who paid rent for land in labor.
Guaira: Small kiln used by Indians for smelting silver.
Ingeniero: Owner or operator of an *ingenio*.
Ingenio: Large water-powered mill that ground silver.
Juez reducidor: Official responsible for returning native people to their reducciones.
Juicio de residencia: Official review conducted after a colonial official's term of office.
Kajchas: Workers participating in kajcheo.

Glossary

Kajcheo: The practice of excavating another's mine for one's own profit, common in Potosí in the late eighteenth century.

Kuraka: Leader of an Andean community; also called *mallku*.

League: The distance a horse could walk in an hour, approximately five kilometers.

Ley: The silver content of ore.

Liquina: Arid, rugged brushlands between 2,600 and 4,000 meters above sea level.

Llactarunas: Temporary Indian agricultural colonists in valley zones.

Maestro: Master artisan.

Mazo: Hammer attached to the grinding wheel that pulverized the silver ores in an *ingenio*.

Merced de tierra: Land grant.

Minga or Mingado: A voluntary Indian worker.

Mita: In Quechua (*mit'a*), a shift or turn. Under the Spanish, a rotating system of forced labor.

Mitayo: A worker performing *mita* service.

Mitimaes: Pre-Columbian agricultural colonists from highland settlements who cultivated crops on lands held by their communities at lower altitudes.

Negrillos: Dark-colored sulphur complexes with high silver content.

Oidor: A judge of an *audiencia*, a colonial governing body.

Originario: Resident of a community or *reducción* created in the 1570s who had access to land there and was required to pay tribute and often to serve in the *mita* for the Potosí mines.

Pacos: Soft, light-colored ores from which silver was extracted relatively easily.

Padrón: Census return.

Palliri: Indian who sorted ore according to its silver content.

Partido: Share of ore that mine workers in Mexico took from the mines as part of their remuneration.

Peso ensayado: A peso worth about twelve and a half reales.

Piña: Refined block of silver ore.

Próximo: In colonial censuses, males fourteen through seventeen years of age.

Pulpería: Small grocery store or stand.

Pulpero/pulpera: Someone who ran a *pulpería*.

Puna: Arid tableland; see also *altiplano*.

Quintal: 100 pounds.

Quinto Real: The "royal fifth," or one-fifth tax paid on silver assayed at the royal treasury office.

Real: One-eighth of a common peso.

Reducción: Nucleated village to which native population was forced to move under Viceroy Francisco de Toledo. See also *congregación*.

Repartimiento: From *repartir*, to distribute, it can refer to the distribution of Indian communities to *encomenderos* or to the distribution of workers to employers.

Repartimiento de mercancías: A system whereby Indians were forced to buy goods distributed by the *corregidor*.

Repasiri: Indian worker in an *ingenio* who kneaded a mixture of crushed metal, salt, and mercury with his feet.

Rescatador: Individual who bought silver from laborers who carried it out of the mines.

Socavón: Mining tunnel connecting a number of galleries.

Teniente de corregidor: Assistant to the *corregidor*.

Trapiche: Small human-powered mill used for grinding silver ore.

Trapichero: Owner of a *trapiche*.

Vara: Measurement approximately equal to one meter.

Vecino: A landowner in a colonial town or city.

Visita: An inspection or survey made by a colonial official.

Visitador: Colonial inspector.

Yanacona: Derived from *yana*; during the colonial period, an Indian who was not clearly identified with any *ayllu*. *Yanaconas* were usually resident laborers on estates owned by Spaniards or worked in various capacities in cities.

Yanaconaje: The state of being a *yanacona*; also *yanaconasco*.

Yungas: Warm tropical valleys formed by breaks in the central portion of the Cordillera Real.

Bibliography

Archival Material

Two major subdivisions of the Archivo General de la Nación in Buenos Aires had indispensable documentation for this study. These were *Contaduría* (Sala XIII) and *Gobierno* (Sala IX). The former supplied the records of the Royal Treasury of Oruro (*Caja Real*) and most important the tributary censuses (*padrones*) analyzed in this study. Although most of the material in Sala XIII is of a quantitative nature, often included in the *legajos* of padrones are letters discussing them, official instructions to local magistrates, etc. Sala IX, Gobierno, also has some census material, but in general contains more qualitative materials such a records of the Society of Jesus, official correspondence between colonial officials, and Intendency reports for the later colonial period. Although Sala IX is a richer source for the eighteenth century than for the seventeenth, it nonetheless provided important materials for this book, such as the "Representaciones y quejas" collected after the enumeration ordered by the duque de la Palata. Below are listed the most important legajos consulted in the AGN with brief descriptions of some of the documentation they contain.

Sala XIII, Contaduría

8-2-4. Contaduría, Oruro, 1625–1673. Accounts of the Caja Real de Oruro (Royal Treasury), including the one-fifth tax (quinto) on silver minted.

8-2-5. Contaduría, Oruro, 1674–1789. As above.

8-2-6. Contaduría, Oruro, 1689–1699. As above.

8-2-7. Contaduría, Oruro, 1700–1703. As above.

17-1-4. Oruro, Padrones, 1604–1786. Enumerations of Indian tributaries. Tribute assessments for 1689.

17-3-2. La Paz, Padrones, 1683–1684.
18-4-1. La Plata, Padrones, 1589–1683.
18-4-2. La Plata, Padrones, 1596–1689. Also contains the duque de la Palata's instructions for conducting the enumeration.
18-4-3. La Plata, Padrones, 1616–1725. Paria.
18-5-1. La Plata, Padrones, 1725–1754. Pilaya y Paspaya.
18-7-4. Potosí, 1670–1694. Padrones, Chichas and Tarija, 1670–1788, Porco, 1684–1687. Representaciones y Quejas for Porco, Chayanta, Paria, Carangas. Tribute assessments based on the numeración of la Palata.
23-10-2. Potosí, Padrones, 1611–1690. Distribution of mita workers by the mills to which they were assigned in Potosí from 1630s and 1665. Canillas de Torneros's interviews with captains of the mita in Potosí in 1690.

Sala IX

5-1-1. Intendencia de La Plata, 1724–1750.
5-1-2. Intendencia de La Plata, 1751–1752.
5-1-3. Intendencia de La Plata, 1753–1759.
5-1-4. Intendencia de La Plata, 1760–1766.
5-1-5. Intendencia de La Plata, 1767–1771.
5-1-6. Intendencia de La Plata, 1772–1777.
6-5-3. Atacama, Carangas, Challapa, Chayanta, Chichas, Poopo. Porco, Potosí. Documents from eighteenth and nineteenth centuries.
6-9-3. Jesuitas. 1595–1675.
6-9-4. Jesuitas. 1676–1702.
7-7-1. Atacama, Padrones 1683–1777.
7-10-5. Indices of viceregal correspondence.
10-3-7. Representaciones y quejas de provincias, 1689–1691.
26-4-2. Ordenanzas de Alfaro, 1611–1623.
21-8-6. Temporalidades de La Plata, 1768–1785.
21-9-1. Temporalidades de La Plata, 1786–1802.
22-6-2. Temporalidades de Potosí, 1799–1809.

The Archivo Nacional de Bolivia (ANB) in Sucre has invaluable correspondence, trial records, and decrees of the Audiencia of Charcas. Although for the seventeenth century most of the documentation in the ANB is what is considered qualitative rather than quantitative, often included in the records of a court cases or reports from the audiencia are detailed accounts of silver minted, wages paid, taxes collected, etcetera.

Libro manual de esta caja de Oruro que corre desde 1 de marzo de este año de 1678
Libro real manual de esta real caja de Oruro de 1684
Libro manual de esta caja real de Oruro que empieza a primero de mayo de 1694
Libro manual de esta caja de Oruro que empieza a primero de mayo de 1695
Libro de contador de esta caja real de Oruro que empieza a primero de mayo de 1699.

Finally, civil and criminal court cases in the Archivo Histórico de La Paz (ALP) provided substantial qualitative material about urban indigenous life, women's participation in the market, and links between urban residents and members of their ayllus in the countryside. These documents are identified by the title in the catalogue, box number, *expediente* (case) number, and year.

In the Archivo General de Indias (AGI) in Sevilla, I found the most information for this study in *Gobierno, Escribanía de Cámara* and *Contaduría*. From *Gobierno* very important was the correspondence between officials in Oruro and the Consejo de Indias. This dealt with various subjects of interest in the metropolis: official visits to and recommendations for government action on the mining center, letters commending outstanding citizens of the city for reward, accounts of the effects the new center was having on Potosí. Also *Gobierno* contains much information about the Numeración General de la Palata.

The subsection of *Escribanía de Cámara* entitled *Pleitos de La Plata* contains volumes of court cases that were important enough to be forwarded from the Audiencia de Charcas to the Consejo de Indias. In *Residencias* are found the judicial reviews conducted of corregidores when they left office. Several of these for Oruro have telling information on the repartimiento de mercancias and other inproprieties committed by the magistrates. One extremely important manuscript in *Pleitos* is 868A, which contains the case brought by Don Fernandez Guarache, cacique for the town of Jesús de Machaca in Pacajes in 1663, against the guild of azogueros of Potosí. This enormous document contains information on Indian labor, migration, social change in the seventeenth century, and a variety of other topics of interest to colonial historians. It was used by Canedo-Arguelles Fabrega in her thesis on the effects of the mita, which is cited in the bibliography.

Finally, *Contaduría* provided some information on the *quintos reales* for Oruro that I did not find in Oruro itself or in the AGN.

The following is a list of the most important legajos consulted in the AGI:

The ANB is cataloged by subject, and two of the most useful indices for this book were *Minas* and *Tierras e Indios*. *Minas* provided varied material on Oruro: information on wages, numbers of workers, refining processes, the fortunes of individual miners and refiners, the depth of mines, religious instruction in the center, the Indians' practice of taking shares of the ore to sell as part of their remuneration, and so forth. *Tierras e Indios* was most useful for the province of Pilaya y Paspaya, providing records of litigation about land sales, *composiciones de tierras*, wills of landowners, suits brought by Indian laborers against their employers, and other matters. Court cases in both Minas and Tierras e Indios had material on indigenous women in Upper Peru and the life of urban migrants, forasteros, and yanaconas. Also consulted for Pilaya y Paspaya in the ANB were mortgage records of the Caja General de Comunidades de Indios.

In *Minas* there is occasionally some confusion because manuscripts are catalogued several different ways and index entries give not only the number assigned the manuscript within the *Minas* collection but also a call number for each document according to the original archive to which it belongs. There is some variation in which number researchers use to request a document. In notes, to avoid confusion I have used the Minas volume (*tomo*) and document number as well as the title of the document as given in the catalogue.

Tierras e Indios manuscripts are identified in the notes by year and number, along with the title as recorded in the card catalogue.

In Oruro, the Biblioteca Municipal (BMO) has some of the city's colonial records of the Royal Treasury. These included data on the one-fifth tax paid by silver producers. The following record books were consulted in the BMO:

Libro real manual de la real hacienda de la Villa de San Felipe de Austria desde 9 de marzo 1611 hasta 29 de marzo de 1612
Libro de thesorero de este año de 1637
Libro de thesorero del año 1638
Libro comun de este año de 1639
Libro del tesorero de este año de 1640
Libro de contador que corre desde abril de 1646
Libro del contador de este año de 1648
Manual de la caja del año de 1649, Libro de contador de 1656
Libro real del cargo de contador Alejo Roman oficial real de esta Caja de Oruro que corre desde 20 de dic. de 1664 hasta 12 de julio de 1665
Libro real contador de esta caja de Oruro 1667-1668
Libro real de contador de esta caja de Oruro que corre desde 3 de marzo de 1673

Gobierno: Charcas, legajos 17–25, 31–32, 35, 37, 44, 54, 60–62, 101, 104–05, 113–17, 128–29, 132, 150, 154, 200, 219, 270. Lima, legajos 38–39, 45, 56. Indiferente General, legajos 1525–27, 1699.
Escribanía de Cámara: *Residencias*: 857A, 857B, 858A, 859A, 859C. *Pleitos*: 868A.
Contaduría: 1775, 1788, 1818, 1829, 1830, 1831, 1832, 1833, 1887.

The Biblioteca Nacional (BN) in Madrid has a good collection of viceregal memoranda and disposiciones in its manuscript section. Many have now been published, but nonetheless there are interesting documents in the collection on mining, the Potosí mita, and tribute regulations. I consulted the following manuscripts in the BN: 859, 3035, 3040, 3041, 3042, 3107, 3178, 6225, 8990, 9963, 19512, 20065.

Published Documents

Acosta, José de. *Historia natural y moral de las Indias*. [1590] Biblioteca de Autores Españoles, vol. 73. Madrid: Ediciones Atlas, 1954.
Agia, Fr. Miguel de. *Servidumbres personales de indios*. Seville: Escuela de Estudios Hispano-Americanos, 1946.
Alcedo, Antonio de. *Diccionario geográfico de las Indias occidentales*. Biblioteca de Autores Españoles, vol. 207. Madrid: Ediciones Atlas, 1967.
Arzans de Orsua y Vela, Bartolomé. *Historia de la Villa Imperial de Potosí*. Ed. Lewis Hanke and Gunnar Mendoza. Providence, R.I.: Brown University Press, 1965, 3 vols.
Ayans, Antonio de. "Breve relación de los agravios que reciben los indios que hay desde cerca del Cuzco hasta Potosí." [1596] ed. In Rubén Vargas Ugarte, *Pareceres jurídicos en asuntos de indios*, pp. 35–88. Lima, 1951.
Barba, Alvaro Alonso. *El arte de los metales*. Madrid, 1729.
Capoche, Luis. *Relación general de la Villa Imperial de Potosí* [1585]. Ed. Lewis Hanke. Biblioteca de Autores Españoles, vol. 122. Madrid: Ediciones Atlas, 1959.
Cieza de León, Pedro. *Parte primera de la crónica del Perú*. Biblioteca de Autores Españoles, vols. 91–92. Madrid: 1853.
———. *El senorio de los Incas* (2a parte de la *crónica del Peru*). Lima: 1967.
Cook, Noble David, ed. *Tasa de la visita general de Francisco de Toledo*. Lima: Universidad Nacional Mayor de San Marcos, 1975.
"Descripción de la villa y minas de Potosí. Año de 1603," in *Relaciones geográficas de Indias*, ed. Marcos Jiménez de la Espada. Biblioteca de Autores Españoles, vol. 183. Madrid: Ediciones Atlas, 1965.

Diez de San Miguel, Garci. *Visita hecha a la provincia de Chucuito en 1567*. Ed. Waldemar Espinosa Soriano. Lima: Casa de la Cultura del Perú, 1964.

Fuentes, Manuel A., ed. *Memorias de los virreyes que han gobernado el Perú durante el tiempo del coloniaje español*. 4 vols. Lima: Felipe Bailly, 1959.

Godoy, Felipe de. "Relación de asiento, minas y población de San Felipe de Austria, llamados de Oruro (1607)." *Boletín de la Oficina Nacional de Estadística* 7 (La Paz, 1912): 114–64.

Jiménez de la Espada, Marcos, ed. *Relaciones geográficas de Indias: El Perú*. Biblioteca de Autores Españoles, vol. 183. Madrid: Ediciones Atlas, 1965.

Konetzke, Richard. *Colección de documentos para la historia de la formación social de Hispanoamerica, 1443–1810*, vol. 1: 1493–1590. Madrid: Consejo Superior de Investigaciones Científicas, 1953.

Levillier, Robert, ed. *Gobernantes del Perú: cartas y papeles, siglo XVI*. 14 vols. Madrid: Sucesores de Rivadeneyra, 1921–1926.

———. *Don Francisco de Toledo, supremo organizador del Perú: su vida, su obra (1515–1585)*. 3 vols. Buenos Aires: Colección de Publicaciones Históricas de la Biblioteca del Congreso Argentino, 1935–42.

———. *La Audiencia de Charcas: correspondencia de presidentes y oidores*. 3 vols. Madrid and Buenos Aires: Colección de Publicaciones Históricas de la Biblioteca del Congreso Argentino, 1918–1922.

Lizarraga, Fray Reginaldo de. *Descripción breve de toda la tierra del Perú*. Biblioteca de Autores Españoles, vol. 15. Madrid: Ediciones Atlas, 1909.

Lorente, Sabastian, ed. *Relaciones de los virreyes y audiencias que han gobernado el Perú*. 3 vols. Lima: Imprenta del Estado, 1867–1872.

Matienzo, Juan de. *Gobierno del Perú*. Ed. Guillermo Lohmann Villena, ed. Paris-Lima: Institut Français D'Études Andines, 1967.

Poma de Ayala, Felipe Guaman. *El primer nuevo corónica y buen gobierno*. Mexico: Siglo XXI, 1980.

Solorzano y Pereyra, Juan de. *Política indiana* [1647]. 5 vols. Madrid: Compania Ibero-Americana de publicaciones, 1930.

Spain. Archivo General de Indias, Seville. *Virreinato de Nueva España y Perú durante los siglos XVI–XVII: correspondencia de los virreyes, años 1552–1657*. 41 reels. Madrid: Centro Nacional de Microfilm, 1975.

TePaske, John J., and Herbert Klein. *The Royal Treasuries of the Spanish Empire in America*. Vol. 2: *Upper Peru (Bolivia)*. Durham, North Carolina: Duke University Press, 1982.

Vázquez de Espinosa, Antonio. *Compendio y descripción de las Indias occidentales*. Biblioteca de Autores Españoles, vol. 231. Madrid: Ediciones Atlas, 1969.
Zavala, Silvio. *El servicio personal de los indios en el Perú*, 3 vols. Vol. 1: *(Extractos del siglo XVI)*; vol. 2: *(Extractos del siglo XVII)*; vol. 3: *(Extractos del siglo XVIII)*. Mexico City: El Colegio de México, 1978–1980.

Books and Articles

Acosta, Antonio. "La extirpación de las idolatrías en el Perú: Origen y desarrollo de las campañas a propósito de *Cultura andina y represión*, de Pierre Duviols." *Revista Andina* 5:1 (1987): 171–95.
———. "Religiosos, doctrinas y excedente económico indígena en el Perú a comienzos de siglo XVII." *Histórica* 4:1 (1982): 1–34.
Andrien, Kenneth. *Crisis and Decline: The Viceroyalty of Peru in the Seventeenth Century*. Albuquerque: University of New Mexico Press, 1985.
Aquí. (La Paz) Friday, August 9, 1991.
Arrom, Silvia Marina. *The Women of Mexico City, 1750–1857*. Stanford University Press, 1985.
Assadourian, Carlos Sempat. "Modos de producción, capitalismo y subdesarrollo en América latina." In *Modos de producción en América Latina*, ed. Assadourian et al., 47–81. Buenos Aires: Siglo XXI, 1973.
———. "La producción de la mercancía dinero en la formación del mercado interno colonial." *Economía* 1:2 (Lima, 1978): 9–55.
———. *El sistema de la economía colonial: mercado interno, regiones y espacio económico*. Lima: Instituto de Estudios Peruanos, 1982.
Bainton, Roland H. *Women of the Reformation: From Spain to Scandinavia*. Minneapolis: Augsburg, 1977.
Bakewell, Peter J. *Antonio López de Quiroga: industrial minero del Potosí colonial*. Potosí: Universidad Boliviana "Tomas Frias." División de Extensión Universitaria, 1973.
———. *Miners of the Red Mountain: Indian Labor in Potosí, 1545–1650*. Albuquerque: University of New Mexico Press, 1984.
———. "Registered Silver Production in the Potosí District, 1550–1735." *Jahrbuch für Geschichte von Staat, Wirtschaft und Gesellschaft Lateinamerikas* 12:67–103. Cologne and Vienna, 1975.
———. *Silver and Entrepreneurship in Seventeenth- Century Potosí: The Life and Times of Antonio López de Quiroga*. Albuquerque: University of New Mexico Press, 1988.

———. *Silver Mining and Society in Colonial Mexico: Zacatecas, 1546–1700*. Cambridge: Cambridge University Press, 1971.
———. "Technological Change in Potosí: The Silver Boom of the 1570s." *Jahrbuch für Geschichte von Staat, Wirtschaft und Gesellschaft Lateinamerikas* 14:57–77. Cologne and Vienna, 1977.
Bargallo, Modesto. *La minería y la metalurgia en la América española durante la época colonial*. Mexico City: Fondo de Cultura Económica, 1955.
Barnadas, Josep M. *Charcas, 1535–1563: Orígenes históricos de una sociedad colonial*. La Paz: Centro de Investigación y Promoción del Campesinado, 1973.
Basadre, Jorge. "El régimen de la mita." *Letras* (Lima, 1937): 325–64.
Belaunde Guinassi, M. *La encomienda en el Perú*. Lima: Ediciones Mercurio Peruano, 1945.
Belote, Jim, and Linda Belote. "The Limitation of Obligation in Saraguro Kinship." In *Andean Kinship and Marriage*, ed. Ralph Bolton and Enrique Mayer. Washington, D.C.: American Anthropological Association, 1977.
Borah, Woodrow. *New Spain's Century of Depression*. Ibero-Americana, no. 35. Berkeley and Los Angeles: University of California Press, 1951.
Bouysse-Cassagne, Thérèse. "L'espace Aymara: Urco et Uma." *Annales* 33:5–6 (1978): 1057–80.
Bowser, Frederick. *The African Slave in Colonial Peru*. Stanford: Stanford University Press, 1974.
Boyer, Richard. "Mexico in the Seventeenth Century: Transition of a Colonial Society." *Hispanic American Historical Review* 57:3 (1977): 455–78.
Brading, David. "Government and Elite in Late Colonial Mexico." *Hispanic American Historical Review* 53:3 (1973): 389–414.
———. *Miners and Merchants in Bourbon Mexico*. Cambridge: Cambridge University Press, 1971.
Brading, David, and H. Cross. "Colonial Silver Mining: Mexico and Peru." *Hispanic American Historical Review* 52:4 (1972): 545–79.
Burkett, Elinor C. "In Dubious Sisterhood: Class and Sex in Spanish Colonial South America." *Latin American Perspectives* 4:4 (1977): 18–26.
———. "Indian Women and White Society: The Case of Sixteenth-Century Peru." In *Latin American Women: Historical Perspectives*, ed. Asunción Lavrin, 101–27. Westport, Conn.: Greenwood, 1978.
Burzio, Humberto F. *Diccionario de la moneda hispano-américana*. 2 vols. Santiago: Fondo Histórico y Bibliográfico José Toribio Medina, 1958.

Canedo-Arguelles Fabrega, Teresa. "Efectos de Potosí en la estructura de una provincia mitaya: Pacajes a mediados del siglo XVII." Tesis de Licenciatura, Universidad de Sevilla, 1976.

Cardoso, Ciro F. S. "Sobre los modos de producción coloniales de América latina." In *Modos de Produccion en América Latina*, 7th ed., ed. Carlos Sempat Assadourian. Mexico City: Cuadernos de Pasado y Presente, 1979.

Cardoso, Fernando Henrique, and Enzo Faletto. *Dependency and Development in Latin America*. Berkeley and Los Angeles: University of California Press, 1979.

Carmagnani, Marcello. *El salariado minero en Chile colonial: el Norte Chico, 1690-1800*. Santiago: Universidad de Chile, Centro de Historia Colonial, 1963.

Cespedes del Castillo, Guillermo. "Lima y Buenos Aires: Repurcusiones económicas y políticas de la creacióndel virreinato de La Plata." *Anuario de estudios americanos* 3 (1946): 667-874.

Chayanov, A. V. "Peasant Farm Organization." In *The Theory of Peasant Economy*, ed. D. Thorner, B. Kerblay, and R.E.F. Smith. Homewood, Ill.: Irwin, 1966.

Chevalier, François. *Land and Society in Colonial Mexico*. Berkeley and Los Angeles: University of California Press, 1966.

Choque Canqui, Roberto. "Los caciques aymaras y el comercio en el Alto Perú." In *La participación indígena en los mercados surandions: Estrategias y reproducción social, siglos XVI- XX*, ed. Olivia Harris, Brooke Larson, and Enrique Tandeter, 357-77. La Paz: Ceres, 1987.

———. "Pedro Chipana: cacique comerciante de Calamarca." *Avances* 1 (1978): 28-32.

Clayton, L. A. "Trade and Navigation in the Seventeenth-Century Viceroyalty of Peru." *Journal of Latin American Studies* 7:1 (1975): 1-21.

Cobb, Gwendolyn Ballantine. *Potosí y Huancavelica: bases económicas, 1545-1640*. La Paz: Academia Boliviana de la Historia, 1977.

Cole, Jeffrey A. "An Abolitionism Born of Frustration: The Conde de Lemos and the Potosí Mita, 1667-1673 ." *Hispanic American Historical Review* 36:2 (1983): 307-33.

———. *The Potosí Mita, 1573-1700: Compulsory Indian Labor in the Andes*. Stanford: Stanford University Press, 1985.

———. "Viceregal Persistence versus Indian Mobility: The Impact of the Duque de la Palata's Reform Program on Alto Perú, 1681-1692." *Latin American Research Review* 19:1 (1984): 37-56.

Cook, Noble David. *Demographic Collapse: Indian Peru, 1520-1620*. Cambridge: Cambridge University Press, 1981.

———. "Migration in Colonial Peru: An Overview." In *Migration in Colonial Spanish America*, ed. David Robinson, 41–61. Cambridge: Cambridge University Press, 1990.

Crespo Rodas, Alberto. *Esclavos negros en Bolivia*. La Paz: Academia Nacional de Ciencias, 1977.

———. "La fundación de la Villa de San Felipe de Austria y asiento de minas de Oruro." *Documentos orurenos*, 1:46–50. Oruro: Editorial de la Universidad Boliviana Técnica de Oruro, 1976.

———. "La mita de Potosí." *Revista Histórica* 22 (Lima, 1955–56): 169–82.

———. "El reclutamiento y los viajes en la 'mita' del cerro de Potosí." *Minería hispana e hispano-américana*, 1:467–81. Leon, Spain: Catedra de San Isidoro, 1970.

Cushner, Nicholas P. *Lords of the Land: Sugar, Wine and Jesuit Estates of Coastal Peru, 1600–1767*. Albany: State University of New York Press, 1980.

D'Altroy, Terence N., and Timothy K. Earle. "Staple Finance, Wealth Finance, and Storage in the Inka Political Economy." *Current Anthropology* 26:2 (1985): 187–206.

Dobyns, Henry F. "An Outline of Andean Epidemic History to 1720." *Bulletin of the History of Medicine* 37 (1963): 493–515.

Duncan Baretta, Silvio R., and John Markoff. "Civilization and Barbarism: Cattle Frontiers in Latin America." *Comparative Studies in Society and History* 20:4 (1978): 587–620.

Elliott, J. H. "The Decline of Spain." In *Crisis in Europe, 1560–1660*, ed. Trevor Aston. New York: Basic Books, 1965.

———. *Imperial Spain, 1469–1716*. New York: New American Library, 1977.

Espinosa Soriano, Waldemar. "El fundamento territorial del ayllu serrano, siglos XV–XVI." In *Etnohistoria y antropologia andina*, ed. Amalia Castelli, Marcia Koth de Paredes, and Mariana Mould de Pease, 93–130. Lima: Museo Nacional de Historia, 1981.

———. "El reino Aymara de Quillaca-Asanaque, siglos XV–XVI." *Revista del Museo Nacional* 45:175–274.

Evans, Brian. "Census Enumeration in Late Seventeenth-Century Alto Perú: The Numeración General of 1683–1684." In David J. Robinson, ed., *Studies in Spanish American Population History*. Dellplain Latin American Studies, no. 8, 25–44. Boulder, Colo.: Westview Press, 1981.

———. "Migration proceses in Upper Peru in the seventeenth century." In *Migration in Colonial Spanish America*, ed. David Robinson, 62–85. Cambridge: Cambridge University Press, 1990.

Ezquerra Abadia, Ramón. "Problemas de la mita de Potosí en el siglo XVIII." *Minería hispana e hispano-americana*, 1:483–511. León, Spain: Catedra de San Isidoro, 1970.

Fifer, J. Valerie. *Bolivia: Land, Location and Politics Since 1825*. Cambridge: Cambridge University Press, 1972.

Flores Ochoa, Jorge A. "Pastores de alpacas de los Andes." In *Pastores de puna*, ed. Jorge A. Flores Ochoa, 15–49. Lima: Instituto de Estudios Peruanos, 1977.

Foster-Carter, Aidan. "The Modes of Production Controversy." *New Left Review* 107 (1978): 47–78.

Frank, Andre Gunder. *Capitalism and Underdevelopment in Latin America*. New York: Monthly Review Press, 1967.

Gade, Daniel W., and Mario Escobar. "Village Settlement and the Colonial Legacy in Southern Peru." *Geographical Review* 72:4 (1982): 430–49.

Gibson, Charles. *Spain in America*. New York: Harper and Row, 1967.

Gill, Lesley. "Painted Faces: Conflict and Ambiguity in Domestic Servant-Employer Relations in La Paz, 1930–1988." *Latin American Research Review* 25:1 (1990): 119–36.

Gisbert, Teresa, Silvia Arze, and Martha Cajías. *Arte Textil y mundo andino*. La Paz: Gisbert y Cia., 1987.

Glave, Luis Miguel. "Mujer indígena, trabajo doméstico y cambio social en el virreinato peruano del siglo XVII: La ciudad de La Paz y el Sur Andino en 1684." *Bulletin de l'Institut Français d'Etudes Andines* 163-4 (1987):39–69.

Golte, Jurgen. *Repartos y rebeliones: Tupac Amaru y las contradicciones de la economía colonial*. Lima: Instituto de Estudios Peruanos, 1980.

Góngora, Mario. *Origen de los "inquilinos" de Chile central*. Santiago: Editorial Universitaria, 1960.

———. *Studies in the Colonial History of Spanish America*. Cambridge: Cambridge University Press, 1975.

Grice-Hutchinson, Marjorie. *Early Economic Thought in Spain, 1177–1740*. London: George Allen and Unwin, 1978.

Hamilton, Earle J. *American Treasure and the Price Revolution in Spain, 1501–1650*. Cambridge: Harvard University Press, 1934.

Harris, Olivia. "Complementarity and Conflict: An Andean View of Women and Men." In *Sex and Age as Principles of Social Differentiation*, ed. J. LaFontaine, 21–40. London: Academic Press, 1978.

Hennessy, Alistair. *The Frontier in Latin American History*. Albuquerque: University of New Mexico Press, 1978.

Isbell, Billie Jean. " 'Those Who Love Me': An Analysis of Andean Kinship and Reciprocity Within a Ritual Context." In *Andean Kinship and Marriage*, ed. Ralph Bolton and Enrique Meyer, 81–105. Washington, D.C.: American Anthropological Association, 1977.

Israel, J. I. "México y la 'crisis general' del siglo XVII." In *Ensayos sobre el desarollo económico de México y América latina, 1500–1975*, ed. Enrique Florescano. Mexico City: Fondo de Cultura Económica, 1979.

———. "Response to Henry Kamen." *Past and Present* 91 (May 1981): 170–80.

Julien, Catherine J. *Hatunqolla: A View of Inca Rule from the Lake Titicaca Region*. Berkeley and Los Angeles: University of California Press, 1983.

Kamen, Henry. "The Decline of Spain: A Historical Myth?" *Past and Present* 81 (1978): 24–50.

———. *Inquisition and Society in Spain in the Sixteenth and Seventeenth Centuries*. Bloomington: Indiana University Press, 1985.

———. *Spain 1469–1714: A Society of Conflict*, 2d ed. London: Longman, 1991.

Kaufman, Gloria. "Juan Luis Vives on the Education of Women." *Signs* 3:4 (1978): 891–96.

Klein, Herbert S. *Bolivia: the Evolution of a Multi-Ethnic Society*. New York: Oxford University Press, 1982.

———. "Hacienda and Free Community in Eighteenth Century Alto Perú: A Demographic Study of the Aymara Population of the Districts of Chulumani and Pacajes in 1786." *Journal of Latin American Studies* 7:2 (1975): 193–220.

———. "The State and the Labor Market in Rural Bolivia in the Colonial and Early Republican Periods." In *Essays in the Political, Economic and Social History of Colonial Latin America*, ed. Karen Spalding. Newark, Del.: Latin American Studies Progran, University of Delaware, 1982, 95–106.

Klein, Herbert, and John TePaske. "The Seventeenth Century Crisis in New Spain: Myth or Reality?" *Past and Present* 90 (February 1981): 116–35.

Kriedte, Peter. *Peasants, Landlords and Merchant Capitalists: Europe and the World Economy, 1500–1800*. Cambridge: Cambridge University Press, 1983.

Laclau, Ernesto. "Feudalism and Capitalism in Latin America." *New Left Review* 67 (1971): 19–38.

Ladd, Doris. *The Making of a Strike: Mexican Silver Workers' Struggles in Real del Monte, 1766–1775.* Lincoln: University of Nebraska Press, 1988.

Lambert, Bernd. "Bilaterality in the Andes." In *Andean Kinship and Marriage*, ed. Ralph Bolton and Enrique Mayer, 1–27. Washington, D.C.: American Anthropological Association, 1977.

Langer, Erick D. *Economic Change and Rural Resistance in Southern Bolivia, 1880–1930.* Stanford: Stanford University Press, 1989.

———. "Labor Strikes and Reciprocity on Chuquisaca Haciendas." *Hispanic American Historical Review* 65:2 (1985): 255–78.

———. "Mano de obra campesina y agricultura comercial en Cinti, 1880–1930." *Historia Boliviana* 3:1 (1983): 71–93.

Larson, Brooke. *Colonialism and Agrarian Transformation in Bolivia: Cochabamba, 1550–1900.* Princeton: Princeton University Press, 1988.

———. "Exploitation and Moral Economy in the Southern Andes: A Critical Reconsideration." Paper presented at the New York University/Columbia University Conference on Patterns of Social Change in the Andes, December 1988.

———. "Rural Rhythms of Class Conflict in Eighteenth Century Cochabamba." *Hispanic American Historical Review* 60:3 (1981): 407–30.

Larson, Brooke, and Robert Wasserstrom. "Coerced Consumption in Colonial Bolivia and Guatemala." *Radical History Review* 27 (n.d.): 49–78.

Lavrin, Asunción. "Women in Spanish Colonial Society." In *The Cambridge History of Latin America*, ed. Lesley Bethell, 2:321–55. Cambridge: Cambridge University Press, 1984.

———. "In Search of the Colonial Woman in Mexico: The Seventeenth and Eighteenth Centuries." In *Latin American Women: Historical Perspectives*, ed. Asunción Lavrin, 23–59. Westport: Greenwood, 1978.

López Beltrán, Clara. "Envejecimiento y migración en una comunidad andina: Livitaca en 1689." *Revista de Historia Económica* 5:2 (1987): 245–70.

Lynch, John. *Spain Under the Hapsburgs.* New York: Oxford University Press, 1969.

Mallo, Nicanor. *Diccionario geográfico del departamento de Chuquisaca.* Sucre, Bolivia: Imprenta "Bolivar" de M. Pizarro, 1903.

Mallon, Florencia. *Defense of Community in Peru's Central Highlands: Peasant Struggle and Capitalist Transition, 1860–1940.* Princeton: Princeton University Press, 1983.

Maravall, José Antonio. *Estado moderno y mentalidad social*. Madrid: Ediciones de la *Revista de Oriente*, 1972.

Martínez, Gabriel. "Espacio Lupaqa: algunas hipotesis de trabajo." In *Etnohistoria y antropologia andina*, ed. Amalia Castelli, Marcia Koth de Paredes, and Mariana Mould de Pease, 264–80. Lima: Museo Nacional de Historia, 1981.

Medick, Hans. "The Proto-industrial Family Economy:The Structural Function of Household and Family during the Transition from Peasant Society to Industrial Capitalism." *Social History* 3 (1976): 291–315.

Mellafe, Rolando. "The Importance of Migration in the Viceroyalty of Peru." In *Population and Economics: Proceedings of section V of the Fourth Congress of the Economic History Association*, ed. Paul Déprez, 303–13. Winnipeg: University of Manitoba Press, 1970.

———. "Evolución del salario en el virreinato peruano (esquema y sugerencias)." *Ibero-Americana Pragensia* 1 (1967): 91–107.

Mesa, José de, and Teresa Gisbert. "Oruro: origen de una villa minera." In *Documentos orurenos*, 1:59–68. Oruro, Bolivia: Editorial de la Universidad Técnica de Oruro, 1976.

Metraux, Alfred. *The History of the Incas*. New York: Schocken Books, 1970.

Money, Mary. *Los obrajes, el traje y el comercio de ropa en la Audiencia de Charcas*. La Paz: Instituto de Estudios Bolivianos, 1983.

Moreno Cebrián, Alfredo. *El corregidor de indios y la economía peruana en el siglo XVIII*. Madrid: Consejo Superior de Investigaciones Científicas, 1977.

Mörner, Magnus. *Perfil de la sociedad rural del Cuzco a fines de la colonia*. Lima: Universidad del Pacifico, 1978.

Morris, Craig. "From Principles of Ecological Complementarity to the Organization and Administration of Tawantinsuyu." In *Andean Ecology and Civilization: An Interdisciplinary Perspective on Andean Ecological Complementarity*, ed. Shozo Masuda, Izumi Shimada, and Craig Morris, 477–90. Tokyo: University of Tokyo Press, 1985.

Moscoso, Maximiliano. "Apuntes para la historia de la industria textil en el Cuzco colonial." *Revista Universitaria* (Cuzco, 1962–63): 67–94.

Mujia, Ricardo. *Bolivia-Paraguay*. La Paz: Empresa Editora de "El Tiempo," 1914.

Mujica, Elias. "*Altiplano*-Coast Relationships in the South-Central Andes: From Indirect to Direct Complementarity." In *Andean Ecology and Civilization: An Interdisciplinary Perspective on Andean Ecological Complementarity*, ed. Shozo Masuda, Izumi Shimada, and Craig Morris, 103–40. Tokyo: University of Tokyo Press, 1985.

Muñoz Reyes, Jorge. *Geografía de Bolivia.* 2d ed. La Paz: Academia Nacional de Ciencias de Bolivia, 1980.

Murra, John V. "La correspondencia entre un 'capitán de la mita' y su apoderado en Potosí." *Historia y Cultura* 3 (1978): 45–58.

———. "The Economic Organization of the Inca State." Ph.D. diss., University of Chicago, 1956.

———. *Formaciones económicas y políticas del mundo andino.* Lima: Instituto de Estudios Peruanos, 1975.

———. "The Limits and Limitations of the 'Vertical Archipelago' in the Andes." In *Andean Ecology and Civilization: An Interdisciplinary Perspective on Andean Ecological Complementarity,* ed. Shozo Masuda, Izumi Shimada, and Craig Morris, 15–20. Tokyo: University of Tokyo Press, 1985.

———. "Notes on Pre-Columbian Cultivation of Coca Leaf." In Deborah Pacini and Christine Franquemont, eds., *Coca and Cocaine: Effects on People and Policy in Latin America.* Cambridge, Mass.: Cultural Survival, Inc. and the Latin American Studies Program, Cornell University, 1986.

Nash, June. *We Eat the Mines and the Mines Eat Us: Dependency and Exploitation in Bolivian Tin Mines.* New York: Columbia University Press, 1979.

O'Callaghan, Joseph F. *A History of Medieval Spain.* Ithaca and London: Cornell University Press, 1975.

Pease, Franklin. "Ayllu y parcialidad: reflexiones sobre el caso de Collaguas." *Etnohistoria y antropología andina,* 19–33. Lima: Museo Nacional de Historia, 1981.

Perry, Mary Elizabeth. *Gender and Disorder in Early Modern Seville.* Princeton: Princeton University Press, 1990.

———. " 'Lost Women' in Early Modern Seville: The Politics of Prostitution." *Feminist Studies* 4:1 (1978): 195–214.

Phelan, John Leddy. *The Kingdom of Quito in the Seventeenth Century.* Madison: University of Wisconsin Press, 1967.

Phillips, William D., Jr., and Carla Rahn Phillips. "Spain in the Fifteenth Century." *Transatlantic Encounters: Europeans and Andeans in the Sixteenth Century.* Berkeley and Los Angeles: University of California Press, 1991.

Pike, Ruth. *Aristocrats and Traders: Sevillian Society in the Sixteenth Century.* Ithaca: Cornell University Press, 1972.

Platt, Tristan. "Acerca del sistema tributario pre-toledano en el Alto Perú." *Avances* 1 (1978): 33–46.

———. *Estado boliviano y ayllu andino: tierra y tributo en el norte de Potosí*. Lima: Instituto de Estudios Peruanos, 1982.
Polo, José Toribio. "Apuntes sobre las epidemias del Perú." *Revista Histórica* 5 (1913): 50–109.
Portugal Ortiz, Max. *La esclavitud colonial y nacional en Bolivia*. La Paz: Instituto Boliviano de Cultura, 1978.
Powers, Karen M. "Indian Migration and Sociopolitico Change in the Audiencia of Quito, 1534–1700." Ph.D. diss., New York University, 1990.
Presta, Ana Maria. "Hacienda y comunidad: un estudio en la provincia de Pilaya y Paspaya, siglos XVI–XVIII." *Andes: antropologia e historia* 1 (1990): 31–45.
———. "Ingresos y gastos de una hacienda jesuitica altoperuana: Jesús de Trigo Pampa (Pilaya y Paspaya), 1734–1767." *Anuario del Insituto de Estudios Histórico-Sociales* (Universidad de Centro de la provincia de Buenos Aires) 4 (1989): 85–114.
Rance, Susanna. "The Hand That Feeds Us." *NACLA Report on the Americas* 25:1 (1991): 30–35.
Rasnake, Roger. *Domination and Cultural Resistance: Authority and Power among an Andean People*. Durham: Duke University Press, 1988.
Rivera, Silvia. "El Mallku y la sociedad colonial en el s. XVII: el caso de Jesús de Machaca." *Avances* 1 (1978): 7–27.
Rostworowski de Diez Canseco, Maria. *Étnia y sociedad: costa peruana prehispánica*. Lima: Instituto de Estudios Peruanos, 1977.
———. "La voz parcialidad en su contexto en los siglos XVI–XVII." In *Etnohistoria y antropologia andina*, ed. Amalia Castelli, Marcia Koth de Paredes, and Mariana Mould de Pease, 35–45. Lima: Museo Nacional de Historia, 1981.
Rowe, John H. "Absolute Chronology in the Andean Area." *American Antiquity* 10:3 (1945): 265–84.
———. "The Incas Under Spanish Colonial Institutions." *Hispanic American Historical Review* 37:2 (1957): 155–99.
Saignes, Thierry. *Los andes orientales: Historia de un olvido*. Cochabamba: CERES, 1985.
———. "Ayllus, mercados y coacción colonial: El reto de las migraciones internas en Charcas (siglo XVII)." In Olivia Harris, Brooke Larson and Enrique Tandeter, eds., *La participación indígena en los mercados surandinos: estrategias y reproducción social, siglos XVI a XX*, 111–58. La Paz: Centro de Estudios de la Realidad Economica y Social, 1987.

———. "De la filiation a la residence: les ethnies dans les valles de Larecaja." *Annales* 33:5–6 (1978): 1160–81.

———. "Une frontière fossile: la cordillere chiriguano au XVIII siècle." Thèse de 3e cycle, Université de Paris, 1974.

———. "Políticas étnicas en Bolivia colonial, siglos XVI–XIX." *Historia Boliviana* 3:1 (1983): 1–30.

———. "Valles y punas en el debate colonial: la pugna sobre los pobladores de Larecaja." *Histórica* 3:2 (Lima, 1979): 141–64.

Salomon, Frank L. "Indian Women of Early Colonial Quito as Seen Through their Testaments." *The Americas* 44:3 (1988): 326–30.

———. "*Pochteca* and *Mindala*: A Comparison of Long-Distance Traders in Ecuador and Mesoamerica." *Journal of the Steward Anthropological Society* 9 (1978): 231–46.

Sánchez-Albornoz, Nicolás. "La denomination des personnes en Amerique Latine." *Noms et prenoms. Apercu historique sur la denomination des personnes en divers pays*, 15–20. Dolhain: Ordina Editions, 1974.

———. *Indios y tributos en el Alto Perú*. Lima: Instituto de Estudios Peruanos, 1978.

———. "Migración rural en los Andes: Sipesipe (Cochabamba), 1645." *Revista de Historia Económica* 1:1 (1983): 30–36.

———. "Migración urbana y trabajo. Los indios de Arequipa, 1571–1645." *De historia e historiadores. Homenaje a José Luis Romero*, 259–81. Mexico City: Siglo XXI, 1982.

———. "Migraciones internas en el Alto Perú. El saldo acumulado en 1645." *Historia Boliviana* 2:1 (1982): 11–19.

———. "Mita, migraciones y pueblos. Variaciones en el espacio y en el tiempo." *Historia Boliviana* 3:1 (1983): 31–59.

———. *La población de América latina. Desde los tiempos precolombinos al año 2000*, 2d ed. Madrid: Alianza Editorial, 1977.

———. "El trabajo indígena en los Andes: teorias del siglo XVI." *Historia económica y pensamiento social. Estudios en homenaje a Diego Mateo del Peral*. Madrid: Alianza Editorial, 1983, 19–44.

Sanderlin, George, ed. and trans. *Bartolomé de Las Casas: A Selection of His Writings*. New York: Alfred A. Knopf, 1971.

Scott, James. *The Moral Economy of the Peasant: Rebellion and Subsistence in Southeast Asia*. New Haven: Yale University Press, 1976.

Semo, Enrique. *Historia del capitalismo en México: los orígenes, 1521–1763*. Mexico City: Ediciones Era, 1973.

Silva Santisteban, Fernando. *Los obrajes en el virreinato del Peru* Lima: Publicaciones de Museo Nacional de Historia, 1964.

Silverblatt, Irene. "Imperial Dilemmas, the Politics of Kinship, and Inca Reconstruction of History." *Comparative Studies in Society and History* 30 (1988): 83–102.
———. *Moon, Sun and Witches: Gender Ideologies and Class in Inca and Colonial Peru.* Princeton: Princeton, University Press, 1987.
———. "Women in States." *Annual Review of Anthropology* 17 (1988): 427–60.
Simpson, Lesley Byrd. *The Encomienda in New Spain.* Berkeley and Los Angeles: University of California Press, 1950.
Spalding, Karen. *De indio a campesino: Cambios en la estructure social del Perú colonial.* Lima: Instituto de Estudios Peruanos, 1974.
———. *Huarochirí: An Andean Society Under Inca and Spanish Rule.* Stanford: Stanford University Press, 1984.
———. "Hacienda-Village Relations in Andean Society to 1830." *Latin American Perspectives* 2:1 (1975): 107–21.
Stern, Steve J. "Feudalism, Capitalism, and the World-System in the Perspective of Latin America and the Caribbean." *American Historical Review* 93:4 (1988): 829–72.
———. *Peru's Indian Peoples and the Challenge of Spanish Conquest.* Madison: University of Wisconsin Press, 1982.
———. "The Rise and Fall of Indian-White Alliances: A Regional View of Conquest History." *Hispanic American Historical Review* 61:3 (1981): 461–91.
Stubbe, Carlos F. *Vocabulario minero antiguo. Compilación de terminos antiguos usados por los mineros y metalurgistas de América Ibérica.* Buenos Aires: El Ateneo, 1944.
Tandeter, Enrique. "La producción como actividad popular: 'Ladrones de mina' en Potosí." *Nova Americana* 4 (1981): 43–65.
———. "La rente comme rapport de production et comme rapport de distribution. Le cas de l'industrie miniere de Potosí, 1750–1826." Thèse de 3e cycle, Ecole des Hautes Etudes en Sciences Sociales, 1980.
———. "Trabajo forzado y trabajo libre en el Potosí colonial tardio." *Estudios Cedes* 3:6 (1980).
Tandeter, Enrique, and Nathan Wachtel, *Precios y producción agraria: Potosí y Charcas en el siglo XVIII.* Buenos Aires: Centro de Estudios de Estado y Sociedad, 1983.
Thompson, E. P. "The Moral Economy of the English Crowd in the Eighteenth Century." *Past and Present* 50 (1971): 76–136.
Urbano, Henrique. "Cristóbal de Molina, el Cusqueño: Negocios eclesiásticos, mesianismo y Taqui Onqoy." *Revista Andina* 8:1 (1990): 265–83.

Varón Gabai, Rafael. "El Taki Onqoy: las raices andinas de un fenómeno colonial." In *El retorno de las huacas: Estudios y documentos del siglo XVI*, ed. Luis Millones, 331–405. Lima: Instituto de Estudios Peruanos y Sociedad Peruana de Psicoanálisis, 1990.

Vassberg, David E. *Land and Society in Golden Age Castile*. Cambridge: Cambridge University Press, 1984.

Vicens Vives, Jaime. *An Economic History of Spain*. Princeton: Princeton University Press, 1969.

Villamarin, Juan A., and Judith E. Villamarin. *Indian Labor in Mainland Colonial Spanish America*. Newark: University of Delaware, Latin American Studies Program, 1975.

Wachtel, Nathan. "The *Mitimas* of the Cochabamba Valley: The Colonization Policy of Huayna Capac." In *The Inca and Aztec States, 1400–1800*, ed. George A. Collier, Renato I. Rosaldo, and John D. Wirth, 199–235. New York: Academic Press, 1982.

———. "Hommes d'eau: Le problème uru (XVI–XVII siècle)." *Annales* 33:5–6 (1978): 1127–59.

———. *The Vision of the Vanquished*. Hassocks, Sussex: Harvester Press, 1977.

Wallerstein, Immanuel. *The Modern World-System: Capitalist Agriculture and the Origins of the European World-Economy in the Sixteenth Century*. New York: Academic Press, 1974.

———. *The Modern World-System II: Mercantilism and the Consolidation of the European World-Economy, 1600–1750*. New York: Academic Press, 1980.

Watson, Foster, ed. *Vives and the Renascence Education of Women*. New York: Longmans, Green; London: Edward Arnold, 1912.

Wayne, Valerie. "Some Sad Sentence: Vives' *Instruction of a Christian Woman*." In *Silent But for the Word: Tudor Women as Patrons, Translators and Writers of Religious Works*, ed. Margaret Patterson Hannay, 15–29. Kent, Ohio: Kent State University Press, 1985.

Wightman, Ann M. *Indigenous Migration and Social Change: The Forasteros of Cuzco, 1570–1720*. Durham: Duke University Press, 1990.

———. " ... residente en esa ciudad ... ": Urban migrants in colonial Cuzco." In *Migration in Colonial Spanish America*, ed. David J. Robinson, 86–111. Cambridge: Cambridge University Press, 1990.

Williams, Raymond. *Marxism and Literature*. Oxford: Oxford University Press, 1977.

Yamamoto, Norio. "The Ecological Complementarity of Agro–Pastoralism: Some Comments." In *Andean Ecology and Civilization: An Interdisciplinary Perspective on Andean Ecological Complementarity*, ed. Shozo Masuda, Izumi Shimada, and Craig Morris, 85–99. Tokyo: University of Tokyo Press, 1985.

Zavala, Silvio. *La encomienda indiana*, 2d rev. ed. Mexico City: Editorial Porrua, 1973.

Zulawski, Ann. "Frontier Workers and Social Change: Pilaya y Paspaya (Bolivia) in the Early Eighteenth Century." In *Migration in Colonial Spanish America*, ed. David Robinson, 112–27. Cambridge: Cambridge University Press, 1990.

———. "Social Differentiation, Gender and Ethnicity: Urban Indian Women in Colonial Bolivia, 1640–1725." *Latin American Research Review* 25:2 (1990): 93–113.

———. "Wages, Ore Sharing and Peasant Agriculture: Labor in Oruro's Silver Mines, 1607–1720." *Hispanic American Historical Review* 67:3 (1987): 405–30.

Index

acculturation, 6, 9, 87, 125, 148, 203; of women, 151
Achatta, Pedro, 163
acllas, 24
Agia, Miguel de, 56
agriculture, 168–98; and colonialism, 41; and migration patterns, 73; impact of decline of mining on, 59–60; around Oruro, 97, 125; payment for labor in, 55; in pre-Columbian Andes, *see* mitimaes; and regional economic development, 49–52; in Spain, 27–28, 31; subsistence, and wage labor, 86, 103
Alba de Aliste, conde de, 106
alcabala, 106–07
Aldana, Lorenzo de, 41, 46
Alfaro, Francisco de, 78–79
Alos, Antonio de, 239n48
Alumbrados, 33
Alvarez de Nava Revolledo, Alonso, 91, 93
Andrien, Kenneth, 59
anti-Semitism, 27
Arequipa: epidemic in, 109; women in, 151, 161, 165; yanaconas in, 135, 138
Arica, 7
Arrom, Silvia Marina, 244n12
Arze, Josepha, 162
Asanaques, 173
Ayans, Antonio de, 54, 63, 69

ayllus, 6, 16, 18, 84; and encomienda, 43–45; forasteros incorporated into, 173; and Inca state, 21, 24; and surnames, 184; tribute paid by, 148; women's ties to, 157–59, 162
Aymaras, 8, 11–20, 172, 181, 204; ecological complementarity among, 12–18; Inca invasions of, 22; mobilization of labor and social inequality among, 18–20; social change and ideological adjustment among, 12; tribute requirements of, 144, 145
ayni, 19
Azpilcueta, Martín de, 30

Bakewell, Peter, 59
Barrios, Bartolomé de, 168, 177
Becerra, Joseph, 158
Belásquez, Felix, 196–97, 251n53
Berlanga, Tomás de, 227n21
blacks, 74; in silver mines, 110. *See also* slavery
Bolívar, Felipe de, 179
Brading, David, 100
British, competition for colonies between Spain and, 26
Burkett, Elinor, 151, 154, 156, 165, 245n17
Buyan, Captain Agustín, 105

Caba Cajero, Juan de la, 111
cabildos (town councils), 48

Cabrera de Cárdenas, Juan, 91
Calla, Juan, 201–02
Callacopa, Fernando, 167
capitalism, Latin America's transition to, 5
Carangas, 7, 131; yanaconas in, 135
Caribbean, colonization of, 39–40
Carillo, Pascuala, 162
Carita, Christobal, 158, 159
Carmagnai, Marcello, 237n31
Castro y Padilla, Manuel, 37, 87, 236n10
Catari, Pedro, 174
Catherine of Aragon, 31
Catholicism, 25–27, 33, 39, 223n42; and women, 166
cattle, 51-52
Cazalla, María, 34
Chambilla, Diego, 75
Charles II, 58
Charles V, 26, 45, 228
Chayanov, A. V., 103
Chevalier, François, 60
Chambi, Domingo, 139
children: census figures on, 117, 118, 120–21; guardianship of, Spanish law on, 155
Chiriguanos, 8, 9, 42, 51, 74, 169, 172–74, 181, 185–86, 204
Chipana, Pedro, 160
Choque, Juan, 163
Chupaychu, 18
Cipriano, José de, 168, 178
class formation, 200–01, 203; and agricultural labor, 170, 198; in Inca empire, 23, 25; migration as contributor to, 84; and women, 155–56, 165, 166
coca, 51
Colque, 22
Colque Guarache, Juan, 41
complementarity: ecological, 12–18, 116; and gender, 154, 202
conversos, 26, 27, 29
Cook, N. D., 63–64
corregidor de indios, 48
corregimientos, 66–68
Cotes, Cristóbal de, 163

craft production, 115, 121–14, 126–27, 147, 148, 202–03, 224n61
Crespo, Albert, 41, 236n10
Criollo, Pablo, 184
Cross, H., 100
Cruz, Isabel de la, 33
Cuterillo, Joseph de, 103
Cuzco, 7; artisan guilds in, 124; epidemic in, 109; forasteros in, 147, 181; women in, 161; yanaconas in, 135, 138, 139

demographic change, 59, 61, 63; from epidemics, 63–65. See also migration
Diez de San Miquel, Garci, 19
diseases, epidemic. See epidemics
domestic workers, 151, 152, 160–62, 198, 202
Dominicans, 40, 44
Duncan Baretta, Silvio R., 186

Elizondo, Antonio de, 107
Elosu Echevarría, Gaspar de, 103
encomiendas, 39–46, 61, 66
epidemics, 61–65, 84, 187–88; and resettlement, 67; and silver industry, 109, 112, 113
Erasmus, Desiderius, 31, 34
Esmoraca, 7
Esperanza, María, 164
Espinoza, Waldemar, 41
Espíritu Santo, 163
Esquilache, Viceroy principe de, 79
ethnocentrism, Spanish, 26
Evans, Brian, 116–17, 120, 241nn10, 14

Fajardo, Maria, 158
Ferdinand, King, 28, 39
Fernández, María, 173
Fernández Guarache, Gabriel, 126, 139–40, 160, 195–96, 242n31
Fernández Guarache, Lucrecia, 159–60
feudalism, 5, 28–30
Flores, Juan, 195, 196
forasteros, 10, 80–84, 147, 203; mita obligations of, 141–42; in Pilaya y Paspaya, 83, 134, 169, 173, 176–78,

180–92, 194, 197, 235n54; in 1683 census, 114–16, 118, 120, 126–35, 140; tribute paid by, 142–44, 148
Franciscans, 56

Gender, 9, 10, 36; Inca ideology of, 23–25, 35, 200, 202; Spanish attitudes toward, 31–35, 152–54, 165–67
Gisbert, Teresa, 87
Glave, Luis Miguel, 152, 160, 162, 165–66, 198
Godoy, Felipe de, 85, 88–97, 103, 134, 200, 236n6
Gómez de Montemaior, Cristobal, 239n48
Góngora, Mario, 260n47
Granada, 26
Gualpa, Andrés, 161
Guampa, Ursula, 162
Guarache, 22
Guaranis, 204
guardianship of children, Spanish laws on, 155
guilds, 124, 224n61
Gutiérrez, Lázaro, 160–61
Gutiérrez, Pablo, 164

haciendas: migration to, 71; renters on, 38, 176–77; as sanctuary from mita, 178; slaves on, 176; temporary labor on, 68, 168, 177; yanaconas on, 75–79, 193–97, 250n41
Hennessy, Alistair, 169
Henry VIII, king of England, 31
Hispaniola, 39
Holy Roman Empire, 26, 58
huacas (Andean gods), 44–45
Huanca, 44
Huancavelica, forced labor in, 120
Huaquirca, 1683 census in, 120
Huayna Capac, 23
humanism, 31–35

Ibañez, Francisca, 196
idleness: attacks on, 29–30; of women, 34
Ignacio, Joseph, 135

illegitimacy, 137–38
Inca empire, 8, 11, 20–26, 40–42; coca use in, 51; defeat of, 44; gender ideology in, 23–25, 35, 154; migration in, 22–23, 25, 73, 147, 153, 158, 172; road construction in, 28; smallpox epidemic in, 64; women in, 152, 165
influenza epidemics, 109
inheritance: Spanish laws on, 155, 158; from women, 157–58, 167
Inquisition, 26, 27; women in, 33–34
Isabella, Queen, 28, 31, 39
Islamic Spain. See Moors

Jesuits, 62, 64, 170, 172, 173, 198
Jews, Spanish, 26, 27, 38, 223n42; expulsion of, 29

kin groups: in Inca empire, 21; see also ayllus
Klein, Herbert, 193
kurakas, 17–19, 22, 55; and contracts between hacendados, 168, 169, 177; and encomenderos, 40, 43; and mita system, 70, 75; property owned by, 159–60; and resettlement, 68
Kusi dynasty, 19

labor: in Aymara society, 18–20; forced (see encomiendas; mita; repartimiento; yanaconas); free, emergence of, 53–57; on haciendas, temporary, 68; in Inca empire, 22; in Oruro, 93–105; in Pilaya y Paspaya, 176–78; sexual division of, 154; Spanish attitudes toward, 28–31, 37–39; wage, see wage labor
la Cruz, Roque de, 157
Ladd, Doris, 110
Langer, Eric, 203
la Palata, duque de, 71, 114–16, 144, 145, 172, 178, 179, 235n53, 243n41
La Paz, 7, 13; family as productive unit in, 167; tribute requirements in, 145; women in, 152, 153, 158, 162; yanaconas in, 135, 138, 139

La Plata, 38, 41; Jesuit College of, 41; migration to Pilaya y Paspaya from, 181; women in, 153, 157, 162; yanaconas in, 78, 135, 138
Larson, Brooke, 218n5
Las Casas, Bartolomé de, 40, 45
Lemos, Viceroy de, 230n70
Lima, 7, 50, 89; artisan guilds in, 124; epidemics in, 62, 64–65; and forced distribution of goods, 106
Livitaca, 1683 census in, 120, 121
llacturunas, 6, 16, 234n52, 235n53
Llano y Astorga, Baltazar, 160
López-Beltrán, Clara, 120, 188, 250n49
López de Quiroga, Antonio, 51, 52, 102, 168, 174–76, 191, 196
Lupaqa kingdom, 19–20
Lutheranism, 26

Maldonado, Polonia, 161
Maldonado de Torres, Licenciado Alonso, 89, 94, 101, 236n10
Mamani, Julio, 139
Mancera, Viceroy marques de, 81, 179, 250n42
manufacturing, 49, 50, 52–53; in Spain, 28, 58–59
Maravall, José Antonio, 29
market economy: craft production in, 148; and demographic change, 63, 84; emergence of, 5; and human freedom, 30; and identity of urban Indians, 115; women in, 156, 158, 165
Markoff, John, 186
marriage, census figures on, 120
Mary I, queen of England, 31
Matienzo, Juan de, 45
Medrano, Diego de, 91, 93
Medrano, Francisco de, 91, 93
merchandise, forced distribution of, 105–07
mercury, 92–94, 100, 108, 111
Mesa, José de, 87
mesta, 27–28
Mexico, 39, 40, 60; silver production in, 57, 110, 112

migration, 65–84, 120; forced, 65–70; patterns of, 10, 70–79, 127, 129–40, 146; to Pilaya y Paspaya, 169, 179–90, 197, 198; to urban areas, 79–83, 87, 105
mingados, 94
Miranda, Francisco de, 107
Miranda, Luis de, 115, 126, 134
Miranda, Pablo de, 177
miscegenation, 176, 192
mita, 4, 8, 41, 47, 56, 57, 61, 68–70, 81, 112, 198; acceleration of silver production after initiation of, 48; agricultural, 41, 68; and census of 1683, 114, 115–17, 140–42; competition of yanaconaje for labor with, 76, 78, 79; exemption from, 172, 173, 202; haciendas as sanctuary from, 178, 196; and migration patterns, 63, 71, 73–75, 131, 134, 181; and Oruro, 86, 87, 93, 110; in Paspaya, 184, 185; payment for service in, 54, 69; precolonial origin of, 18; task system in, 94, 96
mitimaes, 6, 16, 18–20, 147, 234n52; and colonialism, 41, 42; and ideology of reciprocity, 18; in Inca empire, 22–23, 25, 73, 153, 158; in Pilaya y Paspaya, 169, 172, 184; and resettlement, 68
Moncada, Sancho de, 30
Monclova, conde de, 108
money lenders, 111
Montesclaros, Viceroy marques de, 78, 92–93
Montesinos, Antonio de, 40
Moors, 25–27, 38
Moreno, Jacinto, 173–74
Mörner, Magnus, 119–20
Moslems, 26, 223n23. See also Moors
Murra, John, 20, 221n11

neo-Incas, 44
New Christians. See conversos

Ocana, Andres de, 107
Orcoma, María, 159

originarios, 71, 74–75, 81, 83; of Pilaya y Paspaya, 171–73, 188, 192; in 1683 census, 120, 127
Ortega, Alonso de, 107
Ortiz, Miguel, 101
Oruro, 7–10, 13, 79, 84–149, 156, 169, 170, 173, 181, 198, 204; development of mines in, 87–93; discovery of silver in, 41; economic development around, 50; epidemic in, 109; forced distribution of merhandise in, 105–07; labor in, 55, 93–105, 178; occupational structure among Spaniards in, 97–99; population loss in, 59; 1683 census in, 114–49; tax evasion in, 238n36; trapiches, 107–12; women in, 153, 157, 159, 160; yanaconas in, 80, 202–03
Osorio de Mendoza, Alonso, 176, 184, 249n24
Ovando, Nicolás de, 39

Pachacuti, Emperor, 20
Paco, Juan, 197, 251n53
Pérez, Bartolomé, 135, 136
Perry, Mary Elizabeth, 34
Philip II, 45
Philip III, 56, 58, 78, 79
Philip IV, 58
Philippines, 57
Pichu, Ana, 160
Pilaya y Paspaya, 7–10, 41, 51–52, 55, 60, 68, 79, 84, 168–98, 203–04; forasteros in, 83, 134, 169, 173, 176–78, 180–92; indigenous peoples in north of, 170–74; labor in, 176–78; patterns of migration in, 179–80; Spanish landowners in south of, 174–75; yanaconas in, 168–70, 173, 176, 178, 187–88, 191–98, 202, 203
Pinelo, Valentina, 225n79
Pintado, Juan Crisostomo, 111
Pizarro, Francisco, 226n8
Pizarro, Gonzalo and Hernando, 38
Platt, Tristan, 148, 229n58
Polo de Ondegardo, Juan, 234n52

Poma de Ayala, Guaman, 162
Porco, 7, 38; corregidor of, 37; yanacones in, 81
Portugal, Diego de, 96
Potosí, 8, 43, 85, 127, 146, 164, 170, 175, 191; College of the Company of Jesus of, 170; competition between Oruro and, 93; craft professions in, 124, 126; declining silver production in, 58–60, 102; discovery of silver at, 42; epidemics in, 64, 65, 109; family as productive unit in, 156, 167; forced labor in, *see* mita; market demand in, 7; migration to Oruro from, 129, 135; price for ore in, 92; profitability of mines in, 89; regional economic development around, 49–53; trapiches in, 108, 111–12; tribute requirements in, 145; women in, 158, 160; yanaconas in, 80, 81, 83, 84, 138
poverty: feminization of, 162; and idleness, 30; and prostitution, 32
prostitution, 32, 35
Protestantism, 26, 58
protoliberalism, 28–31
Puno, 7

Qari dynasty, 19
Quechua, 19, 20, 204
Quillaca-Asanaques, 8, 16, 22, 40–41, 131, 172
quinto, 97, 100–02, 104; and trapiches, 108
Quiroga, Andrés de, 184
Quito, women in, 151

Ramos, Bartolomé de, 164
Rasnake, Roger, 172, 184
reciprocity, principle of, 12, 18–19, 116; and Incas, 21; and Spanish, 36, 43; and tribute, 148
redistribution, principle of, 12; and Incas, 21; and Spanish, 36
reducciones, 47, 65–68, 71, 73, 127
Renaissance, Spanish, 28
Renxifo, Fernando, 173

repartimiento, 46–49; efforts to end, 53–57
repartimiento de mercancías, 105–07
resettlement, forced, 65–70
Rizo Valmazeda, Joseph, 110
Robles, Juan de, 160
Rodrígues, Geronimo, 239n48
Ropa, Juan, 184
Rostworowski, María, 221n10
Russian peasants, 103

Sacomecassi, María, 167
Saignes, Thierry, 6, 76, 135, 146, 197
Salinas Ruberto, Antonio de, 102
Salomon, Frank, 151, 152, 167
San Antonio de Nuevo Mundo, 7
Sánchez-Albornoz, Nicolás, 30, 56, 65, 71–73, 80–81, 116–17, 226n6
Sánchez Paniagua, Claudio, 195, 196
Sánchez Paniagua, Gonzalo, 195
San Felipe de Austria. *See* Oruro
Santos, Joseph, 196
Santos, María, 160–61
Sempat Assadourian, Carlos, 60
serfdom, elimination of, 30
silver mining: and class formation, 203; decline in production, 57–61; democratization of production of, 107–12; development of, 87–93; encomiendas in, 41–43; forced labor in, *see* mita; and migration patterns, 73, 74; and regional economic development, 49–50; repartimiento in, 46–48; and 1683 census, 125–26; tax on, 97, 100–01; and wage labor, 93–105; women in, 163–64
Silverblatt, Irene, 21, 23, 24, 159, 162
Sisa, Bartola, 163
Sisa, Antonia, 162
Sisa, María, 161
Sissa, Ana, 158
Sissa, Juana, 158–59
slavery, 8, 30, 161, 192; in Caribbean, 39–40; in Pilaya y Paspaya, 176; yanaconaje as form of, 76, 78
Soras, 131
Spain, 11, 25–35; humanism and attitudes toward gender in, 31–35;

manufacturing in, 28, 52–53, 58–59; mercantilist strategy of, 50; protoliberalism and attitudes toward labor in, 28–31; religious orthodoxy and underdevelopment in, 26–28; secessionist challenges to, 58; silver sent as tax to, 43; town councils in, 48
Spalding, Karen, 19, 40, 46, 124
Stern, Steve, 40

Tacuri, Francisco, 186
Tainos, 39
Taki Onqoy, 44
Tandeter, Enrique, 108, 111–12, 237n29, 243n37
Tarija, Fracisco de, 186
taxes: sales, 106–07; on silver, 97, 100–02, 104, 108. *See also* tribute
textile industry, 28, 52–53, 59, 224n66, 228n38, 229n56
Toledo, Francisco de, 8, 47, 51, 53–54, 65, 68, 71–73, 75–81, 126, 127, 131, 138, 144, 145, 173, 178, 196
transport and trade, 124–26, 157; women in, 164
trapiches, 107–12
tribute, 8, 38, 140, 142–48, 201, 226n8; cash, 54, 55; and censuses, 71, 72, 81, 115, 117; coca paid as, 51; in Pilaya y Paspaya, 172, 177, 184–85; in Potosí, 42, 43; versus reciprocity, 19; in repartimiento, 48
Trujillo, yanaconas in, 135

Uriona, Antonio de, 102
Ursula, Lucia, 157–58
Urus, 144, 145
Uscamayta, Hernando, 158

Valencia, Pedro de, 34
Valverde, Vicente, 226n8
Vázquez de Espinosa, Antonio, 51, 172
Velasco, Luis de, 56
Vicens Vives, Jaime, 27, 223n43
Vives, Juan Luis, 29, 31–34, 154

Wachtel, Nathan, 71
wage labor, 5, 54–56, 61, 199;
  agricultural, 176–77, 198; in Oruro, 55, 85–87
Wallpa, Pascual, 196
Wightman, Ann, 124, 147, 157, 235*n*54
Williams, Raymond, 3, 219*n*1
wine production, 51, 60, 174, 175, 177
Wisijsa people. *See* Yura people
women, 150–67; in domestic service, 160–62, 198, 202; economic ties of, 156–57; legal position of, 154–55; in Pilaya y Paspaya, 187–88, 192; property owned by, 157–60; as retail merchants, 162; in 1683 census, 117–18, 148–49; as temporary agricultural workers, 177
wool production, 27–28, 52

xenophobia, Spanish, 26, 27

yanaconas, 10, 20, 24, 75, 202; acculturation of, 125, 148; exemption from mita of, 142; on haciendas, 75–79; occupational ties among, 157; in Pilaya y Paspaya, 168–70, 173, 176, 178, 187–88, 191–98, 202, 203; property owned by, 158; in 1683 census, 115, 118, 126–27, 135–40; tribute paid by, 142–46
Yucayguaris, 172
Yura people, 172, 177, 184–85

Zapatero, Miguel, 184
Zayas y Sotomayor, María de, 225

Pitt Latin American Series
James M. Malloy, Editor

ARGENTINA

Argentina Between the Great Powers, 1936–1946
Guido di Tella and D. Cameron Watt, Editors

Argentina in the Twentieth Century
David Rock, Editor

Argentina: Political Culture and Instability
Susan Calvert and Peter Calvert

Argentine Workers: Peronism and Contemporary Class Consciousness
Peter Ranis

Discreet Partners: Argentina and the USSR Since 1917
Aldo César Vacs

The Franco-Perón Alliance: Relations Between Spain and Argentina, 1946–1955
Raanan Rein, translated by Martha Grenzeback

Institutions, Parties, and Coalitions in Argentine Politics
Luigi Manzetti

The Life, Music, and Times of Carlos Gardel
Simon Collier

The Political Economy of Argentina, 1946–1983
Guido di Tella and Rudiger Dornbusch, Editors

BRAZIL

The Brazilian Voter: Mass Politics in Democratic Transition, 1974–1986
Kurt von Mettenheim

Capital Markets in the Development Process: The Case of Brazil
John H. Welch

External Constraints on Economic Policy in Brazil, 1899–1930
Winston Fritsch

The Film Industry in Brazil: Culture and the State
Randal Johnson

Kingdoms Come: Religion and Politics in Brazil
Rowan Ireland

The Manipulation of Consent: The State and Working-Class Consciousness in Brazil
Youssef Cohen

The Politics of Social Security in Brazil
James M. Malloy

Politics Within the State: Elite Bureaucrats and Industrial Policy in Authoritarian Brazil
Ben Ross Schneider

Unequal Giants: Diplomatic Relations Between the United States and Brazil, 1889–1930
Joseph Smith

CHILE

Chile: The Political Economy of Development and Democracy in the 1990s
David E. Hojman

The Overthrow of Allende and the Politics of Chile, 1964–1976
Paul E. Sigmund

Primary Medical Care in Chile: Accessibility Under Military Rule
Joseph L. Scarpaci

CUBA

Cuba After the Cold War
Carmelo Mesa-Lago, Editor

Cuba Between Empires, 1878–1902
Louis A. Pérez, Jr.

Cuba Under the Platt Amendment, 1902–1934
Louis A. Pérez, Jr.

Cuban Studies, Vols. 16–24
Carmelo Mesa-Lago, et al., Editors

The Economics of Cuban Sugar
Jorge F. Pérez-López

Intervention, Revolution, and Politics in Cuba, 1913–1921
Louis A. Pérez, Jr.

Lords of the Mountain: Social Banditry and Peasant Protest in Cuba, 1878–1918
Louis A. Pérez, Jr.

Sport in Cuba: The Diamond in the Rough
Paula J. Pettavino and Geralyn Pye

MEXICO

The Dynamics of Domination: State, Class, and Social Reform in Mexico, 1910–1990
Viviane Brachet-Marquez

The Expulsion of Mexico's Spaniards, 1821–1836
Harold Dana Sims

The Mexican Republic: The First Decade, 1823–1832
Stanley C. Green

Mexico Through Russian Eyes, 1806–1940
William Harrison Richardson

Oil and Mexican Foreign Policy
George W. Grayson

The Politics of Mexican Oil
George W. Grayson

Voices, Visions, and a New Reality: Mexican Fiction Since 1970
J. Ann Duncan

NORTHERN AND CENTRAL ANDES

Domestic and Foreign Finance in Modern Peru, 1850–1950: Financing Visions of Development
Alfonso W. Quiroz

Economic Management and Economic Development in Peru and Colombia
Rosemary Thorp

Gaitán of Columbia: A Political Biography
Richard E. Sharpless

Military Rule and Transition in Ecuador: Dancing with the People
Anita Isaacs

The Origins of the Peruvian Labor Movement, 1883–1919
Peter Blanchard

Peru and the International Monetary Fund
Thomas Scheetz

Peru Under García: An Opportunity Lost
John Crabtree

Poverty and Peasantry in Peru's Southern Andes, 1963–90
R. F. Watters

Restructuring Domination: Industrialists and the State in Ecuador
Catherine M. Conaghan

Roads to Reason: Transportation, Administration, and Rationality in Colombia
Richard E. Hartwig

Unsettling Statecraft: Democracy and Neoliberalism in the Central Andes
Catherine M. Conaghan and James M. Malloy

CARIBBEAN

The Last Cacique: Leadership and Politics in a Puerto Rican City
Jorge Heine

The Meaning of Freedom: Economics, Politics and Culture After Slavery
Frank McGlynn and Seymour Drescher, Editors

A Revolution Aborted: The Lessons of Grenada
Jorge Heine, Editor

To Hell with Paradise: A History of the Jamaican Tourist Industry
Frank Fonda Taylor

CENTRAL AMERICA

At the Fall of Somoza
Lawrence Pezzullo and Ralph Pezzullo

Black Labor on a White Canal: Panama, 1904–1981
Michael L. Conniff

The Catholic Church and Politics in Nicaragua and Costa Rica
Philip J. Williams

The Costa Rican Women's Movement: A Reader
Ilse Abshagen Leitinger, Editor and Translator

Perspectives on the Agro-Export Economy in Central America
Wim Pelupessy, Editor

INTERNATIONAL RELATIONS

The Giant's Rival: The USSR and Latin America
Cole Blasier

The Hovering Giant: U.S. Responses to Revolutionary Change in Latin America
Cole Blasier

Illusions of Conflict: Anglo-American Diplomacy Toward Latin America
Joseph Smith

Images and Intervention: U.S. Policies in Latin America
Martha L. Cottam

The United States and Latin America in the 1980s: Contending Perspectives on a Decade of Crisis
Kevin J. Middlebrook and Carlos Rico, Editors

OTHER STUDIES

Adventurers and Proletarians: The Story of Migrants in Latin America
Magnus Mörner, with the collaboration of Harold Sims

Ascent to Bankruptcy: Financing Social Security in Latin America
Carmelo Mesa-Lago

Authoritarianism and Corporatism in Latin America
James M. Malloy, Editor

Authoritarians and Democrats: Regime Transition in Latin America
James M. Malloy and Mitchell A. Seligson, Editors

Business and Democracy in Latin America
Ernest Bartell and Leigh A. Payne, Editors

The Constitution of Tyranny: Regimes of Exception in Spanish America
Brian Loveman

Female and Male in Latin America: Essays
Ann Pescatello, Editor

Latin American Debt and the Adjustment Crisis
Rosemary Thorp and Laurence Whitehead, Editors

Public Policy in Latin America: A Comparative Survey
John W. Sloan

Rebirth of the Paraguayan Republic: The First Colorado Era, 1878–1904
Harris G. Warren

Selected Latin American One-Act Plays
Francesca Colecchia and Julio Matas, Editors and Translators

The Social Documentary in Latin America
Julianne Burton, Editor

The State and Capital Accumulation in Latin America. Vol. 1: Brazil, Chile, Mexico. Vol. 2: Argentina, Colombia, Ecuador, Peru, Uru-guay, Venezuela
Christian Anglade and Carlos Fortin, Editors

"They Eat from Their Labor": Work and Social Change in Colonial Bolivia
Ann Zulawski

Transnational Corporations and the Latin American Automobile Industry
Rhys Jenkins